A Rip in Heaven

A Rip in Heaven

A MEMOIR OF MURDER AND ITS AFTERMATH

Jeanine Cummins

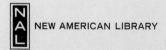
NEW AMERICAN LIBRARY

New American Library
Published by New American Library, a division of Penguin Group (USA) Inc.,
375 Hudson Street, New York, New York 10014, USA
Penguin Group (Canada), 10 Alcorn Avenue, Toronto,
Ontario M4V 3B2, Canada (a division of Pearson Penguin Canada Inc.)
Penguin Books Ltd., 80 Strand, London WC2R 0RL, England
Penguin Ireland, 25 St. Stephen's Green, Dublin 2,
Ireland (a division of Penguin Books Ltd.)
Penguin Group (Australia), 250 Camberwell Road, Camberwell, Victoria 3124,
Australia (a division of Pearson Australia Group Pty. Ltd.)
Penguin Books India Pvt. Ltd., 11 Community Centre, Panchsheel Park,
New Delhi - 110 017, India
Penguin Group (NZ), cnr Airborne and Rosedale Roads, Albany,
Auckland 1310, New Zealand (a division of Pearson New Zealand Ltd.)
Penguin Books (South Africa) (Pty.) Ltd., 24 Sturdee Avenue,
Rosebank, Johannesburg 2196, South Africa

Penguin Books Ltd., Registered Offices: 80 Strand, London WC2R 0RL, England

First published by New American Library, a division of Penguin Group (USA) Inc.

First Printing, June 2004
20 19 18 17 16 15 14 13 12

NEW AMERICAN LIBRARY and logo are trademarks of Penguin Group (USA) Inc.

LIBRARY OF CONGRESS CATALOGING-IN-PUBLICATION DATA:

Cummins, Jeanine.
A rip in Heaven : a memoir of murder and its aftermath / by Jeanine Cummins.
p.   cm.
ISBN 0-451-21053-0
1. Murder—Missouri—Case studies. I. Title.
HV6533.M45C86 2004
364.152'3'0977866—dc22   2003025673

Set in Bembo

Printed in the United States of America

For Robin: my true friend, my blood, my laugh-maker.
And for Julie: my sunshine, my awe-inspirer, my soul-waker.

May God grant us the strength and wisdom
to do your lives a sliver of justice in the telling.

We love you always and miss you every day.
Kisses and Revolution.

ACKNOWLEDGMENTS

There are a number of people without whom, it is no stretch to say, this book might never have happened. To the following people, I want to express my most heartfelt thanks:

To all my friends, colleagues, mos, pokeys and extended New York family—for keeping my daily life fun and (sometimes) sane.

To Dan Slater—for your early wisdom. Your sensitivity and encouragement helped me more than you know. To Kara and Claire—for seeing the potential in a rough, rough draft.

And to Laura—for the incredible insight to spin that roughness into a polish I can feel truly proud of; you made me see things I would never have accepted without your clarity.

To Frank Carlson, Frank Fabbri, and Nels Moss—for taking the time to read the manuscript and share your invaluable advice (both legal and personal) with me. And more importantly, for the things you have all done for my brother.

To Nikki—for being the best live-in therapist a girl ever had. (And to Noel for getting her out of the house in between our sessions so that I could *write*).

To Evelyne—for talking me down from the ledge time after time despite the ocean usually separating us.

To Joe—for chasing the very notion of complacency right out of my life. You are, quite simply, my backbone.

To the Dorks of the Round Table, Anton and Carolyn—for teaching me how to be humble and proud all at the same time. You two are almost as responsible for this book as I am. (Okay, maybe more than "almost.") I very seriously could not have done this without you.

To the best damn sales force in the industry—you guys have been absolutely brimming with confidence and enthusiasm from day one, and I wouldn't want anybody else behind me. I am the luckiest author ever. To Norman and Trish—for becoming my mentors and for teaching me that what's really important in business is the people surrounding you. Norman, you believed in me, and because of that, my dreams are happening. Thank you.

To my family (way too many to name here: all Cumminses, Matthewses, and married variations thereof)—it sounds corny, but it's true: I come from good stock. The strength and love I have witnessed within our family over the years takes my breath away. I am proud to belong to you.

To Jamie—you are the most dignified and courageous young lady I have ever known. You have an amazing willingness to be fully engaged in life, and it is truly an honor to call you my cousin and my friend.

To Ginna—words cannot express what you have done for me. Your daughters planted action in me, but it was your faith and strength that made me unafraid. In my wildest dreams, I could not imagine a more compassionate or generous soul than you have been to me.

To Mom and Dad—for being unconditionally loving and supportive (even when I choose to live in "hostile foreign territories"). For raising me to keep my feet on the ground and my head in the clouds. And for always believing in me, and reminding me of that when I floundered. I hope to make you proud.

To Kathy—what can I say? You will always be my emotional partner in life. We grew up on the same day, and no one will ever understand who I am quite as well as you do. *Eres la mejor hermanita en todo el mundo.*

And to Tom—it's been one hell of a journey, and you have been mostly a pain in the ass. But I love you even more now than I did when we started this dream on Grandma's and Grandpa's back porch all those years ago. Tom, you are my hero.

Author's Note

This is a work of nonfiction. My research materials included court documents, police records, and electronic and print media, as well as interviews I conducted with people who appear in this book. Additionally, because I am part of the story, I used my own personal memories of certain events.

I chose to write the book from a third-person omniscient point of view so that readers could gain an intimate knowledge of each facet of the story. Some supposition was necessary in writing dialogue, though the interactions are all based on real conversations and contain many direct quotes.

Certain family members have requested to be omitted from the book for personal reasons, and I have honored those requests. Apart from these alterations, I have endeavored to maintain the factual and quintessential integrity of both the people and the events related herein.

The river moans and sighs
Swallows my memories
And spits back currents of regret
To drown careless swimmers
'Neath onion's shield
She sheds saltless tears
Howling at the moon

The bridge has long since collapsed
And now the river boasts her danger
For fear of drowning
I no longer cross to meet you
I stand on muddy banks waving
But can't see you clearly
My dreams take me down
To rocks and the cold current below
And I have lost myself
In the water's wailing drone
That lulls me to sleep.

—Julie Kerry

A Rip in Heaven

PROLOGUE

In 1991, I was a sixteen-year-old high-school kid living on the outskirts of the nation's capital and I thought I was invincible. I thought I was tough. Washington, D.C., was the homicide capital of the United States. Roughly one out of every twelve hundred people living there that year was murdered. Our mayor sat in jail after he and a prostitute were caught on video smoking crack in a motel room. But behind this curtain of corruption, D.C. was a shiny, whitewashed city whose streets were lined with world-famous museums, government buildings, and busloads of tourists sporting matching T-shirts and Kodak Discs. This city that was my home thrived in the face of scandal, drew its lifebreath from the mayhem.

So when my parents packed my brother, my sister, and me into the family van and drove us to Missouri for spring break, we brought our East Coast attitudes and our entirely imagined city-hardness with us. We drove through two days' worth of sunshiny American cornfields to get from Maryland to St. Louis, and we were sure we would die from a particularly Midwestern brand of boredom before we even crossed the Mississippi.

The hard truth that we were about to learn was that, in fact, we weren't tough kids at all. In reality, we were fairly sheltered, comfortably angst-ridden, suburban teenagers and we had no idea what "tough" was all about. We lived in the early nineties, during a time when youthful violence still had the ability to shock. Even in the homicide capital of the country, there was nothing that felt commonplace about violence, nothing normal about the metal detectors they began installing in our schools in an effort to quell that violence. We were still several years naïve of Columbine and the kind of terror that a tragedy of *that* magnitude can inspire.

As my family bumped our blue van westward through the heartland of America, we imagined we were leaving urban dangers behind us in the East. We never dreamed of the kind of brutality we were about to encounter, the kind of tragedy that would destroy our lives in a single night. D.C. had not prepared us for anything. Nothing could prepare us for this.

My name is Jeanine Cummins, but I've been called Tink since the day I was born, so that's the name that will appear in the following pages. This book is the true story of a violent crime. And it's the story of my family. By its very nature it is both a true crime and a memoir. I have spent countless hours researching the facts, the evidence, the transcripts, the court documents, the media coverage and the testimony that make up the library of data for this case. And I have made every possible effort to be fair in my portrayal of those facts. But I don't pretend for a moment to be unbiased. This is my *family*. There are victims' voices in this story that have been overlooked and overshadowed by louder, more sensational voices for more than a decade. Now it's our turn.

Julie and Robin Kerry are my cousins. Tom Cummins is my brother. This is *their* story.

CHAPTER ONE

The rickety card table was so heaped with plates and elbows that Tom Cummins was almost afraid to lift his fork and feed himself, afraid that even this slightest movement might threaten to upend the carefully arranged scene. On his right sat the dainty figure of his cousin Julie Kerry, who was devouring her steaming plate of chicken stir-fry without a single thought toward the sturdiness of the quivering table. On his left his two younger sisters, Tink and Kathy, shared their grandfather's organ bench and kicked each other repeatedly under the table, vying for precious knee room. Beside them, Julie's sister Robin was dwarfed in a large blue velvet recliner, and their younger sister Jamie was perched like a bird on the chair's arm. All five of the girls tucked into their plates with a vigor that threatened the trembling little table with every bite, but only Tom seemed concerned.

There was plenty of room at the dining room table for a couple of them to have eaten with the grown-ups, but nobody wanted to be left out of the fun at the kids' table. So they sacrificed elbow room and crowded in together. The six cousins were unusually quiet, maybe because of the good food they were eating, maybe because of the inhibiting presence of parents and grandparents in the adjoining room. More likely, though, their six minds were sharing a faint, unspoken melancholy at the thought of their imminent parting. They all knew that in twelve hours the Cummins siblings would be packed into their parents' van and rolling eastward back to Washington, D.C., leaving St. Louis and their Kerry cousins behind.

Nine-year-old Jamie had finished picking all of the chicken out of her stir-fry and was listlessly shoveling snow peas and broccoli around with her fork. She eyed Robin's plate and waited patiently. When Robin finished scarfing down all her veggies, she switched her plateful of chicken with Jamie's vegetables and the two sisters resumed eating. Tink and Kathy stifled a giggle at this exchange. Jamie and Robin's meat-and-veggie swap still hadn't lost its novelty to them. It was the kind of behavior that their own strict parents would never have allowed, and as such, it had that air of the forbidden that teenagers seem to find so funny.

Nineteen-year-old Robin was a strict vegetarian; Jamie hated vegetables. So the sisters had developed this foolproof system that never so much as raised an eyebrow in their all-girl household — their mother Ginna had always encouraged her daughters to embrace their individual ideals. But to Tink and Kathy, who were raised in a home where free thinking and authority-questioning were *not* actively cultivated habits, the food swap couldn't have been more foreign. In fact, Tink and Kathy found almost everything about their cousins to be a little exotic. The Kerry sisters were the kinds of people that the Cummins kids *wished* they could be.

Sixteen-year-old Tink absolutely idolized the twenty-year-old Julie for her poetry and her passion. The fact that Julie was a brilliant soccer player only furthered Tink's devotion to her; she was a striker — the same position Tink played. And Kathy, who was almost fifteen, similarly idolized Robin. Kathy had even tried vegetarianism a year or so previously, but Tink and Tom had teased her mercilessly, and her mother Kay had explained that, at least while she was preparing the dinners, Kathy would have to eat what was cooked — end of story. So Kathy restlessly obeyed, but she admired her older cousin for her independence and resolve.

Tom was the only male member of the little crew, and Julie was his best friend. It was a fact he was proud of, because Julie was cool in a way that Tom had always wanted to be. She made him laugh, she nourished his self-esteem, and she inspired him. Tom was a practical person, almost pessimistic in nature. Julie had taught him how to dream, how to nurture his ambitions. But he didn't really *know* any of this consciously; he just loved the way he felt around her. She made fun wherever she went. So Tom and Julie were confidantes with a bond so strong that it spilled over onto their siblings. It made all six of them feel like a part of some clandestine, impenetrable society. It was understandable that their last supper together was a gently somber and muted affair.

After the six plates of chicken stir-fry were emptied, rinsed, and stacked in the dishwasher, the six cousins retreated to the game room in the basement while the grown-ups sipped coffee and talked. Downstairs in the musty basement, Simon and Garfunkel was the music of choice and gin rummy was the game. The green-felt-covered game table was as crowded as their dinner table had been a few minutes before. But again, no one seemed to mind. Tink was in dealer persona, complete with green visor and pretzel-stick cigar — and the stakes were high: plastic chips and bragging rights. Eventually, Ginna called down the steps to say that she was heading home and told Julie not to keep Jamie out too late. The games continued, and Tink doodled her name on Tom's arm in capital letters when she should have been keeping score. Ordinarily Tom would have smacked the ballpoint pen right out of her hand for writing on him, but tonight it somehow seemed to fit the atmosphere of the evening. He just laughed at her and shrugged her off as she tried to add a curlicue to the *K*.

After an hour or so, Jamie grew bored, Tom got tired of losing, and Robin was having a nicotine fit anyway, so the group made a collective decision to move the party to the front yard.

It was twilight now on Fair Acres Road. Tink and Kathy barefooted a soccer ball in the dewy grass while the others had a chicken fight — Julie on Tom's back and Jamie on Robin's. A few feet away, Julie's once-blue Chevy Chevette sat in the driveway, a rusty blot on the suburban landscape. Its rear end was completely plastered in bumper stickers, one of which proclaimed, RONALD REAGAN IS A LESBIAN. Gene, the father of the Cummins kids, hadn't found that one particularly amusing.

The six companions laughed and played in the dusky evening with a wantonness that teenagers rarely feel comfortable exhibiting. As was often the case, nine-year-old Jamie seemed to be more mature than anyone else in the group. Her wry sense of humor and easy demeanor made her seem eerily wise and grown-up — so much so, in fact, that her rare moments of childishness sometimes startled the others. But tonight, they *all* romped like children. Together they abandoned self-consciousness and embraced their last vestiges of childhood. So it was with heavy hearts that they brought their merriment to an end when Gene squeaked open the screen door and appeared on the front step. There was packing to do; there were showers to take; there was sleep to get. It was time for good-byes.

Robin threw her arms tragically around Tink and screamed, "Don't go, PLEASE don't go!"

This set off a stream of sarcasm and before long, all six of them were blubbering into each others' necks, "I'll miss you! I love you! I'll write every day!" while Gene stood rolling his eyes and shaking his head. There was a moment or two of authentic gravity and a couple of genuine (if well hidden) tears amidst the mess of sarcasm. And as they all wound down toward the inevitable separation, Julie and Robin suggested that they might make a summer trip out to Washington for a visit. Everyone perked up at the thought. And so, accompanied by a slew of smiles and waves, the three sisters scrambled into Julie's little clunker and buzzed away.

Gene ushered his three children into the house and assigned them to different tasks in preparation for the next day's journey. Tom waited until he was convinced that his two sisters were out of earshot and then asked his father for permission to go out that night. Gene shook his head; they had a long drive ahead of them tomorrow and he wanted everyone in bed early so they would be well rested in the morning. The last thing he wanted to deal with during a two-day road trip was a tired and grumpy teenager.

Tom grumbled bitterly for a few moments and then accepted defeat. "Well, I have to go call Julie anyway and tell her I can't go," he said, glaring at his father with an insolence that only a nineteen-year-old could achieve.

Gene shrugged, unmoved. "I guess you better go call her then," he replied.

Tom's plan to sneak out of the house and meet Julie secretly took shape almost accidentally. He had already managed to sneak out on one previous occasion that week, but he had really been hoping that his father would be reasonable this time. Still, Tom wasn't about to let Gene's refusal spoil the evening. So after a few minutes on the phone, he and Julie had established their secret plans.

Tom had been sleeping on the fold-down bed in the back of the van for most of the week. After spending one long, sleepless night on his grandmother's blue velvet couch, listening to his father snoring through the wood-paneled wall, Tom had convinced his parents that the most logical, most comfortable place for him to sleep would be the van-bed. After all, what was the point in having a van-bed if nobody was ever going to sleep in it? So all that week at bedtime, Tom had taken a house key and a van key, and retired to the driveway. Tonight, he would simply head up the street and wait for Julie at the corner instead.

As Tom replaced the earpiece carefully onto the cradle of the old rotary phone and swiveled around on Grandpa Art's basement bar stool, he came face-to-face with his sister Tink and knew instantly that his plans had been found out. After several minutes of whining and begging, Tink was about ready to give up her hopes of being invited along when Kathy ambled out of the bathroom, towel around head and toothbrush in mouth, to see what she was missing. Tink filled her in on the excitement, hoping for an ally in her arguments, while Tom nervously eyed the staircase and hissed at her to keep her voice down. Kathy returned to the bathroom to spit and when she came back, she started systematically pointing out flaws in the plan. The most obvious and discouraging problem was that Tink and Kathy were sharing the guest bedroom, which was directly across the hall from their light-sleeping grandparents. It would be nearly impossible for either or both of them to sneak out undetected. For Tom the task would be infinitely easier. In fact, he wouldn't really have to sneak *out* at all, he would merely have to sneak *away.* Eventually, Kathy's annoyingly sensible logic won her sister over, and Tink conceded. Besides, she didn't want to be a tagalong, she sniffed as she marched up the stairs, she wanted to be *asked* to go.

This scene was the perfect representation of the two Cummins sisters and their dispositions. Tink never thought about practicalities. She was the dreamer, the comedian, the center forward on her hockey and soccer teams, always seeking the spotlight and usually getting it. Kathy was the shyer and more sarcastic but braver character. She played goalie on both teams and she was more grounded and sensible than her slightly older sister. Tink was the aggressor; Kathy was the defender.

So the sisters wished their brother luck and went back to their assigned chores. Tink more grudgingly of course, pouting for a little while until she started to yawn amidst her folding and packing. Eventually, she even began to think that maybe bed wouldn't be such a bad end to the evening. Shortly everything was made ready for the morning's journey and the lights of the cozy home started to go out, one by one, as its occupants drifted to bed.

Meanwhile, Tom stalled in the basement bathroom. He brushed his teeth twice. He flossed. He brushed again and then looked at his watch. He sat nervously on the closed lid of the toilet, fully dressed and waiting for the sounds of wakefulness to cease above him. He flipped idly through his mother's *Ladies' Home Journal* and tried not to stare at his watch. He was usually the last one to bed, so his parents wouldn't be suspicious if they heard him going out to the van after everyone else was tucked in for the night. All the same, he was hoping the whole house would be asleep before it was time to go. When reading "How to Make the Perfect Bundt Cake" finally became too much for him, he closed the magazine, took one last look in the mirror, and switched off the bathroom light.

At eleven o'clock, Tom closed and locked the front door of his grandparents' brick house feeling a bit stealthy and silly. In the driveway the bright spotlight came on, illuminating the whole yard and, it seemed to Tom, half of the neighborhood. He studied the window of the room where his parents were sleeping. The curtains and shades were pulled tight. Nothing stirred. He approached the van and unlocked it, threw his backpack inside, waited a moment and then slammed the door. Unconsciously, he held his breath as he turned the corner of the van and walked quickly and quietly toward the street. As he arrived at the end of the driveway, he reached into his jacket pocket and drew out a package of cigarettes. He stopped a few minutes and stood at the end of the driveway, smoking and watching the house. If anyone inside was suspicious, they would follow him out now, in the next minute or two. The cigarette was a good alibi — he would much rather get caught smoking than sneaking out. But there wasn't so much as a peep from inside the house, so halfway through the cigarette, he turned on his heel and started walking into the chilly night, thinking how ridiculous it was that he was nineteen and he still felt so sly disobeying his father.

When Tom had asked his father's permission to go out earlier that night, he originally intended to go to Denny's — just for a coffee and a sociable chat with Julie and Robin. But now that he was out, he realized he had no time constraints. When Julie and Robin pulled up in the car that Tom had dubbed "the Hornet" thanks to the high-pitched, moped-like drone of its engine, the three cousins held a quick conference. Shouting over the loud buzz of the little car, they made the collective decision to complete the one item that had been neglected from that week's to-do list: they would go see the poem Julie and Robin had spraypainted on the deck of the Old Chain of Rocks Bridge. They would swing by, go for a moonlit walk, have a quick look at the poem, and *then* go to Denny's for that coffee.

It was fairly easy for Tom to talk himself out of his usual apprehension about such an idea. He told himself that his anxiety was unwarranted, that the Midwest was different from the East Coast, that they would be perfectly safe. After all, he was from Washington, D.C., and St. Louis, Missouri, was hardly competing as the murder capital of *anywhere*. Tom's was a fairly common misconception: St. Louis *had* somehow escaped the reputation it deserved. In 1991, people still thought of the city as the "Gateway to the West," a safe and friendly Mississippi River town. Somehow, the fact that St. Louis had the third-highest metropolitan murder rate in the country had gone largely unnoticed in the realm of public opinion. Certainly it wasn't a statistic that Tom, or even Julie or Robin, knew anything about.

So the atmosphere in the Hornet was excited and chatty. Julie and Robin were elated at the prospect of showing off their hand-iwork to their cousin. Tom was relieved and somewhat exhila-rated by his second home-escape of the week. The conversation, as usual, flipped from politics to religion to sex to music. The three friends changed topics as often and effortlessly as Julie changed lanes on I-70.

CHAPTER TWO

On that night, the fourth of April, 1991, Tom Cummins was nearing the final stages of a fairly major identity overhaul — pretty standard stuff for a nineteen-year-old. He was in transition from awkward high-school screwup to young dedicated fireman/professional. And to his mind, he had the girl seated to his left to thank for much of this change.

Before Julie came into his life, Tom could never have envisioned himself holding an animated intellectual discussion with two other intelligent people. Instead, the pre-Julie Tom would have sat moodily, probably rolling his eyes and shrugging his responses to any questions directed at him, not because he didn't have anything engaging to say, but because he didn't have the confidence to say it. It was thanks to Julie that now he spewed his views on everything from the movie *Dead Poets Society* to Mayor Barry's latest hijinks. He was sure Julie hadn't noticed his substantial personality change because, with her, he had always felt comfortable expressing himself. He wondered if she had any idea at all how much she'd helped him grow up.

Tom's journey through the American public-school system had been a long and arduous one. By the time he reached high school, he had pretty much embraced the version of himself that he saw through his teachers' eyes: lethargic, unresponsive Tom. But as he reached the middle of his teen years, his difficulties became a bit more complicated than some low grades and a lack of educational enthusiasm. Adolescence just didn't seem to agree with him. He was awkward and tongue-tied most of the time; he was embarrassed about being slightly overweight. In fact, he was embarrassed about most everything. And when his first real girlfriend dumped him to start going out with his best friend, he threw up a mighty wall of indifference.

He started hanging out with the punk crowd at school. He admired the girls with the shaved heads and the piercings. He became a die-hard Sex Pistols fan. He took up smoking with vigor. He bought blue hair mascara — but couldn't quite find the courage to wear it, so he ended up passing it on to Tink, who used it to paint her braids for cheerleading. He skipped class periodically, but only at times when he knew he'd get away with it. He tried everything he could, really, to fit in with the out crowd, but he could never quite seem to make it click.

It wasn't long before Tom started spinning stories and telling tales, sometimes to his friends in an effort to seem cool, other times to his parents to cover up the latest report card or a party he wasn't supposed to go to. He walked a fine line, but he seemed to know instinctively where that line was and he did not cross it. He knew the difference between what was regular adolescent disobedience and what was just plain *bad*. So he wasn't a lost cause. His teenage rebellions seemed to follow the same patterns that his schooling had: he screwed up just enough to cause his parents constant disappointment and worry, but never enough that they gave up on him. He really wasn't a bad kid, just a hearty underachiever.

For Gene, the relationship with his son was particularly frustrating. Like Tom, Gene was the eldest sibling in his family. But unlike Tom, Gene had developed a seriousness of purpose and sense of responsibility very early in life. He would never have *dreamed* of disobeying his father, and that fact lent an extra sting to Tom's growing impertinence. Gene couldn't understand his son, couldn't relate to his attitude, and had no patience for his irresponsibilities and juvenile delinquencies.

One night Tom missed his curfew by almost an hour, and when he finally did come home he was sleepy and reeked of peach schnapps. His father dismissed him to bed, agreeing to deal with him in the morning. At seven A.M. the following day, Gene crept into his son's bedroom and silently slipped a Tchaikovsky tape into his stereo. He cranked the volume all the way up, hit the play button, and yanked the quilt off the bed. Then he yelled at his son to peel himself off the ceiling and get dressed — hangover or no hangover, he was going to spend the day cleaning out the garage.

As the daily clashes on the home front escalated, Tom played the game, adopting the characteristics his parents expected of him. The cycle constantly refreshed itself: obnoxious teenager, angry parent; obnoxious teenager, angry parent. Things were looking bleak. And then one day, in Tom's sophomore year at Gaithersburg High, something remarkable happened.

As part of Gene's work as a Catholic deacon, he participated in a lot of community outreach programs. He ministered to the sick at the local hospital and he took communion to the elderly. Most recently, he had been offered the chaplaincy of the local fire department. Gene wholeheartedly embraced the opportunity; he loved the idea of attending to the people who so nobly and courageously gave of themselves to the community. So, with his usual quickness and efficiency, Gene took the required qualification classes and began a rather extensive volunteer program as the fire department's official chaplain. And the job came with an unexpected bonus: Gene impressed his son.

For the first time in years, Tom allowed the well-buried respect he had for his father to cautiously bubble up within him. The common ground that Gene had searched so fruitlessly for had finally, accidentally, appeared. Gene installed a fire radio next to the kitchen table and started carrying a portable radio and a pager. Kay hated the continuous squawking, but both father and son were immediately addicted. Tom tried to appear uninterested, but he silently suspected that his father's new activities were bordering on heroic. It became harder and harder for him to keep his curiosity at bay. Eventually, he started asking questions about the different codes and tones that the dispatchers used, about the different coverage areas, about the squads, and about Gene's own place in the rank and file. Gene answered all of his questions with muted excitement and then one day, as casually as he could, he invited Tom to come with him to the firehouse.

Tom was fifteen years old at the time and after one trip to Station 8 in Gaithersburg, he knew he had found his calling. His parents assumed that it was a phase, but they were so happy with the improvement in his attitude that they naturally encouraged the interest. The next semester when the school issued its course catalogue, Tom was ecstatic to find that they were offering a work-study program in conjunction with the county fire academy. Tom came home so excited that he talked his father into making a call to the sergeant that very night. The next day, Tom was enrolled in the program.

So during his junior and senior years Tom attended Gaithersburg High School in the mornings and then took a bus to the Montgomery County Fire Academy, where he spent his afternoons in qualification classes. His academic grades improved significantly, and at the fire academy Tom graduated near the top of his class.

As a graduation present, Kay and Gene bought Tom a round trip ticket to Florida, where he would spend a couple of weeks of the summer at the home his grandparents had retired to in Clearwater. Julie had just finished her freshman year of college and had decided to spend some time that summer in Florida as well. The two cousins hadn't seen each other in years. Gene and Kay had left their hometown of St. Louis many years earlier to travel where Gene's Navy career took them. Many of his eight siblings had followed suit, scattering across the country. But Julie's mother (and the oldest Cummins sibling after Gene), Ginna, had stayed in St. Louis to raise her family. Nevertheless, when the two cousins arrived at Grandpa Gene's and Grandma Maria's, the bond that grew up between them was instant. They had a couple of basic things in common: they both had an unusual, eclectic taste in music and in movies; they had a similar, offbeat sense of humor; they both liked beer and were too young to buy it. And although Julie didn't share Tom's academic difficulties, she did feel that she could relate to his awkwardness, his sense of not quite fitting in. Tom appreciated that and it amazed him. If she hadn't been his cousin, Tom would have thought she was too charismatic, too pretty and intelligent, to understand what it was like to be him. But he recognized that, in her own way, Julie was really different too. And for the first time, it dawned on him that being different, being a little bit weird, might just be a good thing.

The two cousins went to the beach every day and became reg-ulars at a dive bar where they sipped non-alcoholic cocktails and watched the volleyball players. Their friendship evolved rapidly, changing planes with each new conversation. They shared inti-mate secrets and worked on their tans. They discussed poetry and Julie proudly recited some of her work. Tom confided his hum-ble firefighting ambitions to her and she buoyed him. They dis-cussed their shared family — Julie detailing a colorful history of growing up in close proximity to their grandparents and the rest of their cousins. Tom imagined himself somewhere in each of the scenes she described. They learned about themselves from each other. Tom's own family became more real to him in Julie's words, and in return for that gift, Tom provided her with an outlet. They discussed issues from religion to ecology to politics to marriage. They *debated*. But they never argued. Julie even once joked that, in Zimbabwe, it was legal for first cousins to get married.

On their last night of that summer together they stayed out late and didn't come home until the house was thick with sleep. Tom silently steered his cousin onto the back patio and retrieved an old Tupperware dish from the garbage to serve as a makeshift ashtray. They sat at the deck table and matched the fireflies flicker for flicker with their Marlboro Lights until they had filled the Tupperware twice. They talked about everything, confiding in each other their darkest problems, their most terrifying closet-skeletons. They exchanged smiles and tears with their secrets. The first rays of dawn were glowing back to them on the still surface of their grandparents' pool when they finally lugged themselves inside and fell asleep.

In Tom's life, that week had been a crucial bridge between adolescence and adulthood. It had been a continuation of his coming of age and coming to terms with himself as a person. Through Julie, his family had gained an importance that week that would stay with him and continue to grow. When he left for home, he felt like a grown-up, full of a refreshing maturity and perspective. But as his train headed north out of Florida, he looked south from his window seat and wept like a child.

What the cousins had built that week was a friendship that would remain a constant source of strength and rejuvenation for them both. They began to exchange letters and phone calls on a regular basis. Julie encouraged and calmed her panicky cousin during his struggle through the county fire department's fiercely competitive application process and his subsequent hellish rookie year. They talked about all the problems of their young lives. And although the topics were common, these weren't trivial discussions — these details were the only threads they had to work with, and they stitched their lives from them. In her cards and letters she sent him poetry and song lyrics:

> . . . *Today I was listening to 'Til Tuesday and couldn't help*
> *thinking of you:*
> *Well so long and sorry, darling*
> *I was counting to forever*
> *I never even got to ten*
> *So long and sorry, darling*
> *When we found a rip in heaven*
> *We should have ascended then . . .*

Tom's birthday is November second, but Julie sent his card in early October with this note:

> . . . *I just listened to New Order the other day, for the first time*
> *in months, and it sounded just as sweet and good and real as it did*
> *on a warm June evening with a friend whom I miss very much.*
> *Write me.*
>
> > *Kisses and Revolution,*
> > *Jules*

> *P.S. I know it's early for your birthday, but I usually procrastinate*
> *until it's too late, so I decided to send it now while it was fresh on*
> *my mind.*

So as Tom looked over at his cousin beside him in the Hornet that night, April 4, 1991, he felt an all-encompassing warmth and admiration for her. She was undoubtedly his favorite person in the world; he felt proud to know her. And he felt pleased with himself now too. Because thanks to Julie, he was learning to recognize the good traits in himself. He felt pride in his work. He no longer felt shy or silly about his intelligence — in fact he was beginning to actually like articulating his points and sounding clever. And to top it all off, despite all the years of bickering and the gulf of differing opinions that still existed between them, his parents were finally and utterly proud of him. He had an inkling that somehow, all was right in his world. His metamorphosis was nearing its completion. And if all went according to plan, it looked as if he would emerge from this formerly suffocating, uncomfortable cocoon of adolescence as a happy and healthy young man.

So far the week in St. Louis had been a wonderful vacation, and Julie was just the remedy Tom had needed to keep him going. One evening earlier in the week they had downed several cups of coffee and then, hyped up on caffeine, driven to Lacledes Landing within view of the Arch in downtown St. Louis, and perched themselves on the hood of the near-dead Chevy. They went there because it was the happening place in town — a row of bars where the young twenties set hung out. But they were too young to get in anywhere. So instead they just roosted on the hood of the car, feeling the warm engine through the seats of their blue jeans, and watching the glowing windows of the pubs enviously. Inevitably, Julie turned the topic of conversation to "the sociological ramifications of living in a country that will gladly send an eighteen-year-old off to war, but won't serve him a parting glass on his way to the slaughter." Perhaps it was their environment — the injustice of watching people just a couple of years older than they were drinking and being merry. Or maybe it was just Julie's nature to take up everything around her and shape it into a lively, interesting, and important topic of serious discussion. Either way, these constant chats, these daily deep discussions were the lifeblood of their friendship. So the two friends buried themselves in dialogue while the Mississippi hummed its low song a hundred yards away, accompanied by the music of a hundred clinking glasses throughout Lacledes Landing.

★   ★   ★

At barely over five feet tall and 105 pounds of raw energy, Julie Kerry was busy unfolding into her adulthood alongside her cousin Tom. Her head was covered in a mass of dark, shiny ringlets that hung over her big hazel eyes. This was her trademark look and it hadn't changed much in all the years since Ginna had given up wrestling it into pigtails. Julie had made a few brief childhood attempts at taming the unruly curls, but as she had grown up, she had learned to live with (and maybe even like) her floppy locks.

Julie was a natural leader, inspired even from childhood to seek out and create mischief. She had a strong sense of justice and was never shy about speaking her mind. But she was also prone to spells of pensive quiet. Julie was riddled with inherent contradictions, chock-full of anomalies. She often said, "If I don't look in the mirror, I can go around thinking I'm gorgeous when I'm not." It was that modesty that made her all the more electric.

As an English major at the University of Missouri at St. Louis, Julie was having a full-blown love affair with words. Her poetry was her passion; it helped her to interpret her life, to put things in perspective. She wrote this piece, "Selling Manhattan," for her Native American literature class at UMSL, using what she had learned about the culture and incorporating her own wry wit:

> sure we sold it to them
> biggest scam of the century
> imagine the fools
> thinking they could contain
> the earth
> hold it in their hands
> like gold coins
> thinking they could engrave
> their names across the land

they must have been new
in town
or tourists maybe
we laughed about it afterwards
surprised they didn't ask
to buy the sky too
we would have sold it
to them
could have made a real
killing

Julie was serious about her poetry and her studies, but her friends, including Tom, were equally important to her. They were an outlet for her, an opportunity to put her seriousness and her studies aside and act like a goofy kid sometimes.

For lunch one day in St. Louis, she and Tom went to a shady little sidewalk cafe with plastic furniture, potted trees, and umbrellas over the tables. Tom ordered a triple club sandwich with extra mayo and french fries and Julie had the same. An impossibly Midwestern waitress served them with a smile and a "Y'all enjoy 'em now." They ate and watched the people go by without a care in the world.

A few minutes passed at the table in relative silence, the smacking of lips and slurping of Cokes taking precedence. Julie looked at Tom, who sat with a french fry in one hand and his huge sandwich in the other, and failed to stifle a laugh.

"What?" Tom asked, only mildly defensive.

She covered her mouth with one hand, then thought better of it and showed him her chewed-up food. When she regained her composure, she sipped from her bendy-straw and cleared her throat.

"Our manners," Julie laughed. "You'd think we were raised by wolves."

Tom looked down at himself in his sweat-stained T-shirt and ratty sandals, posture that would make any schoolteacher cringe, mouth stuffed with food and still chewing while he talked. Julie for her part was slumped so far over her plate that her shoulders were almost touching the table. They had both devoured most of their food in under five minutes. And their two cigarettes burnt completely to soot in the little glass ashtray between them. They hadn't even bothered putting them out when the food arrived. So Tom saw her point. And he showed her his own chewed-up food before he swallowed.

But of all of Julie's most valued companions, there was no one whose friendship she treasured more than her sister Robin's. According to Julie, she and Robin had their fair share of typical sisterly aggravations — the odd argument over whose turn it was to do the dishes, or who had used the last square of toilet paper and hadn't replaced the roll. But the outstanding feature of their relationship was that, even in their cantankerous late teens, they recognized and celebrated their similarities, their common interests. Robin shared Julie's love of music and poetry, her sponge-like intellect, and her wit. But it was their shared sense of justice, their passionate activism, that distinguished their lives from the norm. Ginna's friends always marveled at how well the two sisters got along, but Ginna couldn't imagine them any other way. Julie and Robin were best friends, and they spent hours talking, hatching their plans to save the world.

At Christmastime the year before, Julie had read an article in *The St. Louis-Post Dispatch* about the one hundred neediest families in St. Louis and decided that they needed to adopt one of these families for the holidays.

"I'm sorry, honey, but we don't have three cents to spare," Ginna responded when Julie brought up the idea. "I think somebody needs to adopt *us.*"

But Julie and Robin wouldn't let the idea drop. They persisted until their mom gave in, but even as Ginna agreed, she wondered how they would ever come up with the money. When Julie came home the next night and announced that she had adopted *two* families, Ginna threw up her hands in despair. But her anxiety was short-lived. Within days, Julie and Robin had petitioned everyone they knew and raised six hundred dollars. Ginna was absolutely overcome with pride as she helped her daughters deliver five carloads of necessities and Christmas gifts to their two adopted needy families.

Robin was tiny like her sisters, just clear of five feet and not more than a hundred pounds soaking wet. And she was strikingly pretty, but she rebelled violently against anything "cute." She had beautiful high cheekbones and large, darting eyes. Despite her unaffected beauty, she always insisted that Julie was "the pretty one." She had an infectious smile and her hair (at least for the first couple of months of 1991) was straight and shiny and hung in natural-colored chestnut wisps to her shoulders, with the exception of one long tiny braid which came from behind her right ear. It was no more than an eighth of an inch thick, the tip was dyed black, and it hung almost to her waist. That braid was the only section of her hair that remained constantly unchanged. To Robin it was not just a braid — it was an anchor that connected her to her past and her future.

Robin was a nineteen-year-old freshman at the University of Missouri at St. Louis. Just as she had done all her life, she was following in Julie's footsteps — just close enough behind to adopt her sister's good qualities and just far enough behind to command her own unique persona. Robin was bright and defiant. She watched everything Julie did, chose the qualities she liked best, and made them her own. Julie was her mentor, her muse, but Robin was one hundred percent her own person. She was the shier of the two sisters, but her quiet demeanor masked an ever-active wellspring of activity in the mind. She was witty, sarcastic, and passionate.

Her bedroom was a haven of self-expression and artistry. She proudly displayed her sculptures around her room, and sketches of dragons and fairies filled the margins of her notebooks and textbooks. She surrounded herself with things of beauty, things that reflected the abundant goodness she saw in the world. Robin was a believer in karma and in the inherent decency of humanity, and these beliefs outweighed her natural tendency toward cynicism. "Give me a place to stand and I will move the world" was one of the sayings she had adopted from her sister Julie. And that is precisely what both sisters spent their time and energy doing.

Like Julie, Robin was more than active in the community; she was hyperactive. Whenever the two sisters had time off from class, they trekked to the Salvation Army's Family Haven in downtown St. Louis where they tutored first graders, helping them with their homework. They also did volunteer work with Amnesty International and Greenpeace.

One year, early in her elementary-school education, Robin participated in her first food drive, and the experience changed her. The concept of giving food to people who couldn't afford to eat made perfect sense to her. So while the other kids went home to raid their parents' pantries for old cans of beans and the soups they didn't like, Robin went straight to her piggy bank. She cracked it open, took the seven dollars in nickels, dimes, and quarters to Ginna, and asked for a ride to the grocery store. On the way, Robin asked Ginna for advice about what foods to buy. Ginna thought it over and explained that tuna fish and peanut butter would be good choices because they were high in protein, and most people wouldn't contribute these kinds of expensive items. When they arrived at the grocery store, Robin picked out as many cans of tuna fish and jars of peanut butter as her seven dollars would buy. From that year forward the annual food drive became a downright campaign with Robin.

But she wasn't a blind idealist. On the contrary, her natural pessimism was what really triggered her activism. She believed she had a *responsibility* to make a difference. Her reasoning was: if she wasn't going to make an effort to help, who else was going to do it? Robin was a natural fighter — fiercely protective of the things and people she loved — and nothing could dissuade her from standing up for a worthy cause. She believed she could do anything if she tried hard enough.

Robin was only fifteen years old when her parents divorced and Ginna headed back into the workforce after an eighteen-year stint as a stay-at-home mom. Money was tight and Robin was determined to contribute. So she started saving the money she made at her after-school job, and on Christmas morning she gave her mom a teddy bear with a note stuck to his paw that read "The *Bear*er of this note is entitled to the payment of any two bills of choice." Robin knew that paying even one of those bills would wipe out her savings, but that wasn't about to stop her.

So her battles weren't strictly theoretical — Robin recognized the importance of action. One day, in between classes at Hazelwood East High School, she overheard the six-foot-something school bully threaten the class runt. It was an exchange she had witnessed a hundred times, but today she decided that enough was enough. She simply could not stand by while this jerk tormented the little guy day after day. She slammed her locker, marched over to the bully, and punched him in the jaw. She probably didn't do a lick of damage, but the bully straightened up, the runt got off the hook, and Robin earned herself a reputation for fearlessness.

Like Julie and their cousin Tom, Robin was at a crossroads in her life. She was maturing into a remarkable young woman of strong character and passion. Her life was a good and happy one and she valued her family. So when her Cummins cousins came to town for spring break, she spent as much time as she could with them. Julie and Tom were virtually inseparable that week, and she and Jamie had joined them whenever possible. She liked getting to know her cousins — they all got along so well. Tink had a sense of humor like Julie's, and Robin found her easy to laugh with. Kathy admired Robin, which made it easy for Robin to talk to her about her passions and her plans.

So this week in St. Louis had been a good one all around. The Cummins kids were having a great time staying with their mom's parents and catching up with their various cousins from both sides of the sprawling family. But most notably, Robin, Jamie, Tink, and Kathy had built their own friendships on the foundation of Tom's and Julie's. Tom even found his own sisters to be less irritating, almost interesting people when he saw them through the eyes of his cousins. So despite Tom's reluctance for the vacation to come to an end, despite having to return to work and leave his friend behind, he still couldn't stop smiling as he sat in the Hornet beside Julie that early April night. They talked about the things they had done and seen together that week. How they had meandered around downtown one evening and ended up sitting under the Arch looking at the riverboats on the Mississippi. Rush hour had passed and the damp air was cooling and darkening, the river breeze caressing their faces and moving Julie's curls in little tornadoes. They had stretched their legs out under the Arch and plucked at blades of grass, wondering how tiny they appeared to the late-lingering tourists who were still up inside the Arch, peering down at them. It was one of those rare moments of enjoyment for the very here and now, and both friends had sensed that a lifelong memory was in the making.

Julie had smiled from pure contentedness and noticed that her cousin was smiling too. She had breathed deeply and, although the McDonald's french-fry fumes overwhelmed the river's natural scent, Julie had imagined that she was inhaling the very breath of her city, her home. This glorious river was the lifeblood of her town, the river of Mark Twain and William Faulkner and T. S. Eliot. Its currents ran like veins through her consciousness and like sparks through her poetry.

The two cousins had shared a cigarette and watched the smaller boats drift by on the river beyond. That night was April 1 — three days ago now — and Julie had drawn a card out of the inside of her black leather jacket and handed it to Tom, making him promise not to read it until she dropped him off at home. He was deeply touched but not surprised by the gesture. Julie was always doing thoughtful little things like that for her friends.

When Julie had given him the card, Tom had no way of knowing what the next few days had in store for him, or how beautiful and poignant it would seem when he read it again a few weeks later. But when he opened the card before he went to sleep that evening, this is what he found on the front:

We are not lovers
Because of the love we make
But the love we have

We are not friends
Because of the laughs we spend
But the tears we save

I don't want to be near you
For the thoughts we share
But the words we never have to speak

I will never miss you
Because of what we do
But what we are together
      — Nikki Giovanni

Inside, Julie's handwritten inscription read:

1 April, 1991

Tom,

> *I love you — Don't ever forget that, no matter where you are, or how much time passes between us. I couldn't forget you in a million years. Remember me.*

> *Kisses and Revolution,*
> *Jules*

A few miles north of the McDonald's Riverboat, just around a particularly sharp bend in the river, the Old Chain of Rocks Bridge arose from the water. The majestic Mississippi was reduced to insignificance in the presence of the old bridge. The water lapped timidly around the bridge's stalwart ankles, concealing the wreck and tumble deep below the surface.

Perhaps Julie was drawn to the old bridge because, like her, it was steeped in contradictions. It was a place where some people came seeking peace and serenity and others came seeking thrills and danger. It was a place of public solitude, of dilapidated grandeur, of terrible beauty. A place where the carefully painted words of her graffiti were surrounded on all sides by the tangled lines of nature — the dense trees, the gnarled vines, the winding riverbank. It was a place that spoke to her passions, that inspired her. She loved that old bridge with her whole heart and soul, and the poet in her recognized that at this precise moment in time, it probably represented more to her than it ever would again. For she was at a bridge in her own life. She was crossing over from childhood to adulthood, building her future and choosing her

battles. She wanted to share this special place and all of its implications with her cousin before their week together was over.

Julie pulled her little blue car to a stop on Riverview Drive.
She had gotten her wish — she and Robin were here to show
Tom the beloved old bridge and their poem.

CHAPTER THREE

Earlier that evening, forty miles outside the city in Wentzville, Missouri, twenty-three-year-old Marlin Gray had climbed behind the wheel of his girlfriend's Chevrolet Citation. At six-foot-four and over 200 pounds, he more than filled the driver seat of the little white car. He had smooth, deep-brown skin, big eyes, and straight, white teeth. A strong jawline and chiseled chin finished the aristocratic effect. Gray was a head-turner.

In the passenger seat beside him, fifteen-year-old Daniel Winfrey could have been his photonegative. Winfrey was an awkward, scrawny kid who hadn't quite finished growing into himself. In fact, at about five-foot-six and 120 pounds, he had barely started the job. He had pale skin, shoulder-length dirty-blond hair, and acne. Despite his current teenage awkwardness, he wasn't a bad-looking guy.

Winfrey had moved with his father, Donald Winfrey, to Linda Lane in Wentzville only three weeks earlier. He was a freshman at Wentzville High School and an average to below-average student, but his worst school-related problem was skipping class. Everyone described him as a polite and respectful young man both at home and at school, but he was easily bored, the kind of person who could be convinced to try just about anything once.

Winfrey and Gray hadn't known each other long — only a few weeks, in fact — but they talked and laughed like old friends. Perhaps Winfrey's initial attraction to Gray had something to do with the fact that his older friend was able and willing to provide alcohol and drugs. But beyond that, Gray had always had an easy time initiating and fostering relationships, and his burgeoning friendship with Winfrey was no exception. After all, Gray had the qualities of a leader and he was the life of the party wherever he went. Girls giggled at his jokes and guys sought his advice.

But there were a lot of things that Daniel Winfrey didn't know about his new companion — things that Gray tried his best to hide from everyone, including himself. At Winfrey's age, Gray had been small in stature and awkward too, so he had developed a cunning that made up for his size disadvantage. That cunning, combined with the fact that he was the beloved youngest of six children — the baby of the family — meant that he was used to getting his way.

By the time he was eighteen, Gray had begun to construct, in his own mind, an image of himself that he liked. Whenever that image didn't quite correspond with reality, Gray simply altered the reality to suit him. And he was frighteningly good at this deception. He was a gifted man in many ways: extremely intelligent, articulate, persuasive, charismatic, and funny, with great people skills — a natural performer. And everyone around him believed in the act. As far as his friends were concerned, Gray wasn't just a casual weekend member of the Army Reserves, he was a soldier who had heroically served his country. And he wasn't an informant who turned in a friend to save his own butt, but rather "a drug operative who worked with a MAG unit, helping to set up stings and clean up our streets."

His girlfriend Eva was a pretty young girl — tall, slim, and unassuming, with long shiny brown hair and a wan face. She was one of Gray's most ardent admirers. She was also his meal ticket.

Gray's diverse interests didn't include anything that earned a paycheck. He was content to hang out with his friends, driving around in Eva's car while she worked, or relaxing at the friend's house where the couple was currently living.

On the evening of April 4, Gray dropped Eva at a friend's house in Wentzville, telling her he was going to run a few quick errands and he would come back for her in an hour or two. Gray didn't really have anything pressing on his agenda. He had a few friends to see, but really he just wanted a few hours alone with the car, to relax and go for a spin. When he spotted Winfrey on the street not long after he had dropped Eva off, he invited his friend into the car and the two of them set off.

It was a clear day, warmer than usual for early April, the kind of weather when people finally shed their winter coats to go looking for springtime adventures. Gray and Winfrey were bored with the Wentzville routine, with their girlfriends and the same old scene. They wanted to do something different, so they rolled the windows in the Citation all the way down and started driving. When Gray stopped at a gas station for cigarettes, Winfrey stayed in the car. He was too young to buy smokes and he didn't want to arouse questions from behind the counter. Winfrey had been hanging around the neighborhood with Gray since he and his father had moved in a few weeks earlier, but this was their first outing together and he was excited — he didn't want to do anything to jeopardize the evening. The duo headed east on I-70, aiming for Northwoods in St. Louis, with a vague notion of tracking down Gray's old friend Reginald Clemons.

It was just about six o'clock when the oddly matched pair pulled up at Clemons's home. Clemons and Gray had met when they lived in the same neighborhood years before and they'd been friends ever since. Clemons was a shy and quiet young man of nineteen. He was of medium height with a trim build, coal-black hair, and a neat black mustache. His entire appearance could be summed up in the word "tidy"— not at all unlike his life, really.

His parents, Vera and Reynolds Thomas, were both ordained ministers at a Christian church called the Life Victory Center, where Clemons had attended weekly services when he was young. Clemons's childhood had been stable and well balanced; the Thomases were devoted and active parents, loving but disciplined. His mother had married his stepfather when Clemons was just six years old, and Reynolds treated the children as if they were his own. The constant presence of a strong father figure from that young age had been a good influence on Clemons.

In response to their solid parenting, Clemons was an agreeable and respectful child. He had always been fascinated by mechanics and was always dissecting things so he could see how they operated, challenging himself to put them back in working order. When he was nine years old, he had taken apart his stepfather's watch, staying up all night to put it back together. When Reynolds woke up in the morning, the watch was there on his nightstand — as good as new.

That mechanical interest stayed with Clemons throughout his childhood and he aspired to own his own shop repairing lawnmowers, small engines, and motorcycles. But with no job and no capital, he began working from home after graduating from technical school. In March 1991, he ordered business cards for himself: REGINALD CLEMONS: SMALL ENGINE REPAIR.

Harold Whitener, the owner of a small tire and brake shop in Pine Lawn, became a kind of a mentor to Clemons, encouraging his young friend's ambitions. In Whitener's opinion, Clemons was a follower.

A *follower.*

Of all the words and stories that have been employed to describe Reginald Clemons over the years, that one is the most important. It is the key to understanding Clemons's psyche and the role he was about to play in a brutal and vicious crime.

Clemons was the kind of young man who could easily and wholeheartedly accept whatever environment he found himself in. Clemons's parents were good people, Christian people. They supplied their son with rules, with morals, with principles. And what did Clemons do? He followed those rules, adhered to those morals and principles. He grew up with good people, so he was good people. When Clemons's friends and neighbors called him "nice" and "quiet," they were right. He was nice because they were nice; he was quiet because he was unsure of himself. He preferred to imitate and mirror the qualities that surrounded him than dig deep to find out what qualities lay within his own person.

Unfortunately, the very characteristic that led him to embody the goodness that surrounded him also led him to embrace evil when he met it. He adapted to his environment. It's not an unusual phenomenon. It's why sitcom producers include laugh tracks in television programs. When people hear laughter, they laugh.

On the surface Clemons was probably the "nicest guy" among the four companions who were gathering that evening, the most respectful, well-mannered, on-the-right-track young man. But he was also, psychologically, the scariest. And he was treading a very dangerous line. He had surrounded himself with the wrong kind of people — people whose characteristics, when he adopted them as he inevitably would, could get him into a whole lot of trouble. People like Antonio Richardson.

Antonio Richardson was Clemons's sixteen-year-old cousin and, to put it mildly, Richardson was just plain bad news. Although Richardson had grown up just around the corner from Clemons, their childhoods could not have been more different.

Where Clemons had received love, discipline, and constant attention, Richardson had grown up in squalor and neglect.

Richardson was born in September 1974 to eighteen-year-old
Gwendolyn Williams. Richardson was Gwendolyn's second son,
and by the time he was a year and a half old, Gwendolyn had
three children in diapers. Gwendolyn was particularly ill-prepared
for the tasks of single motherhood. She had never finished high
school, and when she was employed (which was sporadically) her
job was a part-time gig at the local White Castle fast-food restaurant. She and her three boys lived in a dirty, one-bedroom,
AFDC-subsidized apartment on Edgewood Avenue. The major-
ity of their meals came by way of food stamps, and at bedtime
each night, the family shared two beds and a couch. Often the
three young boys were left alone in the apartment; Gwendolyn
repeatedly abandoned her sons for weeks on end.

Before he had dropped out of school, Richardson had been
every teacher's worst nightmare. His academic and social progress
were virtually nonexistent. In 1987, when he was twelve years
old, he stopped going to school altogether. He had no interest in
learning anything, he could barely read, and he was fed up with
his teachers' attempts to discipline him. He had been truant for
one month (about the same amount of time as his mother's most
recent abandonment) when a neighbor phoned the Division of
Family Services to report the squalid conditions in which
Richardson and his two brothers were living.

Richardson was re-enrolled in school and then suspended a
short time later for bringing a toy gun to class. His behavioral and
academic problems did not improve. He made his first appearance
before the juvenile court system at age thirteen on a theft charge.
Over the next two years, Richardson's life continued its sad, er-
ratic pattern of occasional schooling, frequent abandonment by
his mother, and constant troublemaking. By the age of fifteen,

Richardson had cultivated a fairly serious drug- and alcohol-abuse problem. In 1990 he was diagnosed as alcohol dependent and he began exhibiting the symptoms of lethargy, confusion, despondency, and stupor that are connected with alcoholic encephalopathy.

That year, the fifteen-year-old Richardson permanently dropped out of school and enrolled in the Job Corps. One year later, on the evening of April 4, 1991, Richardson's future looked as grim as his past, and he couldn't much tell the difference anyway. Spending time with Clemons was a comfort to him; his older and quieter cousin was a calming presence for the rambunctious and angry Richardson. For Richardson, Clemons's home, just around the corner from the cramped and dingy apartment where he had grown up, was like an oasis from another galaxy.

That evening, Richardson and Clemons were wrestling around like two kids on the living-room floor, with the television as background noise, when the doorbell rang. The two cousins, like everyone else in town, had spring fever. So when the two newcomers arrived at the house, they were a welcome diversion. Although Gray had never met Richardson, he still took it upon himself to make all necessary introductions.

The four young men fell in easily with each other, and their group dynamic established itself quickly. Outwardly, Gray was clearly the leader among them. He was the outspoken one, the one from whom all the others took their cues. But Clemons was also a few years older than the two other boys, and he exuded a certain quiet authority — more because of the age gap and his appearance than from confidence or any real leadership abilities. Authority was a role that Clemons wasn't used to, and it was largely a product of the others' imaginations. So while Gray was the mouthpiece, telling his fantastic stories and hatching his crazy schemes, the others glanced to the stable and composed figure of

Clemons for signs of approval before responding. For their part, the two younger boys got along well with each other, joking about girls and what a waste of time school was — the universal realities of teenage existence.

Gray suggested that they move their party out from under the watchful eyes of Clemons's family, and the other three readily agreed. Soon afterward, Gray's friend Mike and his wife Chrissy welcomed the makeshift party into their home; they enjoyed having company and almost always had a full house.

Clemons unwound visibly upon leaving his mother's home; although he was still quiet, when he did speak, his language was noticeably looser, less refined than it had been just a few minutes before, peppered with words he didn't use at home. Even his posture altered — now he sat slumped on the sofa, with a beer between his knees and one arm flung casually across the back of the couch.

While they watched hockey and drank beer, Winfrey remained the shiest of the group, perhaps because he was the smallest, the youngest, and the only white kid. Nonetheless, he felt comfortable with his new companions. Soon, any trace of his former timidity left him and, with the help of the beer and a little marijuana, it wasn't long before he was talking and joking with the others. He even joined one of the others in a game of darts.

Only Richardson appeared completely unaffected by their change of environment, and that was easily explained. He simply didn't possess the "good behavior" mode that the others had felt compelled to employ at Clemons's family home.

So the four companions wiled away most of the evening in Mike's and Chrissy's comfy little home on San Diego Drive. Gray spun stories and sang songs that he had made up or might have heard somewhere. He danced and passed a fresh joint around and did his best to entice a laugh whenever possible. But by eleven o'clock that evening, their hosts were growing tired and they started tossing out hints that it was time for the party to wind down.

Gray was reluctant to abandon the party just yet — he had other plans. Besides, the supply of beer and pot had yet to run short, so he suggested a late night trip to the Old Chain of Rocks Bridge. The two younger boys glanced at Clemons, who said nothing but nodded, almost imperceptibly. And the party was on.

CHAPTER FOUR

The Old Chain of Rocks Bridge first opened in 1929. Serving as the Mississippi River crossing, it was an integral part of America's fabled Route 66. Initially it was privately owned and operated as a toll bridge with a five-cent crossing fee, but it was later bought by the City of Madison, Illinois. The old bridge is a peculiar sight — its fifteen sections stretch to over a mile in length, but it's only twenty-four feet wide, with a curious twenty-two-degree bend in the middle. In 1968, the "new" Chain of Rocks Bridge opened, parallel to the old structure — a modern highway river span and one that was free to cross. The City of Madison had no choice but to shut the old bridge down.

Although it was never officially accredited as a landmark, the Old Chain of Rocks Bridge was widely recognized as one, and the City of Madison was loath to have it torn down. A couple of decades came and went while the old bridge stood silently straddling the Mississippi and gathering rust. Every couple of years, some politician would put forth an idea to renovate the old structure or tear it down for safety's sake, but the cost for any improvement was always prohibitive. Local affection for the old bridge, combined with the enormous price tag of demolishing it, kept it standing. By 1991 the bridge, though structurally sound,

was in a terrible state of disrepair, and it had become a favorite local hangout for teenagers and graffiti artists from both banks.

"I can't wait for you to see the poem," Julie whispered excit-
edly as she dropped her keys into the pocket of her jacket, hopping lightly from foot to foot. Her eyes sparkled in the moonlight
and her dimples seemed deepened by shadows.

"And now, folks," Robin announced in her most game-show-
hosterly voice, "I give you a poet of substantial local acclaim and
unprecedented talent. One whose works have been published in
countless literary journals to glowing reviews by all of academia.
My sister, the brilliant JULIE KERRY! A few words, please, Miss
Kerry."

Julie bowed deeply from the waist. "Why, thank you for that
moving introduction, dahling," she drawled, cooling herself with
an invisible fan. "I just want to say, to all my admirers out there,
that of all my celebrated works, the piece we are about to view is
undoubtedly my favorite, my crowning glory, my pièce de résis-
tance . . ."

"You're a piece of something, all right," Tom retorted. "Can
we just go look at it and get outta here? This place is creepy. How
do we get in anyway?"

There was no traffic on the road now and it was entirely quiet
as Tom studied the treeline. He still saw no visible evidence of the
river, but he thought he could sense it from the dampness in the air.

"Okay," Julie relented, undeterred by Tom's lack of enthusiasm. She bounded over to the chain-link fence and quickly found
the place where she had gotten through so many times before.
There was a gaping hole, an entire section cut out of the fence
that the three of them walked through easily. On the other side,
Julie led them single-file down a well-worn path through the
trees toward the place where her poem shone, its big white letters
bright against the dark concrete deck of the old bridge. She ran

over the now-familiar words in her mind, repeating some of the phrases with whispering lips as she stomped her way through the light underbrush.

They came into the clearing suddenly and the moon opened up above them, lighting the cracked and broken concrete that stretched like the decaying bones of giants between them and the abandoned Old Chain of Rocks Bridge. Tom stopped dead in his tracks, causing Robin to stumble into his back. He willed himself to move forward but he felt stuck, mesmerized by the menacing old bridge that loomed up before him. The massive steel structure was wild with leaves, and the undergrowth near the base was dense and uninviting. A few enormous hanging vines dangled from the top of the bridge's skeleton, and they shifted and swayed eerily in the darkness.

"What's the matter? You're not scared, are you?" Julie teased.

"Course not. Let's go," Tom replied, finding his machismo.

The Mississippi was no longer quiet as the three companions drew near the bridge. It made its rushy music as they went forward, and Tom relaxed a bit, enjoying the conversation and the walk. The two sisters and their cousin laughed and joked as they strolled along together, now three abreast in the moonlight, passing a fresh cigarette among them.

Less than a mile away, Gray, Clemons, Richardson, and Winfrey were nearing the Illinois end of the bridge. They had walked the length of the aged structure, pausing now and again to examine the graffiti. Gray was in a particularly intense mood, almost giddy, like a big kid — St. Louis was his playground and this old bridge was his jungle gym. As they neared the Illinois end, they noticed a campfire on the bank below and realized how far they had wandered. Someone suggested they turn back, so they about-faced and headed toward the Missouri end, toward Julie and Robin and Tom.

As Robin's little black ankle boots took their first resounding steps onto the Old Chain of Rocks Bridge at a couple of minutes before midnight on April 4, 1991, they were accompanied on the right by the petite boots of her sister Julie, and on the left by the dilapidated Nike hightops of her cousin Tom. For a few minutes, the only sounds hanging in the night air were their own footsteps and the low echo of the traffic from the parallel bridge, which they could see — well lit, eighteen hundred feet north of where they now strolled. Tom had grown nervous again when Julie warned him to watch out for the uncovered manholes in the surface of the scarred roadway.

"We wouldn't want you to fall through now," she joked, and Tom tried to join her in a smile.

His eyes were working overtime, constantly scanning the ground in front of him before each careful step. He muttered curses under his breath and wished aloud that they had brought a flashlight. Julie and Robin were used to walking here though, and their nerves and footsteps were unwavering. So they spent their energies on searching the visible surfaces for new and interesting graffiti.

Julie thought of this bridge as a kind of eclectic collection of philosophies, a how-to book for life. And the best part, she thought, was that everyone could add their ideas, so it was an ever-changing, constantly updated handbook of collective wisdom. There was so much to learn and absorb here and she felt so honored, so empowered to have added a piece of her own poetry to the collection. She had a rough idea of the poem's location, but she had never measured it exactly, so as they approached the area, the three slowed their pace from leisurely to barely moving. Tom wished again for a flashlight as the three companions all drew their Bic cigarette lighters from interior pockets and leaned into the pavement with their tiny flames flickering in the river breeze.

They scanned the crowded, overlapping artwork for Julie's words, Tom and Julie taking baby steps, each with one hand on one knee and a lighter aloft. Robin got down on her hands and knees and scooted along beside them, carefully studying the artwork, enthralled by the bridge's spray-painted intricacies.

It was Julie who spotted the first trace of the poem — the peace symbol she always used when she signed her work glowed up at them like a smile in iridescent white. She beamed broadly and wordlessly, elbowing Tom to attention. She tugged at his sleeve and Robin scampered up from all fours to join them, lighting another cigarette to mark the occasion. Then the three friends silently and soberly marched the length of the shining white poem, reading by the light of the stars and the three cigarette lighters.

It was a Spike Lee–inspired poem about the universality of humanity, a plea for understanding and an end to racism. It was Julie's and Robin's wake-up call to their often lethargic, sometimes ignorant generation of peers. Tom had a lump in his throat when he finished reading and Julie, glimpsing her cousin's sentiment, let out a giant whoop and threw her arms out over the water, spinning, embracing the world. Julie knew that the poem wasn't her best in a literary sense, that it wasn't very scholarly. But it was one that very closely represented her life philosophy. Its simplicity, its accessibility were part of its beauty. Inclusion was the whole idea, and nobody who read this poem could miss the point. She knew that Tom really *got it,* and she felt elated.

The three cousins huddled close together there on the bridge with Julie's words under their feet and the wide St. Louis sky above them. Julie was in one of her poetic moods and she spoke dreamily about the bridge, not as a span between two masses of land, but rather as a communion of earth, water, and sky, and as a place of profound peace and contemplation. The moon was

hanging low in the sky over Illinois — a half moon, orange-red
in color. An autumn moon, Tom commented, and how odd that
it should hang so low and so orange at that time of year.

Robin was the first to hear the voices drawing near and she
hushed her sister and cousin. The three stopped in their tracks and
drew instinctively into the bridge's shadows. Julie and Robin had
never gotten in trouble for being here before, but legally they *were*
trespassing and none of them had any desire to spend a night in
jail. Tom's heart raced as he thought of his parents discovering
that he had sneaked out. A moment later Winfrey and Richardson came into view, followed closely by Clemons and Gray. The
three cousins were somewhat relieved at the sight of the four
strangers, but nevertheless they stayed quietly frozen. These four
guys were clearly not the police — they were just teenagers like
them, out to enjoy the fresh air and the night. As they sauntered
up, the tallest one, Gray, stuck his hand out toward Julie and
smiled.

Introductions were made in short order, Gray introducing himself as Marlin, from Wentzville. He asked the three cousins where
they were from. Tom replied, "Maryland," and the two sisters
said, "North County." Gray recommended that they continue out
toward the center of the bridge, and Richardson remarked that
the graffiti was really amazing out there. Someone had painted an
incredibly lifelike dragon right in the bridge's center. Robin's ears
perked up when she heard this and she nodded enthusiastically to
her sister. Winfrey and Richardson bummed cigarettes from the
girls while the two groups stood chatting. When Gray asked if
they had ever partied under the bridge, the three cousins exchanged puzzled glances. He then explained that it was possible to
drop through the uncovered manholes and walk along the bridge's
sub-deck beneath.

"You guys wanna join us underneath for a party?" Gray smiled.
"It's really cool." He turned to Tom while he explained fur-

ther. "You can go down there with your woman and be all alone and just watch the river go by," he finished with a knowing wink.

"I don't think so," Julie responded for the group. "Thanks anyway."

Gray shrugged. Tom and his cousins were friendly to the four young men — they had no reason not to be. But they weren't interested in spending the rest of their evening with them, and they weren't terribly impressed with Gray's apparent idea of fun. Gray sensed that he hadn't quite won over the three strangers, so as the conversation started to wind down, he made one last attempt to capture their interest. In one swift athletic movement, he scaled the bridge's railing and jumped over the side. Julie and Robin both rushed to the railing and leaned over, only to see Gray standing a few feet below. He waved up from the concrete pier before disappearing under the bridge's trelliswork and emerging a moment later from one of the open manholes nearby. Clemons duplicated Gray's antics, disappearing over the side and then popping his head up through the deck a few moments later like a gopher.

Julie and Robin laughed in spite of themselves, more out of relief than amusement, but Tom remained quiet, rolling his eyes. A few more pleasantries were exchanged before the guys said they were leaving and the two groups parted on friendly terms, shaking hands before turning away from each other. Richardson called back over his shoulder to say that he had lost a flashlight — if they found one, it was his.

Once the men were out of earshot, Robin muttered sarcastically that he had probably lost the flashlight while he was busy climbing around the framework of the bridge like a maniac. They laughed and Tom added, "If they think I'm climbing up there to look for it, they can think again." No one questioned Richardson's strange assumption that they would somehow be able to return his missing flashlight to him. Perhaps they didn't think they would really find it, or maybe it was just one of those details that didn't seem important at the time.

The four men headed toward the Missouri bank as the Kerry sisters and their cousin excused themselves and made their way farther out onto the bridge. The men slowed their pace as they approached the end of the bridge and their voices grew soft as they spoke to each other in conspiratorial tones.

"Let's go back and rob them," someone suggested in the darkness.

"Yeah." Gray nodded, smiling and rubbing his hands together. "I feel like hurting somebody," he said.

And it was as easy as that. In a matter of moments, their four minds were made up. The four separate paths that had led them to this moment in their lives all joined and locked together in an instant, with the nodding of their heads in the damp river air. There was no looking ahead and no looking back. The decision the preacher's son, the hoodlum, the entertainer, and the kid made collectively at that moment would alter the course of their lives and others' forever. In a breath, the moment was gone and they moved forward with their plan, completely unconcerned about the horrors they were about to unleash.

Gray reached into his pocket and pulled out a handful of condoms. He handed one each to Clemons and Richardson. Then he turned to Winfrey, proffering the condom to the reluctant fifteen-year-old. Winfrey shook his head timidly. He had agreed to the robbery and maybe a bit of confrontation, but that was as far as his adrenaline would take him. Gray wasn't one for tolerating dissension though, and his glare prompted Winfrey to accept the wrapped condom as it was pressed into his hand. Winfrey stuffed it hesitantly into his pocket and took a deep breath before the foursome set off in pursuit of the intended victims.

⋆   ⋆   ⋆

Approximately fifteen to twenty minutes later, the three cousins neared the far end of the bridge. They didn't realize how far they had come until they spotted the campfire on the bank. They gathered in a clump on the north side of the bridge and lined up quietly by the railing, not speaking — just watching the fire and the water below. The Illinois end of the bridge was not far from where they stood, a dark blotch, covered in the same un-inviting growth as the western end. The two mouths of the old bridge, east and west, were like twin gothic bookends, different in small ornamental ways, but matching in their spooky unwel-comeness.

Tom was more than happy to pause here, to go no farther toward the gaping portal on the black eastern bank. He concen-trated on the campfire below and the animated silhouettes of the people gathered around it. He and Julie and Robin passed a few minutes silently, drinking in the scenery.

It was peaceably quiet on the bridge where the three friends stood enjoying the low murmur of the Mississippi far below them. So they were startled when, once again, they heard voices and footsteps approaching. Robin snapped to attention and they turned their faces west toward Missouri, waiting anxiously for the people attached to those voices to appear. It was misty on the deck of the old bridge, but it wasn't an ordinary fog — over their heads, the stars winked sharply in the cloudless sky. This mist seemed ominous, rising up from the river below them, clinging to their ankles and thinning as it rose, making eye-level visibility hazy. Robin darted her eyes at Julie, looking to her barely older sister for reassurance.

"We're gonna get in trouble," Robin whispered, clutching her sister's arm. "It's gotta be the cops this time."

Julie wordlessly lifted the already-lit cigarette from between Tom's fingers and took a long drag while they waited. In her mind, Julie was already practicing her "I didn't really know we were trespassing" speech, complete with fluttering eyelashes. But she had never been terribly good at buttering people up, and she was really hoping there would be another way out of this.

When the faces of Gray and his three companions came into view through the nighttime mist, the three cousins heaved an audible sigh of relief. Tom was even beginning to feel a little bit empowered by the cycle of needless worry and sudden relief.

"It's just those four guys we met earlier," Julie said, playfully slapping her sister's arm. "Jeez, you scared the life outta me, Robin."

Robin giggled then too, the same tinkling laughter as her sister, and the three companions all relaxed their postures. As the four men drew closer, Antonio Richardson skipped to the edge of the railing and heaved himself up onto the strength of his arms, shouting a friendly greeting down to the people gathered at the campfire below. There was a brief and pleasant exchange from bank to bridge and back again. The campers issued an invitation to the now rather large party on the bridge. Tom, Robin, and Julie knew that they must have been included in the intended invitation, but they still felt like observers.

"We're on our way down," Richardson called. "You have enough extra sleeping bags?"

Someone at the campfire gave the thumbs-up and Richardson laughed, turning away from the railing and rejoining his friends.

As Tom, Robin, and Julie turned westward to head back to the waiting Hornet on the Missouri bank, their four newfound companions fell in step with them, chatting amicably. None of the four men offered an explanation as to why they were still on the bridge, why they hadn't left a half an hour ago as they had said they planned to. But the three cousins weren't nervous. All of their interactions so far had been friendly and uneventful.

It wasn't until the two groups neared the center of the old bridge, where the structure took a sharp bend high above the river, that Julie began to feel uneasy, to really notice for the first time the isolation of their situation. The four men were growing quieter and Julie had noticed the gathering silence. She drew a Marlboro Light out of her king-sized soft pack and lit it, the orange glow of her cupped lighter momentarily illuminating her face. At some point during the walk, Clemons and Winfrey had neatly pulled to the front of the group and Gray and Richardson had dropped to the rear.

While Julie had her hands cupped around her face to light her cigarette, she whispered to her cousin, "I don't like this, Tom. I think these guys are following us or something."

Robin was walking just ahead of them, a few feet off to the left, her hands jammed deep into the pockets of her old brown blazer as she examined the graffiti as best she could in the dim light. Tom's mind started running fast and he was trying not to panic. He hadn't seen any other cars where they had parked on Riverview Drive. Maybe these guys were waiting to steal their car and leave them stranded.

"What do you wanna do?" Julie whispered.

But Tom couldn't see any way out. All three of them successfully making a run for it seemed unfeasible. He shook his head.

"I dunno," he replied. "Just keep going, I guess, stay alert."

Hoping for a unified sense of safety in numbers Julie called Robin over and said something very quietly into her ear. Robin met her sister's gaze with big frightened eyes and nodded wordlessly. Several feet behind them, Gray noticed the furtive dialogue and sensed that now was the moment for action.

The cousins' growing sense of fear had not prepared them for the shocking violence of the attack when it began. In an instant there was a heavy hand on Tom's shoulder and that voice, the one they had been so relieved to hear on the Illinois end of the bridge, said in suddenly ominous tones, "Come here. I need to talk to you for a second."

The hand spun Tom around and he found himself looking up into the sneering face of Gray, who stood six inches taller than him. Gray pulled on Tom's upper arm, drawing him back toward the Illinois side, separating him from his cousins, who, he now realized, were also being seized.

Julie was knocked off balance as one of the men grabbed her from behind by her arms, and the cigarette fell from her grasp in a violent arc, leaving a shower of orange sparks in its wake. Julie and Robin were being dragged struggling and screaming away from their cousin Tom. Robin kicked at her assailant behind her but couldn't make contact. The world turned sideways as Tom found himself cheek-to-concrete, his face squashed against the cold deck of the bridge, with a shoe in the crook of his neck.

"Man, this is not your lucky day," the voice said, though Tom could no longer see the face it belonged to. "You're in trouble. You're in big trouble."

The man instructed Tom to lie perfectly still, said that he would shoot him in a heartbeat if he moved his head or tried to look around. Tom's mouth hung slightly open, but he was speechless. He made himself lie perfectly still despite his heart hammering in his squashed throat. A moment later, the foot was removed cautiously from his neck and Tom struggled to breathe deeply and remain still.

Another voice joined the one that now hovered over him. In the distance, Tom could hear the retreating screams of Julie and Robin, who were being dragged away. Both called out "Stop it!" and "Leave me alone, please don't hurt me." Tom was struck with horror at the realization of what was happening to his cousins. He jerked his head up just in time to see a silhouette forcing Julie down onto the bridge deck. Gray's foot was back on Tom's neck instantly.

"I'll shoot you, motherfucker!" Gray threatened again, pushing Tom's face back into the pavement with his foot. "You move your head again and I swear I'll shoot you, fat boy."

A few minutes later, Tom felt the boot release his neck, and in response he let his muscles go slack, resolving himself to be still. As he lay stretched out on the bridge with the giant Gray towering over him, Tom struggled for calm. *Just stay calm and think,* he said to himself. He had always believed that when people found themselves in situations like this, their only hope for survival was calm, smart thinking. But now he realized how difficult that was. He couldn't think — he could barely come to grips with the reality of what was happening. Only the pebbles embedded in his cheek convinced him that he wasn't caught in some nightmare.

One of the other men came to stand guard over him then, while Gray made his way toward the girls. Tom started to cry as he heard Julie continuing to struggle and scream. Robin had become eerily quiet.

"Do you wanna die?" he heard one of the men asking Julie. "Take your pants off or I'll throw you off this bridge. One. Two. Three."

Tom heard his cousin sobbing and his own shoulders started to heave as well. Whoever had come to relieve Gray from his guard duties now leaned in close to Tom's face, so close that Tom could feel hot breath and spittle as the voice spoke to him.

"I ain't never had the pleasure of poppin' somebody before," it said.

As the attack went on, Tom tried to concentrate on the sounds of the water, or the traffic on the adjacent bridge, anything to block out the muffled noises of his cousins' torture. His watchman changed once again and this time the newcomer was Winfrey, easy to recognize because he was the only white kid in the group. He made himself comfortable, sitting in the small of Tom's back and immediately asking if he had any money. Tom replied that he did and then Winfrey instructed him to empty his pockets very slowly. Tom removed the little bit of money he was carrying from one of the pockets of his nylon ski jacket and the keys to his grandfather's house from another. Winfrey instructed him to put the stuff on the ground in front of him and Tom complied. From his perch on Tom's back, Winfrey could easily feel the lump in Tom's back jeans pocket and decided to help himself to Tom's wallet. Upon opening the wallet, Winfrey panicked.

"What the hell is this fucking badge, man?" he demanded.

"I'm a fireman," Tom replied, as calmly as he could. "I'm a fireman. I'm not a cop."

This seemed to pacify Winfrey, who removed the badge from Tom's wallet and examined it in the moonlight before slipping it into his own pocket. He also pocketed Tom's driver's license and several photographs before sliding the now-empty wallet back into Tom's jeans. Winfrey seemed to be enjoying his role of sentinel, relishing the obvious fear he was inflicting.

"You know," he mused aloud, as he got up from his perch on Tom's back for a stretch, "it's a good thing my buddies aren't faggots or they'd probably fuck you too."

And then he laughed, almost as if he were expecting Tom to laugh with him at the funny joke he had made.

Tom clenched his jaw and his fists, but remained silent. He wouldn't take the bait — wouldn't dignify the monstrous remark with a reply. But despite his resolve to stay silent, bile rose up in Tom's throat and his stomach gave a violent spasm. For a moment he was afraid he would throw up — right there where he was lying with his face pressed into the cold bridge deck and Winfrey's foot on his back. But Tom remembered the threat of the gun and stayed frozen to the bridge, unmoving.

A few more minutes passed and then Tom heard voices, distant but clear, discussing whom to kill first. He heard footsteps as Clemons approached Tom and kicked him hard in the side without warning. Winfrey, now standing nearby, laughed at Tom's writhing and spluttering.

Clemons, encouraged by the audience, announced, "Man, that didn't hurt," and kicked again, harder. Four or five more kicks and Tom was not responding. He knew this was nothing compared to what Julie and Robin had just gone through. Clemons seemed to be getting annoyed at the lack of a suitable response from his victim. So he stopped the kicking and placed his foot instead on the back of Tom's head, crushing his face and lips into the concrete.

"I just fucked your girl," he said then, trying a more calculated approach to his torture. "How does that make you feel?"

The remark was cruel, designed to inflict the maximum pain, and it worked. Tom's stomach convulsed inside him again. But he refused to give Clemons the satisfaction he was seeking.

"They're my cousins," he replied stoically, unashamed of the tears that now trailed down his face.

"Oh, y'all cousins," Clemons drawled, laughing. Removing the foot from the back of Tom's head, he gave his victim one more kick for good measure, and ordered, "Get up."

Clemons and Winfrey got Tom into a standing position and walked him, bent double at the waist, toward where he had last seen his cousins. Tom hadn't heard a peep from either Julie or Robin in quite some time and he was now fearing the worst. The two men walked him about fifty feet down the bridge, toward the Missouri end, and then stopped abruptly. Because of his stooped posture, Tom could clearly see that they were now standing near one of the open manholes. The graffiti leading up to the manhole was a hopscotch board, with the gaping black mouth of a hole as the board's final jumping space. In light of the attacks, the inappropriate childlike quality of the artwork struck Tom bitterly and flooded him with a whole new wave of terror and grief. He still couldn't see any sign of his cousins.

One of the men now guarding Tom kicked him in the foot and asked him what kind of shoes he was wearing.

"Nike Airs," Tom replied.

"What size?"

"Ten and a half."

"You're a rich fat boy and you're gonna die."

Immediately there were hands, grappling at the back of his neck, pulling the collar of his coat up over his head, and forcing him to lie down again on the bridge deck. Tom recoiled and trembled all over, expecting a bullet, waiting for the loud bang that would signal his death. But there was no bang and in a moment he was lying on his stomach again. One of the hands was on the back of his now-hooded head.

"You know what?" a faceless voice declared. "I like you. I'm gonna let you live. I think I'm gonna let you live."

Tom could barely hear the voice and its sugary promises over the hammer of his own heart and the rush of his own blood in his ears. But now there was another voice and they argued. One reasoned that they definitely had to kill him and the other maintained that he had already promised the rich kid that he could live. Tom thought about the eighteen dollars he had given to Winfrey and wondered who this rich kid was they were talking about.

The debate raged above him and then Winfrey's voice was there again, closer and clearer, directed at Tom.

"So, do things like this happen in D.C.?"

Friendly. Tom could almost swear that, in his sick little way, this kid was actually just making conversation with him. The kid who had just helped rape his cousins. The kid who had just robbed him and was about to participate in his murder wanted to have a friendly chat first.

"Things like this don't happen to me," Tom responded. It was all he could think of to say.

"Things like this never happen to *me*," Winfrey replied sardonically. "Well, you're in St. Louis now. Welcome to the city." And Tom could actually hear the kid giggling.

The debate about Tom's death continued nearby but he wasn't listening. Then suddenly there was silence, and it was much louder and scarier than the argument had been. A heavy arm on the back of his shoulder and one or two of the four men maneuvered Tom toward the open manhole, with its demented hopscotch board. Tom could see a little bit through a gap in his coat and he was sitting now, feet dangling into the manhole, as one of the voices commanded him to go through onto the lower deck below. As he descended onto the catwalk, Tom could make out the tiny shivering figures of Julie and Robin, unclothed and lying side by side on the sub-deck below the manhole. Tears of relief started to his eyes and the lump in his throat was instantly massive and constricting, hindering his jagged breath. One of the voices instructed Tom to lie down with his cousins and he did so, grateful to be reunited with them.

There was just light enough to see and Tom could make out the shape of Julie stretched out to the right of her sister Robin, both lying on their backs with their eyes closed. Julie was chanting softly, almost inaudibly, a continuing stream of quiet and comforting words for her sister. A lullaby for Robin.

"It will all be over soon," she kept saying. "It's going to be okay."

Meanwhile, a few feet over their heads, the four assailants were discussing what to do next with their victims. The three cousins weren't listening to the hushed conversation above them — they were too numb and too ravaged to be really alert. Tom lay on his stomach with his right arm along the right side of Robin's little body. She was quivering and Tom was filled with a seething, helpless rage.

"Don't worry, Robin, it will all be over soon," Julie kept repeating. "It's going to be okay."

And Tom took comfort in Julie's encouraging words, although they were meant for her sister. Three or four minutes passed like that before the murmuring voices above them ceased. Clemons and Richardson appeared in shadow, dropping down from the manhole and landing with matching, echoey thuds on the catwalk near where the cousins lay huddled together.

"Get up," one of them commanded.

Tom and Julie both got up slowly. Between them, Robin remained flat on her back, unflinching — rigid with fear and loathing. She didn't move. The men remained a few feet away, cloaked in the bridge's shadowy darkness.

"Let's go. Out onto the concrete," Clemons ordered. Still Robin seemed not to hear. It was as if her ears had shut down, her mind unwilling to be an accomplice to any further victimization of her body.

Tom was out on the concrete now, and his mind was numb. His thoughts felt thick and heavy as he watched the bright brown water moving fast beneath him. It didn't seem that far to him — the distance looked survivable, and for the first time since this horrible ordeal had started, he began to feel that the end was in sight. He heard the two men above, still shouting at Robin to get up, and he turned to go back for her, determined to help her endure these last terrible minutes until it would all be over. But even as he turned, he felt slow, as if we were stuck in one of those terrible dreams where you try to scream but can't, try to run but can't.

As Tom faced the catwalk, Clemons grabbed Robin's little body and literally threw her down to the pier beside her cousin. She appeared tiny, almost weightless, as her body hurtled onto the concrete beside her cousin and she struggled to get to her feet. She staggered toward Tom and tenuously regained her balance beside him on the pier. All of her clothes were gone and she was barefoot, but she didn't even seem aware of these facts. She put both of her arms around her cousin's left elbow and pressed into his side for warmth, for comfort, for a brief moment's delivery from her terror.

He wrapped his arms around her and did his best to shelter her with his body. She stared despondently down at her little toes against the gritty concrete of the pier in the cold April moonlight. The cuts and scratches on her poor battered feet were the least of her injuries.

Behind her, Julie alit on the pier covered by nothing but the green plaid flannel shirt she had been wearing all day. She had aged decades since their family dinner just a few hours before, and Tom was stunned by the change in her. Automatically, Julie moved to her sister's side, cuddling into her, trying to protect and console her.

The three cousins lined up like that and waited, breathlessly, helplessly, for their sentence to be passed down from the shadows. Tom was the farthest out over the water, with Robin beside him, and then Julie closest to the catwalk. Clemons remained safely tucked up into the shadows of the sub-deck, and Richardson ventured only far enough out onto the pier to establish his presence. With one hand he still clung to the steel sub-deck of the bridge.

The three cousins held fast to each other and cooed quietly, but there were no real words exchanged between them, just the barely audible sounds of tenderness. It was Richardson's voice that barked at them to stop touching each other and face forward. The stripping of this last little comfort was almost too much for Robin to bear, and her body seemed to crumple under the weight of despair as she dropped Julie's right arm and Tom's left.

"And spread out!" Richardson added.

The three cousins shuffled apart from each other. And that's when it happened.

Despite the brutality of the last hour, the pushing hand came as a shock to all three of them. The terror on Julie's face as she plummeted over the edge of the precipice was a terrible sight to behold. Robin found herself unable to even cry out as she watched with utter horror as her sister fell. Tom let out a choking gasp and turned to face Richardson, who without a moment's hesitation struck Robin violently on the back and sent her stumbling forward. Screaming, she followed her sister into the muddy water below.

Tom's mouth hung open in silence as he stared at the smug-looking Richardson. Tom's eyes locked onto the merciless face that smirked down at him in the moonlight, the threat of the gun still glinting in those cold, pitiless eyes. Tom was dumbstruck, confused, terrified.

Richardson sneered as he spoke: "Jump, or . . ."

Tom didn't wait for the second choice, the gun. He didn't waste a split second. He didn't answer, didn't even breathe. He stepped soundlessly out over the water and into the air, falling, waiting for a bullet in the back of the head.

CHAPTER FIVE

The Mississippi River is the fourth longest river in the world. As a watershed, it drains about 41 percent of the continental United States, plus two Canadian provinces — that's roughly 1.25 million square miles. Every second, the mighty river spits out 2.3 million cubic feet of water into the Gulf of Mexico, carrying 159 million tons of sediment with it each year. At St. Louis, the old bridge's name, Chain of Rocks, refers to an actual string of huge boulders that jut up from the riverbed, stirring the rushing water into a tumultuous frenzy. Local legend claims that, during dry periods, Native Americans used to cross the river by hopping from boulder to boulder. Today, that same chain of rocks makes the St. Louis stretch of water one of the Mississippi's deadliest. In 1991, it was common knowledge among locals, including Julie and Robin Kerry, that the Chain of Rocks Bridge was a sure thing for local suicide-seekers.

Of course, Tom Cummins, the tourist from Washington, D.C., did not know this as he leapt wildly from a concrete pier, arms and legs flailing, on the north side of the Chain of Rocks Bridge. After he jumped and well before he hit the water, he had time enough to form the thought, *My God, this is a long way down.*

And then, a moment later, *Holy shit, I'm still falling — I still haven't hit yet.*

When he finally did hit the water, he went in feet first and immediately plunged deep into the river, hurtling toward its bed with astonishing speed. Underwater, he opened his eyes and spotted the faintly glowing green of the surface that seemed like miles above his head. He started swimming, executing an overhead pull and kicking with all his might, straining toward the elusive air above. When he broke the surface, he spent a moment just breathing, filling his aching lungs.

The first sight that struck him as he fought to stay afloat was the menacing giant of a bridge above him. The river was swift, moving much more powerfully than he had expected, and as Tom struggled to remove his coat, he realized that the current had already carried him underneath the bridge and he was looking at it from the south side. It was truly a massive beast, that bridge, and the reality of how far he had fallen both terrified and encouraged him. He would never have been able to jump if he had really known how high up he was. They would have had to shoot him.

There was debris everywhere in the water and, now that he had gotten his bearings and assured himself that he had survived, Tom began to scan the water for his cousins. There were logs and branches moving all around him with frightening speed, and in the dimness, as he bobbed up and down in the rapid current, he thought he glimpsed Robin a few feet off to his left. The current rolled up between them and when he looked again at the place where he'd seen her, she, or the log that resembled her, was gone. Julie appeared behind him then, about ten or fifteen feet off to his right, and he spotted her clearly, despite the clash of the rugged water around his face. He shouted to her, receiving a mouthful of dank river water for his efforts, but she heard him and turned her moon-white face toward him, terror-stricken in the frothy water.

"My God, where's Robin?" she screamed.

But Tom couldn't answer her. His efforts at treading water were becoming a losing battle. The current was just too strong for him. He had to get his sneakers off. He tried removing them with his feet and had no luck. When he used his arms, he began sinking. He had a moment of complete and abject panic, convinced that death would be the end result of what had happened to them tonight after all. He screamed as he sank and the water enveloped his head like a slick hood. Two or three feet below the surface he gave up on the sneakers and reached toward the light again. He breathed more calmly now, as if the few moments of panic had been exactly the emotional release he needed in order to find the strength to carry on. His mind became numb — there wasn't much room for a rational thought process here in the river. He had to rely on his body to do the work of survival, and it took every ounce of his physical strength just to stay afloat.

He was vaguely aware of Julie's presence some ten or fifteen feet away, and on that same subconscious plane of thought he supposed that Robin, too, was somewhere nearby, battling mightily against the strong current, obscured from his vision by distance or debris. He wrestled his way onto his back and allowed the current to carry him while he backstroked awkwardly, blindly bumping into debris as he cut his course through the water. All of his concentration was on staying afloat. He hadn't even considered getting to shore yet. In between the constant slap-slap of the water at his ears he heard Julie's voice, crying but not hysterical. It encouraged him. He heard his own voice responding to her.

"We have to *swim, swim, swim, swim, swim, swim!*" he bellowed, in a voice that sounded foreign and distant to his own ears. Between him and the Missouri shore, just past where he thought Julie was, he spotted one of the water-intake towers that belonged to the St. Louis Waterworks. He didn't know what it was, but it was a large structure, stable and well lit, and to his mind it symbolized safety. "Swim toward the lights, Julie! *Swim, swim, swim, swim, swim!*"

"I'm drowning, Tom!" Julie shouted her response with increasing hysteria.

Tom lifted his head out of the water as best he could and yelled at her, "We're not drowning. *You're not drowning.* We're going to get to shore. *Swim, Julie!*"

And she swam. After that, Tom did his best to keep a visual vigil, constantly scanning the water for her at those moments when he swelled on the high side of the fickle current. She was still struggling, getting closer to him as they flowed fast with the mighty river. She drew closer and closer to him as the minutes ticked by, but they didn't waste their energy on speech, their bodies requiring every ounce of strength for their battle with the water. They were only subliminally aware of each other's presence. And then Tom looked up and saw her closer than ever, approaching with startling velocity. In the quick glimpse he got of her eyes, he saw utter fatigue. Julie Kerry did not want to die, but her body was shutting down. Beaten by exhaustion, shock, and trauma, her little frame was giving up, refusing to swim any farther.

Making one last valiant effort to keep herself afloat, she lunged for her cousin Tom, encircling his neck with the strong grip of her tiny arms. They both went under. They sank rapidly, with the weight of two entwined bodies lumped together, unmoving. In a moment they were four or five feet below the surface and Tom had run out of air. He hadn't gotten a proper breath before they went under and he needed one now. He very nearly took one before he realized what he was doing. He knew that he was drowning, but still Julie clung to him, her little arms tense with effort and fear.

Tom wrangled his hands beneath the crooks of Julie's elbows where they stuck out at angles beside his shoulders. In one swift movement, he straightened his arms, pushing Julie up over his head toward the surface and releasing himself at the same time. They both bobbed to the surface.

"We *have* to keep swimming," he shouted over the din of the water. "*Swim, Julie!*"

And again, she swam. The current had swept some distance between the two cousins as soon as they resurfaced, but Tom knew that she was still nearby and he tried to keep her in sight as much as possible. He flipped onto his back again, scanning the water to check on Julie's weary progress whenever the current floated him high enough for visibility. She was clearly exhausted, but she continued to paddle along with the current. Despite the increasing heaviness in his limbs and the spinning thickness of his thoughts, Tom's voice still sounded strong, and he heard it as if outside of himself, encouraging Julie to swim. But even as he cheered his cousin on, Tom's own feet grew heavier in his sopping shoes while he slipped through the mighty river like a ragdoll in the current. About two or three minutes later, when Tom bobbed up and searched the spot that Julie had occupied in the water, she was gone. He became instantly hysterical. He thrashed and flapped savagely in the water, screaming her name, tears joining the river wetness on his face.

"*Julie!*" he cried. "Help us. Help us. *Please somebody help us.*"

Tom's brain still refused to believe that either of his cousins had drowned. He wouldn't even consider it a possibility. *We're just separated,* he kept telling himself. *We're bound to get separated in the roughness of this water.* And so he turned round and round in the water, hoping against hope to spot Julie again. But he sobbed as he turned, and with each moment that passed without his seeing his friend, his heart and his hopes sank toward the bottom of that river. He ceased to swim. He floated on his back, giving himself over to sobs and hysteria.

"I can't do this," he said aloud, and he noticed for the first time how cold he was. He shivered in the icy water and his entire body ached, rigid with the cold and the fear. "*I can't fucking do this!*" he said again.

He was exhausted and terrified and ready to give up. And as he lay floating with the current, body battered and mind ready to submit to the river, he began to experience the strange flashing images that were his life. Water covered his face now and he was drifting down and down slowly, but in his mind, quick and distinct, he saw the snapshots that, strung together, made up his life. First, the guys from his shift at work, out in front of the firehouse on a sunny day, hosing down the big trucks and having a laugh with each other. Next, his family eating a picnic barbecue in the backyard, Blarney the dog sniffing around hopefully for scraps. Next, Julie tickling Jamie on their living-room floor, textbooks and notebooks abandoned on the couch behind them. Tom was markedly absent from all of these images, and that fueled him. He loved his life. He loved his family and friends and he wasn't ready to die. His fingertips broke the surface on the first splash. He hadn't sunk very deep, and now he had a new rush of adrenaline. He was going to make it.

For the first time, then, Tom really studied his position in the water. He was still much closer to the Missouri bank, but it seemed like miles away, and the bridge was rapidly shrinking from his sight. He started to backstroke. He swam like that for what seemed like years. Every few minutes he looked toward the shore and lost hope all over again. He seemed to be making no progress whatsoever. He was sure that the bank was farther away now than it had been before, and he gave up. Then the snapshots would come back to him and he would splash and flail anew, determined to fight his way to the bank.

When he finally did reach the shoreline, nearly an hour after he first entered the water, he found himself facing a whole new obstacle. The bank was only about five or six feet high, but it was almost a straight vertical ascent from the water and Tom looked up at it with renewed despair. Debris had collected in a tangled mess by the bank and Tom had to pick his way among the slimy driftwood before facing his slippery uphill battle with the bank. He grappled with roots and reeds, slipping back into the water with a splash every time he chose an unfixed hold. It took him twenty minutes and several failed attempts before he finally succeeded in surmounting the slick bank. Once atop the muddy hill, he lay on his stomach with his face pillowed in the muck and he wept. It was the truest and purest exhaustion he had ever experienced and he gave himself over to it completely. When his brain kicked in again after those few blank moments, his first thoughts were of Julie and Robin.

I've got to get help, he thought. And he glanced behind him with a shudder at the steep bank and the rushing water beyond, *I've got to get them some help fast.*

And Tom pulled himself up to a standing position and started to make his way through the trees. He had broken his right hip in the fall, his body was generally bruised and battered, and he was in shock, but Tom didn't know any of this. And in the relative comfort of walking on dry land, he ceased to feel any pain at all or concern for his body. He tramped quickly through the dense trees, keeping the river at his back and making for where he thought he might find a road. His eyes were well adjusted to the light by this time, but his tired arms hung limply by his sides, so that as he walked the branches slapped and scratched at his wet and muddy face.

He emerged from the treeline after less than a hundred yards and found himself in a field. There were warehouses nearby, and a pond. He skirted the pond and discovered some railroad tracks with a fence to one side. He followed the tracks for several minutes until he found himself back at Riverview Drive, at the entrance to the St. Louis Waterworks plant. There were lights on the road, but no people and no cars. Tom paced lamely along the road, anxious to find people and help. Several minutes passed and a few cars drove by, their frightened drivers ignoring the desperate and muddy young man as he waved his arms frantically, jumping and shouting at them to stop. When a tractor trailer came into view on the road ahead, Tom walked out into the middle of the road, closed his eyes, and put his hands in the air above him. The truck driver slowed to a stop, blinking with curiosity at the muck-covered teenager in his headlights. Tom drew up gratefully to the driver's window and craned his neck at the man within. His mind spun, overfilled with thoughts and words. He realized that he had no idea what to say to this man.

"We need help," he began simply in a choked and tortured voice. "They raped my cousins. They threw us off the bridge. Please, they need help. We need help."

The man looked confounded and his mouth hung open in confusion or perhaps skepticism.

"All right, wait right here, I'll go get the police," he said.

Tom thanked him and then wandered to the side of the road to await the cavalry. As the truck's taillights disappeared from view and Tom found himself alone again in the silent moonlight, he realized suddenly that he was on Riverview Drive. That he was standing like a target on the side of Riverview Drive, just down the road from where those four men had probably parked their car. They could drive by at any minute, see that their work was incomplete, and finish him off with that bullet they had promised him earlier. In fact, if he hadn't been lucky, he might have inadvertently flagged them down earlier. His breath grew rapid with paranoia and he drew himself into the shadows of the fence, watching the road and shrinking with dismay from any passing headlights. He began to look around him for a more concealed place to hide until the police arrived. The grass was longish and damp with dew, but Tom was already soaked and glad for the cover, however insufficient. He crouched down low in the long grass under an oversized stop sign that had been fastened to the fence. He was several yards off the well-lit road and feeling safer now, tucked into the shadows of the fence-line.

Several minutes and cars passed as he hid there, and he began to wonder if the trucker had let him down, had just kept on driving to Tulsa or Albuquerque or wherever. So he watched out for another truck. When he saw one coming, he sprinted from his grassy hiding place and hurled his body into the beam of the oncoming headlights. He repeated his incredible tale to this second startled driver and the man responded kindly, asking Tom if he wanted to get in, drive with him to a phone. Tom explained that he was already waiting for the police and didn't think he should leave, so the driver said he would go straight to a phone and call for him. Tom thanked him and returned to the fence-line, finding the flat spot that his weight had already made in the wet grass and crouching into it once again.

After ensuring that Robin, Julie, and Tom had all plunged into the Mississippi, presumably to their deaths, Richardson rejoined Clemons on the catwalk and the two of them climbed up through the manhole onto the bridge deck. There they met Gray and Winfrey, who were waiting for them.

"I dumped them hard," Richardson announced gleefully, and looked to Gray for a congratulatory gesture. Gray smiled and nodded, patting Richardson on the back, as if this were some rite of passage that Richardson had accomplished.

"That was really brave of you, Tony," Gray said to the younger kid, who smiled up at him. "Let's get outta here then."

Gray suggested they drive to Alton, Illinois, and climb up the giant boulder there that locals called "the Chair," where they could sit and watch the river for a while. They still had one joint left and the weather, though chilly, was comfortable enough.

Gray had abandoned Eva earlier — she had been expecting a ride home hours ago. He knew he'd be in trouble with her when he finally did make his way home, and that thought was now turning to dread.

Winfrey became panicky while the others talked nonchalantly about what to do next with their evening. He hadn't *really* believed that his new friends intended to murder those three people. He had participated in the rapes by standing guard and by holding the girls down, by covering their mouths and their eyes while they screamed. He had even enjoyed the adrenaline rush, the pure wickedness and momentum of the whole situation. But, he told himself, he *had* been the only one of the four who refused to physically rape the girls, a fact that he would later emphasize to his girlfriend. It wasn't so much out of a sense of goodness or fear that he refrained but, rather, he seemed to possess some subconscious and innate suppressant within him that would not allow him to rape. A suppressant that most normal people must have, he thought, while he tried not to consider how dangerous his companions must be, that they lacked this basic human characteristic. And now that the deed was in fact done, Winfrey began to experience a good dose of panic. So while the others talked about going to the Chair, Winfrey began worrying about "going to the chair" in a different sense. He didn't really worry about Julie or Robin, right now in the process of drowning in the water below, but he did begin to fret about his own culpability in the situation. In short, he started to freak out.

"I'm not in this," he said over and over again. "I'm not in this, I didn't do this."

But the others just laughed at him and soon all four were running down the bridge toward the Missouri end, toward their cars, stimulated by the adrenaline that filled their veins and the sense of self-preservation that urged them all to flee quickly from the scene of their vicious crimes. On the road, they stopped for cigarettes, gas, and sandwiches. Richardson paid for these items with the money they had stolen from Julie and Robin. He tossed one packet of cigarettes to Winfrey and then handed out the sandwiches. Winfrey sat in the passenger seat of Gray's car and immediately lit the first in a chain of cigarettes with his hands shaking, and he continued to mumble, "I'm not in this." His stomach churned a little as he watched the others sitting on the hood of the cars, munching their ham sandwiches and chatting. When they were done eating, the four drove to Alton, ascended the Chair, and lit their joint. From their vantage point, high on the huge rock in the moonlight, they looked out over the rough current of the Mississippi.

"They'll never make it to shore," Clemons stated quietly while he sucked on the joint. There was no emotion in his voice.

"Yeah, they definitely won't make it," Gray agreed. Then, turning to Winfrey, he added, "See, Danny? You should have gotten yourself some pussy. We've got nothing to worry about."

Winfrey was filled with a sick sense of power mingled with relief at the thought that their three victims were all safely dead by now.

At around two A.M., back on Riverview Drive, police officers Sam Brooks and Don Sanders were en route to the water-treatment plant. Their siren was silent and their lights were darkened. They were responding to two strange but fairly routine calls from truck drivers regarding a suspicious man on Riverview Drive telling a wild story about the Old Chain of Rocks Bridge. As they nosed their patrol car toward the fenceline at the St. Louis Waterworks, Tom Cummins cautiously crept from his hiding place in the grass and into the rays of their headlights. The patrolmen were immediately alarmed by Tom's condition.

Mud covered his shoulders and spilled down the front of his shirt and his jeans. His sopping sneakers were caked with silt, and his hands were pruned from the water and trembling. His eyes were glazed over and he approached the officers clumsily, with a visible limp. The young man was obviously distressed, and he attempted to convey a sense of urgency to the officers about getting help for his cousins. Within a few moments, Tom began shivering violently and his teeth chattered audibly as Brooks and Sanders helped him into the back of their patrol car, cranked the heat up for him, and radioed anxiously for backup. From the hasty facts they had gathered so far, they determined that this was the biggest thing that had ever happened on their beat.

Shortly after their arrival on the scene, Officers Brooks and Sanders were joined by what seemed to Tom like half of the St. Louis Police Department. The two partners tried to make Tom comfortable in the back of their squad car, and then they drove him back to the bridge, where there was already a great deal of activity getting underway. Tom felt an unexpected reluctance, a renewal of his terror, as the car he was traveling in approached the bridge for the second time that night. He knew he shouldn't be afraid — there were numerous police cars, a rescue squad, and an ambulance already assembled at the bridge entrance by the time they got there. But he could not assuage his inexplicable fear as the officers slowed their patrol car to a stop on Riverview Drive. The one in the passenger seat turned to face Tom in the back.

"You all right?" he asked.

As Tom nodded his response, a chill spread over his body and sent him shivering and chattering all over again. The officer quickly stepped out of the patrol car and trotted over to the nearby ambulance. He returned a few moments later with a thick woolen blanket. He opened the back door of the squad car and wrapped Tom up in the gray blanket, pulling it tight around his shoulders and tucking it under his chin. This simple act of kindness brought tears to stand in Tom's eyes and he shrunk back against the seat, embarrassed. That officer's small act of compassion sharpened his pain so intensely. The contrast between that kindness and the cruelties he had seen that night solidified his trauma — made his horror all the more real and atrocious. Tom forced a breath past the sharp lump in his throat.

"We've gotta find them," he said quietly to no one, gazing out the far window of the squad car.

The two officers stole concerned glances at each other. They weren't sure if he was talking about his cousins or their attackers, but the chances of finding any of the above at this point seemed rather slim.

CHAPTER SIX

Tink and Kathy Cummins slept soundly, tucked comfortably into matching twin beds in the back bedroom of their grandparents' home on Fair Acres Road, still digesting their chicken stir-fry while they dreamed. The loud banging on the front door of the little house failed to fully rouse them. It wasn't until they heard the strange voices in the living room that they both sat upright in their beds, their hearts hammering. The word "incident" had caught them both in their sleep and wakened them with a rough slap of consciousness. Tink glanced wildly at Kathy as they both leapt out of bed simultaneously. Kathy glanced at the clock: it was 5:32 A.M. Tink reached for the shorts she had discarded on the floor beside her bed a few hours before, tugged them quickly up over her hips, and followed her sister out to the living room.

The front rooms of the house were crowded with people. Two large policemen stood in the doorway, Grandpa Art beside them with his hand still on the doorknob. Grandma Polly stood behind her favorite blue chair, her hands unconsciously wringing the back of the velvet upholstery. Kay and Gene stood blinking sleep from their eyes and asking the officers what questions they could manage in their sleepy confusion.

"I'm sorry, we can't answer any more of your questions right now. We really need you to get dressed and come with us. There's been some kind of an incident at the Chain of Rocks Bridge," the taller of the two officers explained again, "And your son Tom was involved. That's really all we know."

"That's impossible," Gene started to say. "My son is asleep in the van . . ." But his voice trailed off. His mouth closed with a snap as his waking brain finally began to register the limited facts that were being offered to him.

"An incident," he repeated. Then, turning to his wife, "We'd better get dressed."

Tink's blood turned to ice and the room started to spin out from under her feet. An *incident*. And she had known they were going to the bridge. She should have tattled.

"Are they okay?" Kathy asked, alarmed, but more sensible than her older sister. "Is Tom okay?"

"I'm really sorry I don't have more answers for you," the officer responded. "All I can tell you is that he and his two cousins were involved in some kind of incident at the bridge."

Gene stopped in his tracks and turned to face the officer again. "His cousins?" he asked, and he glanced at his guilty-faced daughters.

"Julie and Robin," Tink answered.

"Was this an auto accident?" Gene asked then.

"Not an auto accident, Mr. Cummins. I'm not really sure what the incident entailed," the officer answered. "But to the best of my knowledge, I think your son is okay, I just don't have any details. He was with two of his cousins — that's all I know. I'm sure you'll find out everything you need to know when we get you down to the bridge."

Gene told the officers that he knew the old bridge well and that they wouldn't be needing an escort to find their way. As they left, the two officers tipped their hats to Grandpa Art, who thanked them and closed the door.

"I'm coming with you," Tink declared softly and turned to get her shoes.

"No," her father responded quickly. "You two will wait here and get ready for the trip home while your mother and I go sort this out. We're leaving in a couple of hours, and whenever we get back here with Tom, I want you to be ready to get on the road."

Gene had absolutely no idea what to expect when he got to the bridge, but he did know that the police didn't knock on your door with *good* news at five o'clock in the morning. So whatever it was he was going to have to face at the bridge, he wanted to keep his daughters at a comfortable distance.

Tink briefly started to argue, but it was clear from her father's tone that this particular decision was not up for debate. She walked across the room and fell into a seated position on the long couch with a thud. She folded her arms in front of herself and scowled. Within minutes, Gene and Kay were dressed and ready to go.

Grandpa Art stood waiting by the front door for them, already dressed, with his shoes and his jacket on.

"You two ready to go?" he asked, leaning for the doorknob.

"Oh, Pop, you don't have to come along," Kay responded. "We'll be okay on our own. We can find it."

"No way," her father persisted. "Those kids are in some kind of trouble and they need us. I can be of some help. I know that river and I know that bridge like the back of my hand."

Kay glanced at her husband, then back at her father. She was so moved by his desire to help. He had been sick that past year and had recently undergone treatment for colon cancer; she was worried about him. That had been the whole point of this vacation, really. To visit her father who had been in poor health. She was terrified of what they might find when they got to the bridge and she didn't want to expose her dad to anything that might shock him. But here he stood, completely unconcerned for his own well-being, determined to be a pillar of strength for her and her family. She looked at her two daughters, who were sitting frozen on the couch. She drew in close to her father, put her hand on his elbow, and whispered into his ear.

"Pop, I really think the girls need you here right now," she said.

Grandpa Art looked up at his two granddaughters and silently nodded his head.

"If we need you, I'll call you," she said. "I promise."

Her father nodded again and turned to take his jacket off. Kay kissed him on the cheek and thanked him while he mumbled over her gratitude and waved his daughter off. She opened the front door onto the still-dark yard and stepped out. Gene followed her, but turned as he reached the door.

"I mean it, you two get ready to go," he admonished his daughters. But he added in a softer tone, "I know you're worried. I'll call and fill you in as soon as we figure out what's going on." He looked at the two sullen faces of his teenage daughters and then strode out after his wife, pulling the door shut behind him.

"I can't believe they wouldn't let us go," Tink grumbled as the door clicked shut. She felt her sister nodding beside her but there was no audible response. Tink looked over at Kathy — her younger sister, archrival, and fiercest defender — and saw that her face was red, her eyes and lips twitching. She was terrified.

"Kathy?" Tink said, as the first tears started to slide soundlessly down her sister's face. "It's gonna be okay," she promised. "They're gonna be fine."

At that moment, for the first time in all of their years together, Tink reached out and put her arm strongly around Kathy's heaving shoulders. She wasn't used to being the consoler — she wasn't sure she had the strength. But at the moment she didn't seem to have much choice. Kathy collapsed into her arms and the two sisters sobbed heavily together.

★   ★   ★

At the Kerry house on Petite Drive, Ginna stood at the front window in the living room, peering out into the dark street. She was worried and wild-eyed. With one hand she absently flicked the curtains and from the other one she dangled her car keys. She was fully dressed and her handbag hung loosely at her shoulder. Physically she was still, but her mind was pacing feverishly. She *had* to get to the bridge — that was all the police officers had really been able to tell her. They had used the words "incident" and "Julie and Robin" and "involved," but they hadn't been able to answer any of her questions. She had immediately telephoned someone to come over and stay with Jamie. As the headlights approached and then switched off, Ginna opened the front door and swung out into the chill air of the April pre-dawn.

Shortly after Tom's arrival back at the bridge, the police officers had moved him from the back of their squad car into the more comfortable facilities of an ambulance. Inside, he removed his wet clothes, which were quickly snatched up by the police as evidence, and wrapped himself up in one of the firemen's big yellow running coats, with the blanket over his knees. The universal woodfire-smoky smell of the coat reminded him of work and home; it comforted him. But despite this small consolation, Tom was growing more despairing and despondent with each passing minute. It had been hours now since he had come ashore and there was still no sign of Julie or Robin.

The bridge was a mess of people and activity. The mist hanging in the air was lit red and blue by the lights of all the emergency vehicles that had converged on the scene. Camera crews banged on the back door of the ambulance where Tom sat biting his lip. When he glanced out at them he saw the pampered puffs of hair, the lipstick, and the brightly tailored suits of reporters.

The men and women in the uniforms of the police and fire departments, the plainclothes detectives, the paramedics, the crime-scene photographers, and even the efficient but sloppily dressed cameramen each seemed to be playing an important part here, doing something worthwhile. But the reporters looked gauche and unhealthy in the early-morning light and their presence made Tom shudder. The only footage they would get for their morning newscasts would be a zoom shot of him from a hundred yards away when one of the paramedics opened the back door of the ambulance to check on him. Tom was bent over his lap, resting his elbows on his knees and gripping his dirty hair with his hands.

When Gene and Kay arrived at the Chain of Rocks Bridge sometime between five-thirty and six A.M., they were greeted by roughly two dozen police officers and all the trappings of a bona fide crime scene. Gene was not a panic-prone person. He was, after all, a Navy man, Vietnam veteran, pilot, firefighter, paramedic, and father of three teenagers. He was no stranger to the battle-field. Still, every trial he had experienced before in his forty-six years paled in comparison to this horrible moment in his life. Gene parked the big blue van and surveyed the scene quickly before he and Kay got out and approached the most senior uniformed officer in sight. Gene stuck his hand out to the lieutenant by way of introduction.

"Hello, I'm Gene Cummins, Tom's father. Can you tell me what's going on, please? Where's my son?"

The officer glanced up from his spiral bound notebook and shook Gene's hand. "Mr. Eugene Cummins?" the officer asked.

"Yes."

"Of Gaithersburg, Maryland?"

"Yes, can you tell me what's going on, please?"

"You have a son named Thomas Patrick Cummins?"

"Yes, is he here? Where is he?"

"He's nineteen years old?"

"Yes . . ."

Gene looked around while the officer spoke, which wasn't at all like him. He had always been taught to stand with your head up and look a person in the eye when he or she was speaking to you. It was rude to look around during a conversation and Gene had always been an honorable man, a man with impeccable manners. But his parental instincts were winning out over his sense of decorum now, as he assessed the scene and still couldn't catch any glimpse of his son.

"You've been vacationing here in St. Louis this week, sir? Visiting family, I understand?"

"Yes, that's correct. Where is my son, please?"

Kay stood quietly beside her husband, watching the scene unfold as if she were outside herself, an invisible observer. She could not interject. She felt barely capable of following the volley of answerless questions.

"Your son will be along in a minute, sir. Do you have two nieces named Julie and Robin?"

"Yes — are they here too? Are they with Tom?" Gene continued to ask the logical questions though the officer, up to this point, had seemed either unwilling or unable to hear them.

"Can you give me their full names and ages, please?" the officer asked.

This time Gene didn't answer — he was silent, distracted, examining the scene around him with increasing determination for clues as to his son's whereabouts. Kay answered for him.

"Julie Ann Kerry and Robin Ann Kerry. Julie is twenty and Robin is nineteen. I can give you their exact birthdates if you want them, but *where are they?* Where are our children?" she demanded.

"Your son will be along in a minute, Mrs. Cummins. Do you recognize that blue car across the street?" he asked, gesturing with his ballpoint pen to where Julie's little Hornet sat abandoned in the damp and foggy dawn. Kay turned to look where the pen was pointing, over her shoulder.

"Yes," she responded. "That's my niece's car — Julie's car."

Her tongue felt thick in her mouth as she spoke and the confusion was worse than ever. They had gotten no answers since they arrived — only stranger and more terrifying questions. Her eyes and her husband's were both furiously surveying the scene now, searching for Tom and the girls. There was no sign of them. Gene's patience slipped from thin to nonexistent and he settled his gaze back onto the officer in front of them.

"Where is my son?" Gene demanded. *"Is Tom alive?"*

"Yes, Mr. Cummins, your son is alive," the officer responded, finally looking up from his notepad.

Gene began to breathe again, and his heart beat with renewed vigor.

"Tom is alive. At least we know he's alive," he whispered either to himself or to Kay, whose knuckles and face were rapidly paling to a rather sickly shade.

"Where is he?" he inquired then, in the same persistent tone.

"Right now I believe he is in the back of an ambulance, being driven to a crime scene a mile or two downriver. It seems he has been a witness to an incident," the officer replied.

"What kind of an incident? Exactly *what* is going on here?" Gene demanded further.

The officer cleared his throat and replaced his ballpoint pen in his breast pocket. He flipped the notebook back a couple of pages and cleared his throat again before he started to read. The words flew out of his mouth with sickening speed and Kay gripped her husband's arm for balance as she listened. She couldn't concentrate on the words — she only caught every fourth or fifth one, and those fell on her ears like the staccato crack of ammunition.

"Approximately . . . arrive   at   bridge . . . accosted . . . four men . . . restrained . . . robbed . . . beaten . . ."

At the words "gang rape," Kay's hand flew up to her mouth. Her stomach dropped and she was sure she would vomit, but nothing came. Just the continuing, nauseating stream of words from the officer in front of them who was doing his job.

"Thrown . . . water . . . Tom . . . ashore . . ."

"Tom came ashore." Kay seized on that phrase, interrupting. "Tom came ashore, Tom came ashore. What about the girls? Where are Julie and Robin?"

The officer stopped reading and closed his notebook. He took a deep breath, pausing a moment. "We're looking for them, ma'am," he responded. "So far they're not, uh . . . your nieces are not accounted for."

"Oh my God," Kay said quietly, tears starting soundlessly in her eyes.

"We'll be intensifying the search when the sun comes up and we'll probably have more luck then," the officer explained.

Now that he saw the naked horror of these people, saw their anguish unleashed in front of him, he seemed to want to say something to comfort them.

"It's just been too dark," he continued. "But with the daylight we're sure to have better luck."

He was unconvincing. He didn't even believe his words himself. For a brief moment Gene was speechless. His face drained of color and his voice was mute, while his mind interpreted the fact that although Tom had come ashore, according to this officer, four or five *hours* before, Julie and Robin were still "unaccounted for." It hit him like a sucker punch: his two nieces — his sister's two vibrant and beautiful daughters — were dead.

⋆   ⋆   ⋆

The next hour passed in a blur of pulsing, dreamlike commotion for Kay and Gene. One of the officers asked to see Gene's fireman's badge. Gene didn't understand how this stranger even knew he was a fireman. Had he introduced himself as such? He couldn't remember.

"Is your shield the same as the one your son carried, Mr. Cummins?" the lieutenant asked.

Carried. Why was everything in the past tense around here? Gene still hadn't set eyes on his son.

"Yes, it's very similar to the one Tom carries," Gene responded. "Only his doesn't say CHAPLAIN on it. Other than that it's basically the same."

"Do you mind if I take a look at it?" the officer inquired.

Gene lifted his chunky wallet out of its permanent place in the back pocket of his blue jeans and flipped it open with one hand, displaying his shiny fireman's shield. It looked like a promise in the slanted morning light. The lieutenant quickly called over a crime-scene photographer who pulled in close beside Gene, his camera's giant flash waving boorishly in Gene's face. He snapped several pictures of the shield from different angles while Gene stood holding it out at arm's length to escape the monstrous flash. Gene was now an active player in the evidence-gathering.

Another officer approached Kay and produced a set of keys in a plastic bag, as if this were all some sort of elaborate magic trick. He asked her if she could identify them. They were the keys to her parents' home, where she and her family were staying on Fair Acres Road.

"How did you get them?" she asked tentatively, quite sure she did not want to hear the answer.

"We found them on the bridge, near where the kids were forced off," he responded.

"Forced off," she repeated, unable to make sense of the words.

When Ginna arrived a short time later, Kay was the first person she spotted. She hurried over to her sister-in-law and started speaking immediately. She had a dozen questions and Kay found that she was unable to answer any of them.

"I don't know, I don't know, I don't know," she heard herself telling Ginna.

And she wished with all of her heart that she really didn't.

When the ambulance finally rolled up to the scene, crunching gravel under its big tires, Gene and Kay were over to the back door like a shot. They waited impatiently, fighting back the urge to twist the large metal handles on the double doors, fling them open, and leap inside. They didn't have to wait long. When the door cracked open, they looked up at the tormented face of their eldest child, their son, slouching on a gurney inside. Tom took one look at his parents and was overcome with emotion. He sobbed sloppily and covered his face, shaking. The next moment Kay and Gene were in the ambulance beside him, hugging him tenderly from each side and trying in vain to comfort him.

It took Tom several minutes to tell his parents the most basic facts of the ordeal. He curled and uncurled his muddy toes while he talked and his mother stared at them, and at the dirt caked into his ears. She wanted to take him home and wash him as she had when he was a newborn baby. She kept hugging him while he talked and patting his hair when he would break down and sob into her shoulder. Gene and Kay were scarcely able to conceive of the horror of the ordeal, of what Julie and Robin had been through, of what Tom had witnessed and survived.

"Mom," Tom said as he concluded his account, shaking his head and gazing trancelike at the empty space in front of him, "those four men should be put to death for what they did." He spoke softly now, without any malice, his voice sounding more sorrowful and frightened than angry. "They were so evil, they were the *face* of evil. They really deserve to die."

The tears started to dry on his dirty face and Tom was quiet then, having related the whole horror story, briefly, to his parents. They sat in silence for a couple of minutes, the parents patting and reassuring the son. There was a knock on the ambulance door and Tom jumped at the sound. Gene reached for the door and twisted the handle. His sister Ginna stood outside in a stunned state of breathless suspension, shielding her eyes from the brightening daylight and looking expectantly into the ambulance. Her face fell when she saw Tom seated inside without her daughters, but she struggled to reset her features into some semblance of normality.

"I don't really know what's going on," Ginna said feebly, feeling carefully for each word. "No one seems to be able to give me any answers."

Her mind would not yet allow her to suspect the worst. Of course the police had told her that Julie and Robin were not yet accounted for, but some impossible hope had nestled into her heart that they were mistaken, that she would open that ambulance door and her girls would be sitting inside with Tom, drinking coffee and warming themselves.

"Do you mind if Tom and I talk alone for a few minutes?" she asked Kay.

"Of course not," Kay replied and stepped over her son's outstretched legs, kissing him on the way by. She gripped his hand and looked briefly into his eyes, hoping to convey all of her motherly love in that momentary glance. She and Gene climbed out of the ambulance and Ginna climbed in to replace them. She sat next to Tom, and Gene closed the doors to give them some privacy. He and Kay both tried not to think about what Tom had to tell Ginna right now, that her daughters, both of her beautiful daughters, had been *hurt* in the worst way that anyone's daughter can ever be hurt. Kay tried not to look at the agonizing contortions that Tom's face was making as Gene shut the heavy double doors.

Gene had already put his suitcase into the van the night before, keeping out only his shaving kit and the clothes he had selected for the trip home. He remembered this now, and he and Kay went back to the van together to get Tom some dry clothes. They returned to the ambulance with some jeans that were so big they would have to be duct-taped up, and a checkered button-down shirt that Tom ordinarily wouldn't even have worn to sleep.

Ginna was disembarking from the van as they approached. Her face was ashen and blank. She wasn't crying. She was completely expressionless. She walked past her brother and his wife without seeming to recognize them, as if her mind had mercifully and necessarily turned off.

When Kay called out to her, she turned, unseeing, toward her brother's wife. But after a moment she continued walking toward her car, determined to get home quickly so she could collect some clean, dry clothes to bring back for her missing daughters.

By the time Tom was dressed in the dry, oversized clothes and shoes of his father, a duo of plainclothes officers had approached the ambulance and introduced themselves as Homicide Detectives Gary Stittum and Raymond Ghrist. They were asking Tom if he would accompany them out onto the bridge to walk them through the scenario. Tom nodded eagerly.

"I'll do absolutely anything I can to help," he said.

"Only if I accompany him," Gene interjected.

Over the course of the next hour, Tom walked up and down the bridge deck, pointing out relevant sites and recounting his story yet again. There were markers down all over the bridge now, encircling what seemed to Tom like countless pieces of evidence: a beer label, some change, a cigarette butt, a taffy wrapper, and, most damning — an opened condom.

The detectives listened closely, nodding and prompting Tom, taking notes in their little spiral-bound pads. Gene played the silent observer, staying very close to his son at all times. The detectives were respectful; they seemed sympathetic and friendly. They heavily implied that Gene's being allowed on the crime scene was a professional courtesy they were extending to him only because he and his son were both firemen. Gene nodded his appreciation.

When the group returned to the Missouri bank, they got coffee from the auxiliary van that was set up, and then approached Kay, who was standing waiting impatiently near the van. She was clearly not happy to have been left behind, to have been separated from her son while he was still so fragile, so traumatized. She reached out for him as they approached.

"Tom, we'd like you to come down to the station with us to make a statement, to help with our ongoing investigation," Stittum suggested as he took a swig of steaming coffee.

Tom nodded and curved the fingers of both his hands around his warming paper cup. He was determined to do anything and everything in his power to help catch the monsters who had done these horrible things.

"I think we're going to take him home first," Gene interrupted. "Let him at least get showered and into some clothes that fit him. He's been through an awful lot."

Tom shook his head.

"I want to stay and help, Dad," he maintained. "I want to be wherever they think I can be the most help."

"We can drive you down there afterwards," Kay said. "Don't you want to rest for a little bit and get cleaned up? You'll be more help to them if you're refreshed."

The family's decision-making was abruptly interrupted by one of the detectives. "Mr. Cummins, Mrs. Cummins," Ghrist announced, "you can go home and get freshened up if you want. Do what you have to do. But your son needs to come with us."

When the Cumminses' faces expressed their alarm at these words, Ghrist continued, "We just don't want to contaminate his memory by removing him from the scene right now. If he's exposed to his normal family environment, he may begin to block out important details."

Kay peered into her son's face and Tom nodded to her.

"I *want* to go and help," he assured both of his parents.

They nodded.

"So you're not taking him into custody?" Gene asked, demanding perfect clarity before he agreed.

"Oh, absolutely not, nothing like that," came the detective's reply.

"I'll be right behind you then," Gene said. "I'll swing by the house and pick up some clean clothes for you, and then I'll meet you down at the station."

Tom nodded and his parents hugged him for a moment before turning toward the van.

Back on Fair Acres Road, the Cummins sisters were doing their best, although begrudgingly, to follow their father's instructions. When the phone rang at around seven A.M., they both dropped what they were doing and sprang toward the kitchen. Grandma Polly had already picked it up and was "uh-huh"-ing into it while they stood with their anxious faces trained on her. After a brief conversation, she replaced the receiver softly without out a formal good-bye.

"Well, your parents are on their way home," she announced, her hand still lingering on the phone.

"And what about Tom?" Kathy asked quickly.

"He has to go down to the police station," their grandmother began. "They need him to make a statement."

"What kind of a statement?" Tink interrupted. "And what about Julie and Robin?"

Their grandmother looked up at them with big, watery eyes and bit her bottom lip.

"Well, that's what the statement is about. They're not sure where Julie and Robin are right now. Tom is going to help the police find them," she explained.

Tink clutched the counter to steady herself while her grandmother rubbed her shoulder gently and reached to put her arm around Kathy at the same time. This wasn't right. Something was terribly, terribly wrong. How could the girls possibly be *missing?* Julie and Robin had just eaten dinner with them a few hours ago. At the card table, Tink had sat next to Julie and admired her older cousin's well-developed, soccer player's calf muscle.

"But she was just here. They were just here," Tink muttered, waving her hands in front of her. "How can they be missing?"

The immediacy of such a tactile memory — Julie's leg beside her at the table — would not allow Tink to accept the word "missing." She had just hugged her cousin Robin good-bye a few hours ago. They had shared sarcastic tears, and Robin's braid had brushed her neck as they clung to each other and laughed. Dread spread over the sunny kitchen like a shadow. This was going to be much worse than any of them had at first imagined.

"Don't worry yourselves now," Grandma Polly said. "I'm sure everything's gonna be just fine. Why don't you go ahead and get your showers and I'll make some breakfast. I'm sure your mom and dad will explain everything a bit better when they get here." She patted both of her granddaughters and they nodded glumly.

"I'll go first," Tink said softly to her sister.

Kathy was still silent, staring into the Formica countertop as if she might find some answers there, as if it were a Magic 8 Ball. Tink plodded down the basement stairs, opened the door to the big converted bathroom, and stepped inside. She pulled the string that hung from the wall and a lightbulb lit up over the reflection of her unhappy face in the clean bathroom mirror. This room was so big that Tink thought it must have been an old extra bedroom that had been converted to a bathroom — and that the shower's former life had been that of a walk-in closet.

She shivered and rubbed her goosebumps as she undressed in the orange glow of the naked bulb. She left her clothes in a rumpled pile on the shaggy yellow rug by the sink and turned toward the shower. The damp, musty basement smell permeated everything here, covering even the spicy berry scents of her shampoo and conditioner. Tink listened to the water dripping down her body, splattering onto the floor under her cold feet, and gurgling as it made its way down the echoey drain beneath her. She fell to her knees on the wet stone floor and hung her head in the stream of tepid water, rocking herself and sobbing for her missing cousins.

Gene and Kay Cummins arrived at the house on Fair Acres Road at approximately seven-thirty A.M. and were greeted by a flurry of fearful questions. They faced their daughters' queries with stunned and solemn silence. Tink and Kathy both noticed, suspending their questioning simultaneously with a subconscious desire to postpone the inevitable knowledge. The information they had been waiting so impatiently for all morning suddenly seemed less appealing. They could tell by their parents' faces that this knowledge wasn't going to allay their fears — it would only confirm them.

Gene was abnormally quiet, and he set about his business with determination. His current objective was to grab some clean clothes for Tom and get down to police headquarters as soon as possible. His mother-in-law was scrambling eggs on the stove in the kitchen and their aroma was filtering through the upper rooms of the house. It reached him in the den where he was bent over his son's duffel bag, rummaging around for a complete set of clothes.

"Why don't you have some eggs before you run off, honey," his mother-in-law said a few minutes later, smiling good-naturedly at him, the spatula in her hand hovering over the pan of steaming yellow goo. "You'll need to keep your strength up."

"Just coffee," Gene grumbled, stalking into the kitchen and opening a cabinet to reach for a good-sized mug.

She looked back to the eggs in the pan and stirred them quietly. Gene swallowed the coffee in a few reckless gulps, turned on his heel, and headed for the front door.

He passed his two daughters, who were sitting silently on the blue couch, looking blankly at the television. Their brother was there on the screen, an image from a few hours earlier, before he had dressed in Gene's baggy clothes. On the news, he was still wrapped in the fireman's bright yellow coat. His hair stuck up at angles and he glared at the camera, turning away with a look of disgust at the intrusion. The reporter was saying something about two missing girls and there was a quick image of Ginna, looking terribly distraught, actually wringing her hands.

Gene bent and kissed his daughters on the tops of their heads, and then rushed out the door. Kay closed the front door as he left and went to sit with her daughters, to answer the questions they no longer wanted to ask.

Grandma Polly was still working over the hot eggs in the kitchen, and she glanced worriedly at Grandpa Art seated at the kitchen table with his morning paper. For everyone's sake, he was striving to keep up an appearance of normality. After more than fifty years of marriage, she knew that he was frightened too, but would keep a calm exterior, reading and shuffling around the house, hoping his calm would infect the others.

The steam from the eggs rose into Grandma Polly's face and she heard her daughter's low voice murmuring to Tink and Kathy in the next room. The next moment the two girls erupted into the horrible sounds of grief-stricken hysteria and their mother's voice continued, soft and low, trying to comfort them. Their cries grew louder and more terrible for several minutes but slowly silence fell. There were light footsteps in the carpeted hallway as Tink ran past the kitchen and into the bathroom to throw up.

Gang rape was an awfully difficult fact for a fourteen- and a sixteen-year-old girl to face.

CHAPTER SEVEN

Dr. Richard Ofshe, a Pulitzer Prize–winning professor at the University of California at Berkeley, is one of this country's preeminent experts in the field of social psychology. His research interests include coercive social control and police interrogations. He has been certified as an expert witness regarding police interrogations in over twenty-five civil and criminal trials. In a 1992 article entitled "Coercive Persuasion and Attitude Change," published in the *Encyclopedia of Sociology,* he said:

> *Programs of coercive persuasion appear in various forms in contemporary society. They depend on the voluntary initial participation of targets. This is usually accomplished because the target assumes that there is a common goal that unites him or her with the organization or that involvement will confer some benefit.*

On the morning of April 5, 1991, an unassuming Tom Cummins fit as neatly into Ofshe's category of "target" as he did into the backseat of the unmarked squad car. Tom certainly assumed that his goals of finding Julie and Robin and bringing in their attackers united him in purpose with Detectives Stittum and Ghrist.

The two detectives, for their part, were doing everything they could to nurture these feelings. His assistance was invaluable, they kept saying. With his help, the three of them — the two police-men and the brave young fireman — were going to find Julie and Robin. And the entire uniformed city of St. Louis was behind them. They would unite in a fraternal effort between depart-ments: the police spearheading the examination and investigation, and the fire department leading the physical search. It was a great thing that Tom was a firefighter, Stittum and Ghrist stressed. His kind of hands-on experience with traumatic situations was un-usual among the general population, and they were sure it would prove invaluable to the investigation.

So Tom began to feel a small bit better while he chatted with the two detectives. They were stuck in rush-hour traffic on the way to police headquarters, and Tom was anxious to get moving, to get downtown. He was beginning to believe that maybe he really did have something to offer, maybe he wasn't *completely* helpless and useless. Just maybe, if he was brave and tireless and sharp, maybe if did everything exactly right, everything that was asked of him, maybe then they would find Julie and Robin. Weren't there a couple of islands in that stretch of the Mississippi? Or couldn't the girls be clinging to debris somewhere along the river's edge now, unable to ascend the steep and slippery bank the way Tom had? For the first time in hours, Tom's exhaustion and anguish were defeated by a tiny flicker of hope.

The detective in the passenger seat turned to face Tom while they talked, and the one in the driver's seat kept glancing at him in the rearview mirror. They asked him about his vacation that week, about spending time with Julie, about his family back-ground. Tom told them his father had been in the Navy and they had moved around a lot, that he and Julie had only become close friends in the last year or so. They encouraged him to talk about her and he did so without reserve, with the candidness that Julie had helped him to nourish in himself. And in accordance with his new mood, he spoke about her with the lightness of the present tense.

When he grew quiet, they chatted to him more about his job as a rookie fireman. They asked him what kind of station he worked in and what his crew was like. They asked him about the police department in Washington. How closely did they work with the fire department? Did he have many friends on the force?

"We're gonna do everything we can to find your cousins and catch those bastards," Stittum assured Tom during a lull in the conversation. "We feel just awful about all this. And you're practically one of our own." He shook his head as he said this and turned back to face the windshield.

Tom gazed out the window at the passengers in the stopped cars beside them and he slumped down self-consciously in his seat as he did so, pulling the collar of his father's flannel shirt up closely around his neck. The Midwestern speech patterns were not totally foreign to Tom, but often he still found himself bewildered by the oddness of a phrase or a pronunciation. The detective's words "practically one of our own" rattled around strangely in Tom's head, and the vinyl of the seat squeaked under the movement of his bottom sliding around in the too-big jeans.

The passenger detective had now turned his attention to the radio, flicking it on and judiciously flipping past the news station in search of some music. There wasn't much on but drive-time talk, so he soon grew bored and flicked the radio off again.

Tom stared into his lap and realized that his right index finger was stuck inside the cuff of his left sleeve, rubbing the flannel repeatedly. It was a comfort-seeking habit he'd had since he was a small child. His mother used to tease him about it. "Silkying," she called it. "If you keep silkying that pillowcase, there's gonna be nothing left of it," she would laugh when she caught him in the act. But it had become such an ingrained habit for him that he was usually unaware that he was doing it. He was embarrassed when he caught himself silkying the shirt cuff, and he stopped immediately, jerking his hand out of the sleeve and up toward his face. Then, after a moment, he purposely placed the finger back against the soft material and resumed the rubbing, hoping to suppress the tears that had inexplicably sprung to his eyes.

While their brother sat in the back of a squad car on his way to police headquarters, Tink and Kathy Cummins were returning from walking their dog around their grandparents' neighborhood. Tink had tied the red bandana that Julie had given her the night before around her right wrist and she wrapped Blarney's leash around her left. She didn't know why she was wearing the bandana that way. She usually wore them in her hair. But this one smelled like Julie and she wanted to keep it that way. The phone was ringing as they came in and, as usual, Grandma Polly answered it. Kathy slumped onto the blue couch and was yanking her shoes off when their grandmother appeared in the kitchen doorway.

"Girls," she said to the two of them, "Jamie's on the phone. Which one of y'all wants to take it?"

Kathy shrugged and nodded at her sister.

"I will," Tink said as she bent to release Blarney from her leash.

Jamie was having one hell of a morning. She wanted to know if Kathy and Tink could come over and keep her company.

"We'll be there in ten minutes," Tink said, with an air of authority in her voice that was quite new to her.

Kathy relayed the news to their mother through the basement bathroom door. Kay opened the door in a towel gathered firmly under her arms and followed her youngest daughter quickly up the steps and into the now-sunny kitchen.

"We don't even have a car here, guys," she said to her daughters, who were both determined to get to Jamie immediately. "And we have a million phone calls to make to aunts and uncles, before they all see this on the news . . ."

"There's a phone at Aunt Ginna's house," Kathy stated matter-of-factly. She had already put her shoes back on.

"And of course, you can take my car," Grandpa Art added.

Kay closed her mouth and looked up at the ceiling, weighing the options. She ran one hand through her sopping wet hair, shaking heavy drops of water from her black ringlets and onto her mother's tiled kitchen floor.

"Yeah, okay," she decided. "It will probably do you guys and Jamie both some good to be together right now. But let me at least get dressed first. I can't go like this." Before long, they were on their way.

Petite Drive was quiet, almost abandoned-looking, when the female constituent of the Cummins family pulled into Ginna's driveway. It was close to eight o'clock and most of its residents were at work or school for the day. Tink and Kathy were out of the car before Kay had even managed to put it in park and, after knocking lightly on the front door, they pushed it open and stepped inside. Jamie was sitting cross-legged on the floor in front of the big television in the front room. She gripped the Nintendo controller with both hands and her eyes never left the screen in front of her.

"Hey," she said to her cousins, without looking at them.

"Hey yourself," they both answered her. Kathy left the door open a crack for their mother and sat down on the floor beside Jamie while Tink dropped onto the low comfy couch behind them.

When they arrived at police headquarters, Stittum, Ghrist, and Tom walked shoulder to shoulder down the long linoleum hallway and someone pressed button 4 in the rickety old elevator.

Once upstairs in the homicide squad room, the two detectives offered Tom more coffee, which he gladly accepted.

After a few minutes Gene arrived, and Tom was shown to the bathroom, where he quickly changed into the fresh clothes his father had brought and splashed water on his face. His eyes were beginning to burn from the lack of sleep and his tongue felt downright hairy with river water and coffee. He wished he had asked his dad to bring a toothbrush. He didn't even bother checking his reflection in the mirror before, buttoned and zipped into the new clothes, he banged open the bathroom door and returned to the small company. They were gathered at a messy desk talking seriously when he strode up. His new clothes seemed to have endowed him with a renewed energy and sense of purpose.

"Let's do this," he said.

Gene would not be permitted to remain in the interrogation room during the interview, but the detectives allowed him to have a short look around and satisfy himself that there was nothing out of the ordinary. Once again they emphasized that this was not a courtesy that they would usually allow to the family member of a witness; it was Gene's status as a fireman that motivated them to extend the invitation to him. One of the detectives instructed Tom to make himself comfortable and told him they would be in shortly to conduct the interview. Then they left him alone.

As the door clicked shut, Tom fell into the hard metal chair at the room's empty table and allowed the backlog of tears to drip quietly from his eyes. It was his first moment alone and at rest since he had squatted, panting and terrified, beneath the stop sign at the St. Louis Waterworks a few dark hours before. He spread his arms out on the table in front of him and examined them. Tink had written her name in capital blue ink letters on his forearm the night before — during their poker game — and it was still there. He was surprised that it hadn't washed off in the water, and the sight of the ink there stunned him. His bottom lip trembled as he touched the TINK letters on his arm. With a suddenness that almost made him woozy, he realized how dramatically his life was mutating around him. Just hours before he had been sitting with his sisters and cousins; they had been playing games and harassing each other. And now he had to shake away the images of what Julie and Robin had endured on that bridge. He had to chase away the fact that they were still missing, that they might not have survived their ordeal. He put his head down on the table and battled these thoughts. In a matter of seconds, he was fast asleep, his head cradled into the crooks of his bent elbows, and his ankles crossed loosely under the table.

When Stittum and Ghrist returned to the room some forty-five minutes to an hour later, Tom woke with a start. He snapped his head up in confusion. A moment later, the expression of distress returned to him as he remembered where he was and why he was there. His sleep had been mercifully black and dreamless — the sleep of pure physical and emotional exhaustion.

The detectives sat down opposite Tom and one of them placed a small, handheld tape recorder on the otherwise empty table between them. Tom looked at it suspiciously, not quite sure why its presence made him uncomfortable. He shook his head, trying to clear the cobwebs that had accompanied his sleep. He loosened his cramped arms from their cradled position and brought his hands up to rub his face and hair. After a good yawn and a few stretches, Tom was waking up, but he was still quiet, looking expectantly at the detectives for guidance. He felt comfortable with these cops. He felt they were good guys, smart guys — and they were clearly the only path toward the possibility of finding his cousins.

"Do you need anything before we get started?" one of them asked Tom. "Some more coffee, another trip to the john?"

"Nah, I'm good," Tom said and he took a deep breath.

"Okay. Now, there's nothing to be nervous about," the detective explained. "This is absolutely, one-hundred-percent routine. We do this with potential homicide witnesses whenever possible. It's going to be a great help to our investigation, so just answer the questions as clearly as you can remember, and if at any time you start to feel uncomfortable or you need a break, you just let me know."

Tom nodded, trying to ignore the word "homicide."

"Now, I'm going to have to read you your Miranda rights when the tape starts," he explained further. "Don't let that scare you. It doesn't mean you're in custody, it doesn't mean you're a suspect, it doesn't mean we're arresting you. It's simply the law to protect anyone who is making a taped statement. Again, one-hundred-percent routine — as if I have to tell you all this. I'm sure you're already familiar with the procedure. I just want to reassure you. I know what an awful night it's been."

Tom nodded again and felt a little foolish for all the nodding he seemed to be doing.

"Let's go then," he said.

The transcript of that taped statement begins as follows:

Q: Today is April fifth, 1991, I am Detective Raymond Ghrist, G-H-R-I-S-T. In the room with me, and we're in interview room number two of the Homicide Office, is Detective Gary Stittum, S-T-I-T-T-U-M, seated across from me is Thomas Cummins, for the purpose of this tape it is now 9:02 A.M., and at this time, Thomas, we talked before this tape started, and I told you I was going to advise you of your rights.

A: Yes sir.

Q: Okay, I want to advise you that you have the right to remain silent, that anything that you tell us can and will be used in a court of law. Do you understand that?

A: Yes sir.

Q: Okay. You have the right to an attorney, do you understand that?

A: Yes sir.

Q: If you cannot afford an attorney one will be appointed for you. Do you understand that?

A: Yes sir.

Q: Do you understand that this attorney will be appointed for you at no cost?

A: Yes sir.

Q: Okay. If you consent now to talk to us, Detective Stittum and I in this room, with no one else present, you may stop answering questions at any time. Do you understand that?

A: Yes sir.

Q: And, at any time during this conversation, if you feel you may need a lawyer, you can request one. Do you understand that?

A: Yes sir.

Q: Okay, are you willing to give us a statement about an incident that occurred in the evening hours in, of the fourth of April, into the early morning hours of the fifth of April?

A: Yes sir.

It was disconcerting to Tom, hearing those words he had heard so many times before, on television, in movies, and even on the job. They were offered in such a different tone from the one he had heard them in before — a quiet, sympathetic, and helpful tone. Still, the words themselves were alarming. He took a deep breath and began his story all over again.

The detectives interrupted him occasionally to ask him for further explanations or clarifications of certain points, but by and

large, it was Tom's voice that filled that audio tape — Tom's weary
and miserable voice, recounting the evening's events in all their
horror to these two strangers who sat nodding and prodding him
from across the table. He started by telling them about Julie, by
trying to explain the closeness of their friendship, how uncon-
ventional and good it was. "A real strong bond between us," was
how Tom defined it. At this description, the two detectives raised
their eyebrows at each other, but Tom didn't notice. Ghrist's next
question startled him.

Q: But you've never been physically intimate with her?
A: No sir.

Tom responded emphatically, a bit confused by the query.

Q: You never had sex with her at any time?
A: No. Absolutely not.

Tom was a little annoyed, not to mention somewhat disgusted,
at the suggestion, but he shook it off. They had explained to him
before the interview started that they might have to ask him a
couple of uncomfortable questions. They assured him that this
was purely to rule out every possibility. After all, this statement
would be the beginning of the official police record for the case.
Besides, Tom thought, these guys were professionals — they knew
what they were doing. Upon further reflection, he supposed that
Detective Ghrist probably *had* encountered first cousins who were
sexually involved before. That's probably why he had asked. Still.
Yuck.

Tom continued his statement as carefully and completely as he
could manage in his ever-heightening state of exhaustion. He
racked his brain meticulously for every detail he could grasp,

shuddering at the more physically sickening ones, but pressing on nonetheless.

Outside the homicide room, in a nearby office, Gene Cummins was settling in to wait for his son. His head was still spinning a bit, but the police officers were showing him every courtesy so that, despite the horror of the situation, he found himself at least well looked after. They had seated him at someone's empty desk and offered him the use of the phone there. He was working on his fourth cup of coffee already that morning and agonizing over the decision of whether to telephone his parents in Florida or wait for more definitive news before alarming them. He was, after all, the oldest sibling and he had insisted on being the one to make that call. He had a very special relationship with his father, and if Gene Senior really had to hear terrible news like this about his grand-kids, Gene Junior felt that it was only right that it should come from his eldest son. The family had all agreed wholeheartedly — nobody wanted to make that call. While he sat thinking it over, a passing officer remarked that he must be a glutton for punishment.

"That police-issue coffee is disgusting. You may as well drink a vat of tar," he joked.

"Not at all," Gene responded. "If you want tar, you should try Navy coffee sometime."

Gene smiled to himself as he sipped the cooling coffee. He was remembering an act he used to put on for his kids when they were younger. They would be seated around the breakfast table, heads bent over cereal bowls and backpacks flung down beside chairs, when he would shuffle in. He would still be wearing his glasses, just up out of bed in boxer shorts and a T-shirt, and his three kids would hear him coming. They would all put their spoons down and wait anxiously for their father's comical arrival in the kitchen. He would trudge with closed eyes toward the spot where his timer-efficient pot of warmed coffee was waiting for him on the counter. He would reach for the regular mug in the regular place and pour the coffee into it, still with his eyes shut tightly. Not until he had that first slurp of black, sugarless coffee would he shake his head vigorously and pop his eyes open as if the coffee itself had awakened him. The first time he had done this, it had been almost real, but his three kids had howled with laughter. He enjoyed that so much — the sound of his kids laughing — that the morning coffee trudge had become a ritual in their house. One that had worn away in recent years. They were growing up so fast.

Now, as he brought his thoughts back to the present, his mind flooded with grief for Ginna, and he shook his head, unable to imagine what she could possibly be going through. He set the mug on the desk in front of him, folded his hands, and bent his head for a moment, thanking God for his family, and praying against all hope for the safe return of Julie and Robin.

In the room next door, Tom felt fairly confident that the interview was going well. After he overcame the brief shock at being asked about a sexual relationship with Julie, he settled into a groove and answered all of the detectives' questions in earnest. He was surprised and a little impressed with the sturdiness of his own memory actually, particularly given the fact that he had been awake for over twenty-four hours at this point.

Yet try as he might, he could not come up with any names. He knew that they had been exchanged during the initial conversation with the four men, but Tom hadn't considered them even remotely important at that time, and consequently they had gone in one ear and out the other.

He did, however, remember that the tallest of the four assailants had said he was from Wentzville. Tom was extremely pleased that he had remembered that detail. The only reason he had retained the name of the town, he explained to the detectives, was that his Aunt Lisa and her family lived out there. They had gone to visit her for lunch the day before. By Tom's estimation Wentzville was a tiny town and this must be an extremely important piece of information. What a stroke of luck it was that the name had registered with him, he thought.

Tom's rapport with Ghrist and Stittum remained friendly and professional throughout the interview. He continued to call them "sir." An old-fashioned habit, no doubt, but one that had been successfully and irreversibly instilled in him by his father.

Criminal Interrogations and Confessions by Fred Edward Inbau, John E. Reid, and Joseph P. Buckley is this country's leading manual on conducting police interrogations. It was the textbook most often quoted in Chief Justice Warren's famous Supreme Court opinion on the *Miranda* case. And according to that manual, detectives are warned that: "Any suspect who is overly polite, even to the point of repeatedly calling the interrogator 'sir,' may be attempting to flatter the interrogator to gain his confidence."

But even if Tom had been aware of this fact, it probably wouldn't have done much to change his behavior because, as far as he was concerned, he was not a suspect. He was clearly a victim in this case — anyone could see that. He was an emotional basket case. His lips and hands trembled while he spoke and he had to take deep breaths to complete the more difficult sentences. He was traumatized and dirty and exhausted. The idea that Stittum and Ghrist might actually suspect *him* of some wrongdoing hadn't even entered his brain. Which was why he wasn't terribly shocked at the final questions of the interview. The transcript indicates that it was Ghrist who wrapped things up in this way:

Q: Okay. Now, I'm going to ask you a couple other questions — and we're gonna take a break. Did you do anything to those two girls?

A: No sir. I did not.

Q: Okay. By that I mean did you in any way cause any harm to come to those two girls?

Tom shook his head firmly. These questions weren't accusatory. And Ghrist's tone and manner were still overtly sympathetic. The detectives were just getting his statement on record. This was all standard procedure, as they had explained and explained and explained.

A: No sir. I did not.

Q: Okay. Did you at any time have any sexual relations with either one of these girls tonight?

A: No sir. I did not.

Q: You never have?

A: No sir. I have not.

Q: Okay. Would you be willing to give us some samples for comparison later on? By that I mean hair, saliva, and so on?

A: Yes sir.

Q: Because, as we said now and we explained to you before, you know, we're trying to find out what happened. We have no knowledge of you before today.

A: Yes sir.

Q: And you're telling us a story and we're trying to verify.

A: Yes sir.

Q: Do you understand that?

A: Yes sir, I do.

The transcript of the tape indicates that the interview concluded at ten-thirty A.M. Tom had been questioned for an hour and a half. As the detectives clicked the tape recorder off, Tom let out a deep breath. He felt good about his participation. He was quite sure he had remembered some helpful details. The two detectives smiled and stretched.

"Listen, that was great, thanks a lot for your help, man," Stittum said, reaching across the little table to shake Tom's hand.

"If you would just make yourself comfortable here for a few more minutes, we're going to go check in with our chief and then we'll be right with you."

Tom nodded and tried to suppress a yawn as the two detectives stood to go.

One of them chuckled at Tom's inability to stifle the yawn. "Looks like you could use another cup of coffee. Or a soda maybe?" Stittum asked.

Tom shook his head in response. "I'm all right," he said.

And, within seconds of their departure, he was asleep on the table once again.

It was just after ten A.M., and twenty-six-year-old Jacquie Sweet, the youngest of Gene's and Ginna's six other siblings, was standing bent over her fully burdened desk in the composing room of Missouri's *Columbia Daily Tribune*. Daily deadline was 11:48 A.M. and the atmosphere was tense, as usual. When the only phone in the room rang, Jacquie didn't even notice it until somebody shouted her name. She sighed crankily, grabbed her open bottle of Mountain Dew, and then made her way to the phone desk.

"Jacquie Sweet," she said in her why-the-hell-are-you-bothering-me-don't-you-know-I'm-on-deadline voice.

"Jack? It's Sheila," came her sister's voice from over the phone.

Jacquie dropped her pen and took off her glasses. Her face immediately drained of color and her stomach rolled. Her brothers and sisters never called her at work.

"What's the matter, Sheila? Is something wrong with Dad?" Jacquie asked. She rubbed her forehead with the hand holding her glasses and they hit her in the face.

"No, no. Dad's just fine," Sheila responded. "Jack, I think you better sit down for this one."

By the time Sheila finished relating what she could manage to piece together of the morning's horror, Jacquie was trembling silently while her coworkers buzzed around her. The room seemed to spin in sickening color when Sheila finally broke into sobs and handed the phone to their sister-in-law Kay.

"Jack, I want you to listen to me very carefully," Kay began. "I know this is a lot to take in. Don't just get in your car and drive. You have to get yourself together a bit before you get in your car. You could be here for several days. Go home first and pack some clothes. Make sure you get somebody to take care of your dogs. Can your husband get away from work?"

Jacquie nodded. "Mm-hmm."

"Good. Bring him," Kay said. "You'll need him. And don't worry about trying to call anybody. Sheila and I are at Ginna's house and we're making all the calls from here. Oh, and we haven't told your mom and dad yet. We're leaving them for last. We're hoping for some good news by then."

Jacquie nodded again, and took a swig from her Mountain Dew, clearing the lump in her throat so she could talk. She said good-bye to her sister-in-law and hung up. For a moment she sat frozen to the chair, unable to move. Her coworkers had ceased to take any notice of her strange phone call and were engrossed in their work all around her. She rose unsteadily to her feet and groped around blindly on the table for a cigarette before her legs could find the strength to carry her to the door. The two-hour drive to St. Louis would be the longest of her life.

When the door to interview room number two swung open again nearly forty-five minutes after Stittum and Ghrist had excused themselves, Tom was still fast asleep on the table. There was a puddle of saliva gathering beside his dirty face. He woke with a

jerk when the door banged shut. When he looked up he was startled to see that the two detectives who had entered were not Stittum and Ghrist.

"Detective Richard Trevor," said one of the two men, and
stuck his hand out to the sleepy Tom.

Tom wrestled with another yawn and shook off the urge to
rub sleep from his eyes instead of shaking this man's hand.

"This is my partner, Detective John Walsh."

Tom shook the second man's hand and began to wonder why
none of the detectives around here looked like detectives. He
wasn't sure what a detective was *supposed* to look like, exactly, but
these guys all looked like dentists or software designers or something.

"I understand you were talking to Gary and Ray earlier. They
had to go home — their shift was over hours ago. So I hope you
don't mind our coming in. We're gonna take things from here,
and we'd like to go over some of the details of your statement
with you again. We're going to make a second tape. Nothing major — it won't be as long as the first one. We just want to confirm
and clarify a few of the details, since we weren't here when you
made the first one."

Tom nodded and rubbed his face with both hands.

"Okay, sure. No problem," he replied, still trying to shake
himself awake.

At 11:25 A.M., Tom began his second taped statement. He told
his story again "from the top," as Detective Trevor put it. By and
large, it was the same interview as the first taped statement. As they
finished up the interview, Trevor once again thanked Tom for his
continuing help and they talked about what would happen next:

Q: We appreciate your helping.
A: I'll help in any way I can. Any way.
Q: What I'd like to do is . . . You remember these people?

Trevor meant the four attackers. Tom shuddered and nodded, thinking about how he would never forget a single detail of any of those four faces, no matter how he might like to.

Q: We'd like to have you do a composite drawing. You know, get down with one of our technical artists and do that. What I'll do is just like we've done earlier — just eliminate everything we can now.
A: Uh-huh.
Q: We'll have the artist, you know, draw a little sketch. Do you have any problems with that?
A: No.
Q: Okay.
A: How do you think they'll do a composite?

Tom began to get excited about the prospect of helping in a more concrete way. His frustration with telling the same story over and over again was beginning to make him impatient. A composite drawing would definitely be a step forward, would introduce some new possibilities. Tom's mood lifted ever so slightly at the thought of it.

Q: I don't know how they operate. They're all different. Is there anything else that we left out that you might want to say?
A: No. Just . . . no.
Q: I mean, is there anything that happened that nobody's asked you?

Tom thought very carefully before answering this last question.

A: No, because I've . . . I've really . . . I've tried to cover every single bit.

The transcript of Tom's second taped statement shows that the interview concluded at 12:40 P.M. Again the detectives thanked him for his ongoing cooperation and assured him that his help was really vital to their investigation.

"I mentioned earlier about eliminating your samples from evidence," Trevor said to Tom after the tape was shut off. "You understand what that means?"

"I think so," Tom responded.

"It's basically just us getting all of your samples — hair, blood, fingerprints, et cetera — so that we can eliminate all of your samples as evidence from the crime scene," he explained again.

Tom nodded, "Yeah, I understand."

"You ready to do that then?" Trevor asked.

"Sure," Tom answered in a mildly sarcastic tone, "I don't really have anything else going on."

"All right." The detective smiled. "Let's get you upstairs then."

Eva was *not* happy with Marlin Gray. She had been more than a little pissed off that he had left her waiting for him all evening and then hadn't even come home until five o'clock the next morning. When they got up, well after eleven o'clock Friday morning, he told her he'd gotten into a fight on the Chain of Rocks Bridge. He had won a watch in the fracas, he explained proudly, before tossing Tom's Swatch watch down on the quilt beside her. She picked it up and looked at it somewhat uninterestedly before deciding to put it on.

"It's no excuse, you know," she admonished, as she climbed out of bed and began rummaging around for something to wear. "I was worried about you."

Gray smiled and gave her his best puppy-dog eyes. "Come on, baby," he cooed. "I don't wanna fight with you. I'm here now and everything's fine." He pulled her back onto the bed for a long kiss.

"All right," she relented, smiling up at him happily when the kiss was finished. "But *don't* do it again."

He leaned in for another kiss but she wriggled away from him and stood up.

"No time for that today," she chirped. "Come on, get up. We've got stuff to do."

But Gray didn't get up. He leaned back against his pillow and watched Eva as she picked her way around the room, gathering their clothes together for the laundry. She wore the watch for a few minutes, but took it off before she got into the shower. After a quick bite to eat, Gray and Eva drove over to a friend's house, Gray now wearing his new watch. Eva tugged their heavy load of laundry along behind her as they trudged up the walk. Eva was grateful that Robert Troncalli and his wife Kendra let her and Gray use their washer and dryer. Otherwise, Eva would have had to spend her afternoon off in a laundromat. This arrangement was perfect. Eva could throw the laundry in and then the two couples could sit and chat or watch television while they waited.

Troncalli was sitting watching the noon news when the couple came in, and Kendra was puttering around in her kitchen, clattering plates and silverware while she worked. Eva went straight to the laundry room, while Gray sat down in the recliner.

"Hey," Troncalli said by way of greeting once Gray was settled into his chair.

"Hey," Gray responded.

"Did you see that shit on TV?" Troncalli asked.

"What?"

"Two girls were killed at the Chain of Rocks Bridge last night," Troncalli answered. "And apparently their cousin was with them, but he survived."

Gray lifted an eyebrow, surprised but unconcerned. He took a deep breath and then rocked back in the recliner. "Yeah," he said, grinning, "I did it."

Troncalli darted his eyes at his smiling friend. He was used to Gray's off-the-wall comments, his twisted sense of humor, and his lust for the spotlight. "Marlin," he began in mild exasperation, as if warning a kindergartner to put the forbidden cookie back in the jar, "you shouldn't say things like that. One of these days, somebody's gonna overhear you and take it the wrong way."

"Oh, lighten up," Gray chuckled.

But as the footage of Tom Cummins rolled, a marginally nervous Marlin Gray slid his newly acquired green Swatch watch from his wrist and pushed it down deep into the cushions of Troncalli's recliner.

Tom was fingerprinted first and then allowed to use the bathroom and wash up a little bit before returning to the homicide squad room. Once he was seated back in interview room number two, a detective from the forensics lab showed up with a comb and a plastic bag. She was combing his hair and Tom was trying to stay awake when Gene's face appeared in the little grid-covered window on the room's only door.

Tom's face brightened when he spotted his father. Before today he never would have thought he would live to see the day when the sight of his father's face would cheer him up. Gene smiled at his son as he pushed open the door to the little room.

"How ya holding up?" he asked, sitting down across the table from his son in one of the chairs previously occupied by a detective. "Hungry?" he asked, and handed Tom a paper menu from a sandwich shop across the street.

"Starvin'," Tom replied, glancing through his options. "I guess I'll have a tuna sub," he said, handing the menu carefully back to his father.

He was trying to remain still for the woman who was combing his hair. He pressed his lips together as he looked at his father, but could think of nothing further to say to him. *Our lives are*

changed forever? Thank you for being here with me? Why am I not dead?
I didn't do enough to help the girls? None of these thoughts could
find its way to his lips and it was just as well, because none of
them could even begin to articulate the enormity of what he was
feeling. For the first time ever in his father's presence, Tom felt
like a man. This was a feeling he had been striving for throughout
his teenage years and now that he was here, all he wanted to do
was go back to feeling like a boy. The responsibility of what had
happened to him in the last twelve hours, and what would now
be expected of him in the future, settled on Tom like the weight
of the world.

"Tuna it is," Gene said. He reached over and squeezed his son's
hand briefly before leaving the room.

The sandwiches arrived within a half an hour, and Tom and
Gene ate them together, side by side in interview room number
two, in the company of yet another detective. There wasn't much
conversation at the little table. Both men were too exhausted and
hungry to talk. When they finished, Trevor and Walsh returned
to the little room to introduce the suggestion of a polygraph test.
Tom batted around the wadded-up wrapper from his tuna sub
while the detectives explained the importance of such a test to
Tom and his father — and why it would be helpful.

"Again, I want to stress to you both that this is completely
standard procedure, totally routine," the detective said. "It will
serve to help us establish the fact that Tom is a credible witness —
that's all."

Gene looked dubious, so the detective focused his arguments
on him.

"Listen, Mr. Cummins," he said, "I know your son is exhausted
and you're anxious to get him home — that's completely understandable. We just want to make absolutely certain that he hasn't
forgotten anything or mixed up any of the details. Once you take
him out of here, once he gets home and he's in his family envi-

ronment again, his memories of the event will be contaminated. He may even begin to block some of the more traumatic moments out — and those are probably the most important details. We really have to establish his credibility while all of this is still fresh in his mind. It won't take long and this is the last thing we will ask him to do today — then you will be free to take him home. We can leave the composite drawings until tomorrow. What do you say?"

Gene looked at his son and began to shake his head.

"Dad," Tom interrupted, "I've got no problem with this. I want to do whatever I can to help and I have no reason not to take the test. I've got nothing to hide. I want to do it."

"Well, if you're sure," Gene responded cautiously.

"I'm sure," Tom said.

By the time Jacquie arrived at Ginna's house on Petite Drive, all of the siblings had been notified, and those who hadn't arrived already were en route to St. Louis. The little house was already crowded.

Ginna had arrived home sometime mid-morning and stuffed two pairs of jeans, two pairs of shoes, two sweaters, and four wooly socks into a backpack before returning immediately to the Old Chain of Rocks Bridge. She arrived home with the still-full backpack in the early afternoon to find that her house was filling with supportive brothers and sisters. The Cummins siblings had never been famous for getting along terribly well. There was a lot of love in the family, but when there are eight siblings under one roof, personalities are bound to clash. Yet that day, despite the intensity of emotion in the house, or perhaps because of it, there were no ruffled feathers. Everyone was given a task, and they all worked well together.

Kay and Sheila were on phone detail, both making and taking the difficult calls. Tink and Kathy were charged with keeping

Jamie occupied, which conveniently kept them occupied as well. One of Ginna's sisters stayed close to her, keeping her company and helping her sift through family photos. The police had requested recent pictures of Julie and Robin to aid in the search.

Jacquie was assigned to take care of the first food run. She grabbed one of the kids and disappeared to the grocery store for an hour or so, returning to the house with a trunk full of brown paper bags. There were so many hands there that the car was emptied in one trip.

Jamie, Tink, and Kathy continued to monopolize the television in the front room with the Nintendo, which was probably a good thing because it prevented them from seeing the increasingly distressing news coverage.

In fact, there *was* no news, which didn't seem to discourage the reporters, who were crawling around the crime scene in ever-growing numbers. The only obvious fact was that, in this case, no news was *bad* news. By two o'clock that afternoon, it had been at least twelve hours since Julie and Robin had disappeared into the Mississippi. And there was still no sign of them.

Jacquie came in and stooped to rub Tink's back where she lay on the floor with the game controller in her hands.

"Your mom tells me you haven't eaten anything today, Tink," she said quietly. "How about a blueberry muffin?"

Tink shook her head. "No thanks," she said.

"Okay, I'll just leave it here anyway, in case you want it when you finish your game," Jacquie said, and placed the muffin carefully on the carpet in front of her niece.

Tink continued to play but after a moment she smelled the sweet stickiness of blueberry muffin. She looked down at it sitting at her elbow and her stomach turned. She threw the controller aside, jumped to her feet, and ran to the bathroom. She was relieved to be away from the thick sugary smell of the muffin and even more relieved to find that the bathroom was miraculously unoccupied.

She clicked on the light, took one glance at her ashen reflection in the mirror, and then collapsed to her knees beside the bowl to relieve the rush of bile from her stomach. Sweat trickled down from her hairline when she was finished, and she lay her forehead on her right arm where it was still gripping the toilet seat.

Tink was a bit of a germophobe in ordinary times, and the physical reality that she was now embracing a toilet hit her like a sucker punch. She felt the cold, curved porcelain with her left hand and suddenly realized that this was not a dream. This was not a nightmare. She was not going to wake up. The lingering sourness in her mouth and the bangs matted to her forehead with sweat were proof. Julie and Robin were gone. She stayed on the bathroom floor for fifteen minutes and sobbed.

CHAPTER EIGHT

The polygraph examination room was on a different floor, in a different wing of the building, and Tom was once again separated from his father during questioning. He was pleasantly surprised to find the new room to be considerably more comfortable than interview room number two. The polygraph machine was set up in a nicely furnished office, on a table next to a cushioned vinyl chair with matching cushioned arms.

The detective who was to administer the test was friendly. Again, he was in plain clothes, and Tom wasn't even sure if he was a detective. He introduced himself by first name instead of as *Detective So-and-So,* as all of the other homicide guys had seemed so fond of calling themselves. He began the conversation by telling Tom how sorry he was for everything he had been through. There were pictures covering the walls and desk of the large office, and the examiner led Tom around on a little tour, pointing out his favorites and naming his daughters for him.

"I can't imagine what I would do if anything ever happened to them," he said. "Your poor cousins. I'm so sorry for you."

Tom nodded, but didn't know what to say. Condolences were new to him. He didn't know quite how to respond yet.

"Here we all are out on our family boat last summer. That was taken up at the Lake of the Ozarks. The kids love it out there. We always have such a great time," the man mused.

The idea that just yesterday Tom had been on his own family vacation, one that had gone horribly, tragically wrong, suddenly seemed to dawn on the man. "Oh, how insensitive of me," he began.

But Tom cut him off. "No, no it's fine. You have a lovely family," he said.

The examiner thanked him and led him over to the vinyl chair and the contraption on the table. He spent the next several minutes explaining the physiology of the machine to Tom. One cord would be strapped around his midsection to record his breathing. A second would be attached to his finger to record perspiration. And lastly, a cuff around his arm would measure both blood pressure and heart rate. Any major or rapid fluctuation in these measurements would indicate that a lie was being told. Tom said that he understood.

"We don't want the questions themselves to shock a response out of you, so what we'll do is go over the list of questions together before I administer the test," the examiner explained. "There will only be ten to twelve questions total. Some of them will be extremely straightforward. Your name, your age, things like that, to kind of establish a baseline. And then, interspersed with those questions, I will ask you the more difficult questions, the meaty things, like 'Did you do anything to hurt your two cousins?' And when you respond, I want you to do so slowly and quietly. You should keep your eyes closed during the exam and relax — breathe as deeply as you can. I don't want the physical act of answering the questions to be recorded on the machine. Just answer slowly and methodically. Got it?"

Tom nodded.

"Now before we get started," the examiner continued, Velcroing Tom into all the appropriate devices, "we have to calibrate the apparatus. In other words, I need to see how the machine reacts to you specifically when you tell a lie. So here's what we're gonna do."

He picked up a deck of cards from the corner of his tidy desk and lifted the top ten cards off the deck.

"I want you to pick one of these cards, look at it, and then put it back in the pile. Then I'm going to show you each card individually and ask you: 'Was it this one?' I want you to respond 'No' every time. Afterwards, I will be able to tell you which card was yours because the machine will indicate to me which time you were lying."

"Okay," Tom said. "Sounds easy enough."

Tom was absolutely stunned a few minutes later when the examiner correctly identified his secret card. Tom had not perceived any physical change in his body during his lie, yet the examiner had identified his card without hesitation. Never in a million years would Tom have suspected that a straight shooter like this guy, a family man with a boat in the Ozarks and a vinyl chair in his office, would mark a deck of cards in order to trick a witness into a false sense of security. Tom was completely convinced that the polygraph was infallible. And he was more eager than ever to begin.

At no time during the examiner's description of the polygraph did he tell Tom that the machine's accuracy rating falls anywhere between 48 percent and 90 percent, depending on which study you read, or that the rate of false positives has been found to be as high as almost one in every four. He also didn't tell Tom that, among the factors contributing to the lie detector's unreliability, sleep deprivation is by far the worst — that virtually no one in a heightened state of sleep deprivation could feasibly pass a polygraph test.

So Tom closed his eyes as he had been instructed and began to breathe deeply, in through the nostrils and out through the mouth. The first thing he noticed with his eyes closed was how much quieter it was in this section of the building than up in the busy, squawking homicide room. He wondered why he hadn't noticed that before. The machine was humming quietly on the table beside him and the sound of his own deep breaths soon began to lull him into semi-consciousness. The volume and suddenness of the examiner's first question startled Tom fully awake.

"Is your name Thomas Patrick Cummins?"

"Yes," Tom spluttered.

Everything was quiet again, but Tom could hear his own heartbeat in his ears. He considered stopping the test, telling the examiner that he had been asleep before the first question. But he wasn't sure what the protocol was or if it would be inappropriate to interrupt the test. So instead he tried not to worry about being startled by that first question and he tried to distract himself by thinking about other things. He wondered if he would get in trouble if he opened his eyes. He simply couldn't stay awake with them closed like this. He had been awake for over thirty-four hours by now. The lull between questions couldn't have lasted longer than fifteen or twenty seconds, but it was long enough for Tom to drift off again.

"Did you murder your cousins?"

The question actually scared him this time. It wasn't just the startle response of being roused either. There was something in the questioner's tone. Something accusatory. Tom tried to regulate his breathing. The palm of his free hand was now damp with sweat, he noticed, and he was sure that the little perspiration tester strapped to his finger was sucking up plenty of liquid. He told himself to relax, take a deep breath, and answer the second question.

"No," was his response.

He had regained control of himself, he felt. *This guy must know how tired I am,* Tom thought. His head lolled while the seconds ticked by and he awaited the next question. In a moment he was asleep again and the test continued like that for the duration. When it was over and the last question was answered, Tom knew how badly it had gone before he even opened his eyes. He looked over at the examiner on the other side of the machine for reassurance.

"Well, it looks like we've got a real fucking problem here," the detective spat.

Tom opened his mouth to speak but found nothing to say. He watched as the examiner threw his notepad and pen down on the table and stood up. He came around the machine and bent to within inches of Tom's face. He was red with rage.

"You heard me. I said we've got a real fucking problem here," he shouted. "I want you to tell me the fucking truth *right fucking now.* You can lie to the boys upstairs all you like, but you can't lie to the machine, and you can't fucking lie to me, you cock-sucking piece of shit. I *will* get the truth outta you, so you may as well start telling it now."

Tom shook with fear and the machine hummed and scratched a little more loudly on the table beside him. Tears sprang to the corners of his eyes and all thoughts of manhood or bravery or helpfulness fled from him. He broke into childish sobs.

"I . . . I don't know what you mean," he pled. "I swear, I am telling the truth. They hurt us — they hurt all of us — they threw Julie and Robin in the river. I swear. I was just trying to help."

The detective sneered at Tom in disgust and pushed back from the vinyl handles of the chair as he spun away.

"You make me sick," he said, and returned to his seat on the far side of the table. "Now we're gonna do this again, scumbag. Except this time you're gonna tell me the truth."

In Ginna's house on Petite Drive, the overall mood was becoming increasingly desperate. Jamie, Tink, and Kathy had developed sore thumbs from the hours and hours of Nintendo and had decided to kick a soccer ball around in the front yard for a while.

It had grown into a warm and sunny day, yet the three cousins had managed to avoid the outdoors entirely. Somehow the festiveness of the sunshine seemed to further illuminate their grief. Once outside, all three of them sat down on the front step, lethargic. Tink bounced the soccer ball up and down on the concrete between her knees.

"Julie's really great at soccer, you know," Jamie said quietly.

"Yeah, I know," Tink answered, squeezing tears from her eyes and putting her arm tightly around her little cousin.

Gene had been calling the house periodically throughout the day to inform his wife of any updates down at police headquarters, but by and large there was very little to report. Jacquie, Sheila, and Kay had all been seated at the kitchen table during Gene's most recent call. It seemed that he was mostly just sitting around waiting for Tom to finish answering a growing list of questions. Tom was exhausted, definitely, but he was determined to help and there was no way Gene would be able to convince him to come home if he felt he could still be of some use for the police. Kay agreed that they should stand by their son, allow him to do what he felt he had to do. But still, she worried about him and a part of her wanted to insist that he leave and come home. Sheila and Jacquie exchanged nervous glances during the conversation.

"Can I talk to you alone for a minute?" Jacquie mouthed to Sheila.

Sheila nodded and stood. She bent and hugged Kay for a moment, kissing the top of her head before following her little sister out of the room. Finding a quiet corner in the house was no easy feat at this stage. Jacquie shuffled down the long hallway into Robin's room, where she waited for Sheila and then closed the door behind them.

"Tommy's been down at that police station for an awfully long time," Jacquie began, searching her sister's face for agreement as she spoke. "Sheila, I really think we should get him a lawyer."

"I couldn't agree more," Sheila said. "It's so awkward though — I don't want Kay and Gene to think *we* suspect him of something. Getting Tommy a lawyer might just panic everybody."

The two youngest of Gene and Ginna's siblings stood quietly in the little room, with their arms folded in front of them and the wings of all of Robin's ceramic and paper creatures surrounding them on every wall and surface. There was nothing more to say. The subject that everyone was avoiding had finally been broached.

"I think we have to do this," Sheila resolved.

"We do," Jacquie answered firmly.

Just then Sheila's face fell as she gazed over her sister's shoulder and out the front window of Robin's room. Jacquie turned to see what she was looking at.

"Oh my God," they both gasped, and before Jacquie could even turn around, Sheila had flung open the door of the room and was running down the narrow hallway. She jumped across people seated on the living-room floor and grabbed the door-knob on the front door. She stepped out into the blinding sunlight and stalked across the lawn to where Tink, Kathy and Jamie stood huddled together, surrounded by a reporter and a camera crew. Their soccer ball sat motionless on the grass a few feet away.

"And how are you holding up? The dead girls were your sisters, is that correct?" the reporter was saying, waving a padded microphone in little Jamie's confused face.

"Dead?" she was saying.

Tink stood behind her cousin with her arms on Jamie's shoulders. She was horrified but stunned. She didn't know what to do. Kathy was trying to maneuver her body in between the cameramen and Jamie, but they were persistent and she was having trouble.

"Girls, get in the house," Sheila hollered as she came storming across the lawn.

The three cousins turned toward their aunt with relief and scampered into the house.

"What the hell is wrong with you people?" Sheila shouted. "Don't you think that little girl is going through enough right now? You want a quote for your evening news? How about this for a quote: Get the fuck out of here and leave my family alone!"

Sheila was glad her two little boys weren't there to hear her cursing like this, but this kind of anger was completely new to her. And the bitterness of her language didn't even begin to express the raw fury she was really feeling.

"You're just sick. You didn't get enough footage down at the bridge, no bodies to show on the six o'clock news, so you come to a little girl's house and accost her on her own front lawn where she's in the middle of trying to comprehend the most devastating tragedy that can ever befall a family. We are grieving here. Leave us alone. *Get out, get out, get the fuck out of here now!*"

She was screaming now and waving her arms over her head at the quickly retreating news team. Jacquie had followed her out the front door and closed the girls inside, but had stayed on the front step when she saw that Sheila needed no help in chasing them off.

Sheila felt like finding a big rock and heaving it through the back window of the white news van as it squealed its tires and drove away. Her shoulders slumped as the van drove off and she felt the emotional exhaustion that follows such an outburst. The prickle of tears didn't come until after the van was out of sight, but she still stood staring into the street.

"Well, I don't think they'll be coming back here in a hurry," Jacquie commented from the front stoop.

Sheila turned and marched toward the house, where Jacquie put her arms around her big sister and used her sleeve to dry Sheila's tears.

"*Get out, get out, get the fuck out of here now!*" Jacquie mimicked her sister as the two of them laughed and cried with their foreheads together for a moment. "Well, I think we've found one homicidal maniac, anyway."

"Oh God, Jacquie, that was awful," Sheila responded. "Was I completely nuts?"

"You were perfect," Jacquie answered. "Absolutely perfect. And I don't think they'll be able to use any of that footage — it was so strewn with profanity."

They both laughed again and spent a few minutes composing themselves and drying their faces before they returned to the house.

Inside, Tink and Jamie had recovered from their brush with fame and were now re-entrenched at the Nintendo, sore thumbs and all. Kathy was a bit more shook up and she sought a quiet corner where she could be alone and think for a while. The ground floor was completely crowded — there were people in every room. Kathy crept quietly through the kitchen and creaked open the door to the basement. It was dark downstairs. She heaved a sigh of relief, glanced around at all the chatting grown-ups to make sure no one was noticing her, and then slipped inside the stairwell, closing the door behind her. She felt along the wall in the dark to find the light switch and stepped gingerly down the stairs toward Julie's room.

Julie had been newly installed in this room just a few months before. It was an unfinished basement, and only Julie's corner had a nice new wooden door, cool white tiles on the floor, and drywall covering the beams and boards of the house's frame. She had wasted no time stamping her personality on the room.

Kathy stepped inside and turned the light on. She knew that Julie wouldn't mind her being there. She thought about listening to music but she didn't feel right about going through Julie's tapes, so she avoided the radio altogether and went to lie down on the bed. She lay with her hands laced together behind her neck and her legs stretched out, studying the walls. She knew with a sickening suddenness that she would remember this day every day for the rest of her life. She was filled with a desire to absorb every detail of her cousins. She sat up silently cross-legged on the bed and began trying to mentally catalogue and memorize the room.

Julie's desk was heaped with pages and pages of poetry, which she had proudly shared with Kathy and Tink when they visited earlier in the week. Kathy stood up now and approached the little desk; she wanted to read some of her cousin's poems again. When she did, she was stunned at how much the meanings of Julie's words had changed in one day:

She remembers the unwelcome hands
The stranger
The safety that is now a threat
The cold sky, white with snow
Her hands before her
Becoming an old woman's
The leaves cover the front yard
The wind a bitter chill

She loves you in her own uncertain way
Fiercely
Desperately
It may just be the fear
That clings to her back
Stiffens her shoulders
It may just be the loneliness
The letting go of hope

But she thinks of you often
She loves you fiercely, doubtfully

Wonders if she'll ever see you again,
Even though sometimes
She can't bear the thought of you
She dreams of riverbeds, rocks and bridges
And remembers sadly a lost symphony

Kathy shuddered as she let the words sink in, and decided that one poem was her limit for the day. She avoided reading the ones that were tacked up to the walls, hanging alongside the political slogans and Greenpeace posters. Her eyes came to rest on the focal point of the room: the cork bulletin board that hung above the tidy but crowded desk. In the center of the board was a royal-blue bumper sticker stuck up with a pin, and in large white block letters, it read GEORGE BUSH IS A TRANSVESTITE. Kathy chuckled in spite of herself. There were strings of red, orange, and yellow beads that Julie had probably strung herself hanging from the top two corners of the board. But amid the clutter, the next thing that caught Kathy's eye was a plain and simple yellow index card with an ink drawing on it of a candle wrapped in barbed wire.

That candle was a symbol that resonated with Kathy. The first time she had seen it was ten years before, and it was one of her earliest vivid memories. It had been a beautiful early spring day in 1981 and Dad had angrily shushed the whole family during the evening news. Young Kathy had turned wide-eyed to the television screen and watched the silent, solemn protesters, each one carrying a large placard bearing a picture of that candle wrapped in barbed wire. At the time she hadn't known what Amnesty International was, or what *hunger striking* meant. She hadn't understood why her father had cried and told them all that this was a day of terrible grief for Catholic and Irish households all over the world. But the grim newscaster had reported that, after sixty-six days on hunger strike in an English prison, civil-rights leader Bobby Sands was dead.

She had always remembered that name, Bobby Sands. When she had gotten old enough, she had looked him up at the public library and read about his life. She had learned about how he had earned that candle wrapped in barbed wire. And now here, on the bulletin board above Julie's desk, was that same strong image. Kathy drew connections in her own mind. She wasn't yet fifteen, but she suddenly felt like a very old woman, bent with the weight of wisdom. From that day forward, she would forever associate that Amnesty International candle with deaths of great importance and the unbearable grief that accompanies them.

Tom's second polygraph had gone just as badly as the first one, or worse, if possible. His relief when the examiner called the homicide squad room to tell the detectives they were finished was enormous.

Sergeant Michael Guzy was the detective who appeared in the polygraph office a few minutes later to escort Tom back up to homicide. Tom felt goosebumps prickle his skin as he passed the desk where the examiner sat glaring up at him. The man's hatred for Tom was almost tangible.

The footsteps of Tom and Guzy echoed down the long corridor toward the elevator. Tom was still shaken, but the physicality of relief was starting to settle on him and he felt like hugging this new detective for getting him out of there. He remembered Trevor saying that he would be free to go after the polygraph and, for the first time that day, Tom was actually looking forward to going home. Things were getting scary around here and, besides, he felt he had done everything he could to help at present. He was simply too exhausted to keep going.

"That guy was really mean to me," Tom said to Guzy as the elevator doors slipped shut. "I don't know what his problem was, but he really scared me. I mean, he was really, really mean to me."

Tom looked up at the detective next to him, who didn't say

anything, but just kind of nodded. Tom took it as a reassuring gesture. He was so relieved to be headed away from that maniac and back to the homicide room, where his father was, and the team of detectives who had been so nice to him all day, so sympathetic and helpful. Tears still threatened his eyes and he realized that his face was soaked with them. He started to feel a little babyish, and spent the remainder of ride up in the elevator drying his face with his sleeve and generally trying to pull himself together.

"Right this way." Guzy motioned Tom into a small room with a window, a desk and two chairs.

It looked like an office, but there were no personal artifacts that Tom could see. The room was tiny, claustrophobic, despite the curtainless window and the mirror on one wall. Tom peered over his shoulder back into the squad room and tried to catch a glimpse of his father, but Guzy was mostly blocking his view. He turned and sat down in the hard metal chair in front of the desk.

"I guess we've got some problems with this polygraph," the sergeant said.

"Yeah, I guess so," Tom began. "I guess maybe that's why that guy downstairs was so mean. I don't know what went wrong, but I couldn't stay awake and . . ."

"All right, let's cut the bullshit," Guzy interrupted. "What the fuck did you do to those two girls, you sick little shit?"

Tom stopped talking in mid-sentence and his mouth hung open. There was a moment of silence in the tiny room.

"I . . . I didn't do anything to them. They're my cousins . . ." he stammered.

Guzy lost it. He slammed his open hands down on the tiny desk and popped out of his seat. His face was suddenly red and there was a vein throbbing visibly in his forehead. How had he become so angry so fast? Tom wondered. His entire demeanor had changed. Even his physical appearance seemed to alter. He seemed huge, more cumbersome, and his skin seemed to glow red with fury.

"I'm sick and tired of your little-innocent-boy act," he shouted. "Nobody's buying it. You're a liar, and we all know you're a liar, so you may as well drop the charade, you twisted fuck."

Guzy was around the desk now, standing beside Tom's chair, screaming into his ear. Tom had a history of bad ears. He had burst his eardrums before, and he shrank away from the sergeant now. The tears were coming so fast now that Tom couldn't even feel them and, after looking briefly at the throbbing, contorted face of his accuser, he turned and focused his eyes on the window. It was a sunny day out and, through the blur of his tears, Tom watched the sunlight glinting off the chrome and glass of the passing cars. He wished he were in one of those cars, driving away. With Julie. He tried to make himself small in the chair. "I didn't do it," Tom said lamely through his tears. "I couldn't do a thing like that."

Before long Tom ceased to even hear Guzy's accusations. The voice screaming beside his head became like a siren, loud and shocking, but just a noise. Tom's entire body was wracked with fear and grief and exhaustion, and the only words he could manage to string together were, "I didn't do it, I didn't do it, I didn't do it."

Around dinnertime, when Kay announced to her two daughters that it was time to head back over to her parents' home, she met the resistance she had expected from Tink and Kathy.

"We wanna stay with Jamie and everybody else," Tink stated emphatically.

But their mother was just as emphatic. "Grandma Polly and Grandpa Art are worried too, guys," she explained. "It's not fair to leave them all alone either."

Both daughters nodded glumly, their Catholic sense of guilt predictably defeating their personal desires.

"Maybe we can come back later on," Kay said. "Besides, we have to talk about a few things."

Leaving Ginna's was an emotional affair and it took the better part of a half an hour for Kay to drag her two daughters out to the driveway. They hugged and kissed everyone in the house countless times and promised to come back as soon as they could. It was Kathy's turn to sit in the front seat, and for the first time that Kay could ever remember, Tink didn't complain. She opened the back door and buckled herself in quietly. Kay backed out of the driveway and took a deep breath. She shifted to drive and started the car rolling as slowly as possible. It was only a five-minute drive to her parents' home, but she had to draw it out. There were things she needed to discuss with her daughters in private. Tink leaned as far forward as she could within the constraints of the seat belt when her mother started to talk.

"Okay guys, here's what's happening. Your father called a while ago to tell me that they've asked Tom to take a polygraph test — a lie detector," she explained.

Kathy didn't think it was possible to feel any more stunned or distraught than she already did, but as her mother talked her head began to reel and she clutched the dashboard in front of her dizzily.

"Why would they do that?" Tink asked.

"I'm not sure exactly, but your father seemed to think that they will be coming home soon. The police told them that the polygraph was the last thing they would ask him to do today. He'll probably be home after dinner sometime. But I have to tell you that, as a precaution, Sheila has been talking to a lawyer, a Mr. Frank Fabbri. We are probably going to hire this man to represent Tom."

"A lawyer?" Kathy asked. "Why would he need a lawyer? He hasn't done anything wrong. This doesn't make any sense."

"Unless they think he did something," Tink said, giving up on the seat belt and unbuckling herself to bring her face in between her mother's and her sister's. "They don't think that, Mom, do they? They can't possibly think that."

Kay shook her head but couldn't answer. She hadn't cried in front of her daughters yet. She couldn't cry in front of her daughters. She had to be strong for them.

"Oh God, Mom," Kathy said. "They don't, do they?"

Kay shook her head again, but the lump in her throat was too restrictive. She couldn't speak. The girls both started to cry and Tink flopped back against the seat. Kay sped up a bit, wanting to get off the road now, needing to get home and park the car and hug her daughters.

"It's gonna be okay," she managed to say.

But Tink and Kathy had been hearing that phrase all day and it wasn't okay. It was nowhere near okay. In fact nothing in the world had ever been *less* okay. Julie and Robin were gone, and with each passing hour, each passing minute, it seemed less and less likely that they would ever come back. And now Tom was at police headquarters taking a polygraph test and their mother was talking about lawyers. It was not going to be "okay."

"Mom, can you pull over?" Tink asked quietly from the backseat. "I think I'm gonna throw up again."

Meanwhile, in an office adjoining the homicide squad room, Gene was seated across a cluttered desk from the senior officer on duty that day, Lieutenant Steven Jacobsmeyer. Jacobsmeyer had called Gene into his office while Tom was down taking the polygraph test. Gene sat up straight, rigid in the chair, with his hands resting loosely on his knees. He was nodding solemnly at Jacobsmeyer while the lieutenant spoke.

"It's simply . . . impossible, Mr. Cummins. It is simply *too fantastic* to be true. Your son would have had to have fallen ninety feet from that bridge. *Ninety feet,* Mr. Cummins. I don't have to tell you that there's no way he fell from a height like that without sustaining more serious injuries. Not to mention the fact that the Coast Guard tells us the water speed at that particular section of the river is at least five knots. Come on, now, you're a Navy man. Do the calculations. He simply could not have survived the ordeal he is describing. The Coast Guard also mentioned that the current in that stretch of river leads toward the Illinois bank. According to his story, he came out on the wrong bank."

Gene's face was a mask of disbelief. His nostrils flared wildly while he tried to take in all the facts being thrown at him. He was a quick-minded individual — he always had been. And he was qualified to within a thesis paper of a doctorate as an engineer. No, he didn't need to be told that a drop of ninety feet would likely result in death, that a drop of ninety feet would, at the very least, have broken a few bones.

"Now I want to stress to you again that we do not suspect your son of actually *committing* these crimes himself. I don't think he's capable of murder any more than you do. But when you review the facts of the case, Mr. Cummins, your logical conclusion must be that something is amiss here. Something doesn't add up. He's not telling us the truth."

Jacobsmeyer picked up a paper clip from his desk and sat back in his swivel chair, fidgeting and watching Gene struggle with all this new information. Jacobsmeyer paused a few moments to allow it all to sink in.

"When we spoke earlier, you mentioned that your son had a history of lying."

Jacobsmeyer let that sentence hang in the air for a moment as if expecting Gene to arrive at some sort of next logical step from it. Gene responded by looking at him blankly.

"Lying about report cards and parties where the parents weren't home," Gene explained. "That's what I told you. All kids lie about that kind of stuff from time to time. This is a whole new ballpark. My son is not capable of this. He is a fine young man, a good young man. I can't . . . I don't . . ." Gene ran out of things to say.

"Ninety feet, Mr. Cummins. Just think about that for a few minutes," Jacobsmeyer replied tartly.

Now Gene started to get annoyed. He didn't need to think it over. He understood the implications. But this simply wasn't a situation a parent could be prepared for. *Okay, so ninety feet. Now what? My son's a liar and a murderer? No.* Gene shook his head.

"I don't know what you want me to say," he said flatly.

"I want you to say that you'll help us." Jacobsmeyer looked pleadingly at Gene and leaned forward in his chair, resting his elbows on his army green desk blotter. "Mr. Cummins, we really need your help. We need to get at the truth here. If we have any hope of finding those girls, or finding any potential attackers, we need to know everything that really went down on that bridge last night. Maybe everything happened the way Tom says it did, up until the point where these guys pushed them off the bridge. Now suppose that somehow Tom got away, he escaped, and he's not sure exactly what happened to the girls after he ran. Now once he gets away and he's safe, he's starts feeling ashamed that he abandoned his cousins and didn't do more to help them. So naturally, he runs down to the water's edge and splashes around, maybe looking for the girls. When he can't find them, he goes up to the road to find help and he concocts this story along the way so he won't look like a coward.

"Or maybe it's even simpler than that. Maybe he was so traumatized by what happened up there that he blacked out. He can't remember what happened and he's ashamed to tell us that. He needs to know that whatever the truth is, it's okay. But we *need* to know the truth."

Gene was silent and his jaw worked back and forth while he

listened. He stared at the checkered floor tiles in the small office and considered Jacobsmeyer's hypotheses. The lieutenant was quiet for a few minutes, leaning back again and flicking the paper clip back and forth between the knuckles of his right hand. He swiveled ever so slightly in his chair.

"He didn't fall ninety feet, Mr. Cummins," Jacobsmeyer said. "And if there's anybody in this building right now who can get the whole truth out of him, it's you. He respects you and he'll listen to you. He's obviously petrified. He's exhausted. But I think he has a very real desire to help. He probably doesn't understand that making up this story to cover up some more embarrassing truth could destroy our entire investigation. The sooner he tells us what really happened, the sooner you can take him home and we can get the investigation moving in a more appropriate direction. At this stage, it seems to me that you are our only hope of finding any trace of what happened to those girls."

Gene was silent. He felt uneasy — he didn't trust this man. Gene was sure that Jacobsmeyer was more suspicious of Tom than he was letting on. It was true that either one of his hypotheses sounded more plausible than Tom's version of events, but Gene felt pretty sure that Jacobsmeyer wasn't buying his own theories. He was simply trying to win Gene over, trying to make him feel comfortable so that he would participate in questioning Tom. *Ninety feet,* he thought. *There must be more to this than Tom has remembered or told us.*

He glanced up at Jacobsmeyer, whose face was stern and patient. Gene knew that, if he cooperated, he would remain in the good graces of the police department. And that, in turn, would allow him access to his son, and with it, at least some degree of tenuous control over the situation. He was determined to do what was best for his son, to remain intimately involved. Gene lifted his hands from his knees and, lacing his fingers together, almost in a gesture of prayer, placed them in his lap. A flicker of loathing passed through Gene as he looked at the man seated across from him, the man who thought his son was a murderer. *I'm gonna prove you wrong,* Gene thought.

"I'll do it," he said.

In the article "Coercive Persuasion and Attitude Change," cited at the beginning of this chapter, Ofshe also states that:

> *Under unusual circumstances, modern police-interrogation methods can exhibit some of the properties of a thought-reform program . . . Although they rarely come together simultaneously, the ingredients necessary to elicit a temporarily believed false confession are: erroneous police suspicion, the use of certain commonly employed interrogation procedures, and some degree of psychological vulnerability in the suspect . . . Tactics used to change the suspect's position and elicit a confession include maneuvers designed to intensify feelings of guilt and emotional distress . . .*

Certainly the circumstances surrounding Tom Cummins on the afternoon of April 5, 1991 could be described as utterly unusual. Bizarre, even. And secondly, as Tom sat in Guzy's office, staring longingly out at the waning afternoon sunshine, his psychological vulnerability, feelings of guilt, and levels of emotional distress were off the charts. He had been awake for over thirty-six hours, but he no longer even felt tired or aggrieved. His head simply nodded into his chest whenever there was a moment of quiet. But despite his exhaustion and extreme emotional distress, Tom was unbending.

"I didn't do it," he repeated to himself, alone now in the quiet room.

In 1988, Ofshe, along with his colleague Dr. Richard A. Leo, conducted a further study for the Northwestern University School of Law. The study was entitled "The Consequences of False Confessions: Deprivations of Liberty and Miscarriages of Justice in the Age of Psychological Interrogation," and it was published in the *Journal of Criminal Law and Criminology*. In that study, Ofshe declared that:

> *Interrogators sometimes become so committed to closing a case that they improperly use psychological interrogation techniques to coerce or persuade a suspect into giving a statement that allows the interrogator to make an arrest.*

Ofshe further warned that:

> *American police are poorly trained about the dangers of interrogation and false confession. Rarely are police officers instructed in how to avoid eliciting confessions, how to understand what causes false confessions, or how to recognize the forms false confessions take or their distinguishing characteristics. Instead, some interrogation manual writers and trainers persist in the unfounded belief that contemporary psychological methods will not cause the innocent to confess — a fiction so thoroughly contradicted by all of the research on police interrogation that it can be labeled a potentially deadly myth.*

By the late afternoon hours of April 5, the St. Louis Metropolitan Police Department was under heavy scrutiny from the community, and their desire to close the case was indeed great. Two gifted and beautiful young girls were missing, and the police couldn't produce any answers about their attackers. They couldn't even produce bodies. The media had devoured Tom's wild story about four brutal rapist/murderers, and the sensationalism surrounding the case was reaching heights never before experienced in St. Louis. Julie and Robin were already being caricatured into downright saintly personas in the media. In short, the case was turning into a circus, and the police department was in the center ring. The spotlight was on. They needed answers fast.

When Guzy returned to Tom in the small office, a new detective accompanied him. His name was Christopher Pappas, but Tom couldn't remember how he had learned the new detective's name. The niceties that included introductions had now ceased — he must have heard Guzy call the man by name.

"You ready to tell the truth now?" Guzy asked.

Tom nodded. Guzy stood across the desk from him, leaning toward Tom on his fists. The new man, Pappas, now stood behind Tom, who could feel hands gripping the back of his chair. Tom sat forward a bit.

"Good. Now. You didn't go off that bridge, did you?" Guzy began quietly.

Tom swallowed hard and nodded cautiously.

"*God damn it!*" Guzy erupted and slammed his two hands against the desk again. "This *did not* happen! There is no way you went off that bridge. We *know* you're lying. You're just making this harder on everybody. The Coast Guard has told us there is no way you could come out on the Missouri side."

Pappas threw his two cents in from over Tom's shoulder.

"I'll bet you didn't know there are water-intake valves out there in that stretch of river. You would have come up with a better story if you had known that. If you had gone off the bridge where you say you did, you'd be stuck in a pipe somewhere by now, sucked right in." The closeness of the man's voice made Tom cringe, but at least he wasn't shouting.

"Look, I've told you what happened, I don't know what else . . ."

"Shut up," Guzy interrupted him. "Just shut the fuck up, scumbag."

"I want to see my father," Tom stated then.

Guzy laughed. He actually seemed to find humor in Tom's request.

"Oh, you want to see your daddy! How quaint," Guzy mimicked in an unnaturally high and whiny voice. "Well I'm afraid there's nothing Daddy can do for you now, sonny boy. You're fucked. We know what you've done and you're not going to see your precious daddy or anybody else in your sick family for a long, long time unless you start telling the truth."

Tom bit back a sob, shook his head, and remained silent. Guzy pointed to the door, and he and Pappas both shuffled out without further conversation, leaving Tom alone once again. When the door reopened, Pappas was back, and this time it was Jacobsmeyer who was with him. Pappas immediately resumed his position behind Tom's chair, while Jacobsmeyer sat down on the edge of the small desk, dropping his manila folder theatrically beside him. He sat directly in front of Tom on the little desk and leaned into his face while he spoke.

"Guess who's here," Jacobsmeyer said to Tom.

Tom felt a flicker of hope as his mind raced with possibilities. Julie and Robin? Dad?

Jacobsmeyer smiled. "You know the four guys who you say raped and killed your cousins, the four guys you met on the bridge? Well, lucky day for us! We've found two of them. Of course, their story is a little different from yours and there are *two* of them. In a situation where we have their word against yours, we have to take into account the fact that your story is, of course, physically impossible. Stand up a second there, son."

Tom's heart felt as if it were lunging around inside him, beating against his rib cage one minute, ready to come up his throat and out his mouth the next. His heartbeat was so strong and rapid he could feel it in his skin, in every extremity. His knees trembled as he pulled himself to his feet.

"See that mirror over there?" Jacobsmeyer indicated the mirror on the wall behind him. "Well, it's not really a mirror, and if you could just stand over there and let those nice young men on the other side get a good look at you."

"You mean you found those guys? They're . . . they're . . ."

"That's right, they're right through that mirror. And they told us what really happened up there. We know that you're the sick fuck who killed those two girls. So stand in close there and let them look at you."

Tom's feet were planted firmly on the floor and he twisted hysterically, refusing to move toward the mirror.

"Don't worry about a thing, they can't get to you in here. Of course, if you don't start telling the truth and we're forced to let you go home, I can't promise you they might not wait around outside for you. And I couldn't blame them, really. I think you're a sick fuck, they think you're a sick fuck. Only difference is, I can't really do much to you myself because I'm a police officer."

"You can't let them go!" Tom erupted. "If you've got them, you *can't* let them go, you have to believe me. They *raped* my cousins."

Tom was shaking before the mirror, but Jacobsmeyer merely rolled his eyes at the boy's terror. They made him turn left and then right for a nonexistent audience before they allowed him to sit down again. There was nobody on the other side of that mirror. Clemons, Richardson, Gray, and Winfrey were still at large; there hadn't been so much as a hiccup in their daily routines, and they were all quite busy getting on with their lives.

"So what do you think now, brave boy? You ready to tell the truth?" Jacobsmeyer asked as Tom tried in vain to control his trembling.

Tom nodded.

"All right. Here's what I think happened," Jacobsmeyer began, opening the folder from the desk beside him. "You went to that bridge last night because you wanted to have sex with Julie, didn't you?"

"*No,*" Tom said, but Jacobsmeyer continued as if he hadn't even heard.

"You went to the bridge to have sex with Julie and when she refused, a struggle ensued. According to our two witnesses" — Jacobsmeyer accompanied the word "witnesses" with a flourishing wave toward the mirror on the back wall — "Julie fell and then Robin jumped in to try and save her."

"No. No, no way," Tom started. "Those guys are lying. *They* did it . . ."

"You didn't mean for Julie to fall, but it happened and you panicked," Jacobsmeyer continued, increasing the volume of his voice to be heard over Tom's protestations.

Tom continued to shake his head and murmur his denials, but Jacobsmeyer went on to list various sick and twisted plots, each one incriminating Tom in his cousins' deaths. Eventually, Jacobsmeyer grew angry and threw the folder to the floor.

"You know what? We've been trying to help you out here but we're not gonna get anywhere as long as you refuse to cooperate," Jacobsmeyer shouted, looking at Tom with disgust. "You make me sick," he added, before storming out of the room.

It was dinnertime at Fair Acres Road but nobody was interested in food, least of all Tink. Grandma Polly was desperate to do something helpful and, as was her habit, she sought solace by trying to feed her loved ones. Her petite figure was cast in silhouette as she stood in the kitchen doorway, looking into the darkening dining room where her daughter Kay sat at the table with her head resting in one hand. She was trying to fill her mother in on what had taken place that afternoon, but she couldn't seem to construct a chronological sequence of events. Every moment since the rude five A.M. awakening was a kind of blur of surreal activity. Grandma Polly wiped her hands on the clean apron she wore and went to hug her daughter.

"How about we make some dinner for these kids, hon?" she asked. "They still need to eat."

Kay smiled weakly.

"That's a great idea. Mom, listen, I'm not quite sure how to say this, but I think maybe I should make dinner tonight. The girls love your cooking, but they are really screwed up and I want to try and make things as normal as possible for them. I'm thinking of making something really simple and plain — at least try to trick their bellies into thinking things are normal. Tink hasn't eaten a bite all day and both of them have been throwing up."

"Of course, doll baby," Grandma Polly answered, squeezing her daughter's hands. "Whatever you think is best. But only if you promise to let me help."

"Thanks, Mom."

Kay went into the living room, where her father and her two daughters sat glued to the television. Kay's two brothers had also arrived and were doing their best to lighten the mood without seeming insensitive. Their family tragedy had been advertised every hour of the day on the television as "breaking news" with announcements to "tune in live at six for detailed coverage." Kay glanced at the clock. It was about five minutes to six, and breaths all over St. Louis were being drawn in. She went and sat between her two daughters on the blue velvet couch, hoping to get a few words with them before the ugly newscast and the inevitable upset that would follow.

"I'm gonna make some dinner." she said. "What are you guys in the mood for?"

Kathy shrugged and Tink said nothing.

"Tink?"

She shook her head.

"Honey, you've gotta eat something. You haven't eaten all day," Kay said.

"I can't eat," her daughter responded quietly. "I'm not hungry anyway."

"I'll make whatever you want — anything you want. Just name it."

Tink shook her head again.

"I can't," she said. "I'll only throw it up."

"How about hot dogs? Pancakes? Ice cream? *Anything,* honey," Kay pleaded, brushing the bangs away from Tink's forehead.

Her daughter's eyes were swimming with tears but she held them in check.

"Okay, I'll try, Mom," she finally conceded. "Just make whatever."

The newscast ended up coming and going rather uneventfully. The media simply had nothing to report. Somehow, one of the local network affiliates had gotten ahold of one photograph of each of the girls and they flashed them at the top of the story, with the names reversed — Julie's name under Robin's picture and Robin's name under Julie's. It was almost too infuriating to comment on, but Tink wouldn't let the opportunity pass.

"They could at least get their names right," she said. "If they insist on invading our privacy and stalking Jamie and making a public spectacle out of our family, they could at least get Julie's and Robin's names right."

Her jaw was set at a hard angle and no one contradicted her. Grandma Polly made supportive *tsk*-ing noises and Kay rubbed the back of Tink's hair.

Grandpa Art added, "Now that's just awful," and Kathy slipped out to throw up.

Kay's brother Skip, the family comedian, followed Kathy down the hall to the bathroom door. He waited for the retching sounds to taper off inside and then he knocked loudly, shouting through the closed door. "No point in flushing that — just a

waste of water. Your mother is cooking, so we'll all be in there after dinner anyway. You may as well leave it."

That did the trick. When Kathy opened the door, she had
tears of laughter in her eyes and the living room was erupting in
a much-needed case of the giggles.

"Turn this crap off, shall we?" Tink said, in a more normal
tone of voice than she had commanded all day.

Grandpa Art hoisted himself out of his chair and flicked off
the big television. "Yeah, let's get some dinner," he agreed.

As Gene Cummins was led into the room where his son sat
trembling at yet another empty table, he felt a fleeting pang of regret for agreeing to participate in this debacle. But he steeled
himself for the task at hand. He knew that Tom was incapable of
harming anyone, least of all Julie and Robin. Sure, he had a kid's
history of lying and there was a good bit of evidence to suggest
that he wasn't being *entirely* truthful now. But whatever the truth
was, Gene felt one-hundred-percent positive that it would not
implicate Tom in any way. He was determined to procure the entire truth from his son once and for all, to prove to Jacobsmeyer
and the rest of these guys that, though Tom may have been confused or ashamed, he was certainly *not* a murderer.

Gene sat down next to his son and they gazed at each other
levelly. It was an awkward moment, with all the shifting eyes and
heavy silence of the detectives in the room. Gene wished that
they could be alone for a minute, that he could just hug his son.
Tom's eyes were full and shining and his cheeks were red and
streaked, but he looked composed. He was clearly relieved to see
his father. Gene took a deep breath and exhaled his words quickly.

"Tom. We have a real bad situation here," he began. "I know
we've had our differences in the past, you told a lot of tall tales when
you were a kid and I was awfully hard on you. But all that's changed

in the last few years. That was just regular kid stuff and you grew out of it like I always knew you would. Now you've got your life in order and we're all so proud of you — your mother and your sisters and I. That's why I want you to know that no matter what happened up there last night on that bridge, you can tell me. I know you wouldn't have done anything to hurt anybody on purpose."

Tom had dropped his father's gaze somewhere in the middle of the little speech and his breath was coming in short quick gasps now. He looked around from the face of one detective to the next and his eyes screwed up again, his cheeks flushing deeper red than before. His lips worked into a tight little bow and he couldn't speak. He was sure he would vomit but his stomach was empty. His own father didn't believe him. His mind started to slip away from him and the sound that emanated from him was deep and low, so inhuman that Gene and the detectives didn't realize, at first, that it came from Tom. It was a low wail that started in the pit of his stomach and caught wind as it moved up and out through his body. It was the sound of pure grief and it broke Gene's heart to hear it. He put his arms around his son but he couldn't stop the wailing.

"Son, listen to me," Gene tried, speaking directly and urgently into Tom's ear, raising his voice to be heard over the cries. "It's okay, whatever happened it's okay. Just *tell* me. You don't have to be ashamed."

But Tom was hysterical now and, even if he had had another truth to tell, he would have been unable. His tongue felt thick and he inhaled a torrent of tears through his nostrils and mouth when his wail broke long enough for him to gasp a breath. The episode lasted a few minutes and Tom fought helplessly to regain control of his senses and his body. When he finally steadied his breathing and the tears had slowed to a constant trickle, he spoke erratically. His sleeves sloppily covered his nose and mouth, but everyone in the room caught the thick words.

"I've told you the truth. *My God,* why doesn't anyone believe me?"

His voice was full of desperation and his arms were clenched in front of his stomach as if to quell the nausea. Gene tried in vain to comfort his son, who was rocking back and forth now with his father's arms around him. It was quiet for a few moments. Then Gene quickly relayed the facts as told to him by Jacobsmeyer, the main reasons why the detectives were doubting his story.

"The drop from that bridge was ninety feet, son. You couldn't have fallen from that height. There's just no way. You probably wouldn't even have survived," Gene said softly.

Tom shook his head dumbly. "I don't know what to tell you. I don't know what else to tell you. That's what happened," he said and he gave up control again.

To quote the previously cited police training manual, *Criminal Interrogations and Confessions:*

> *Trickery and deceit are at times indispensable to the criminal interrogation process. It was stressed that they do not present the risk of false confessions.*

This manual, the very book used nationwide to train our police officers in how to properly conduct an interrogation, discusses at length the fact that the United States Supreme Court has sanctioned the use of deceit and trickery in interrogation settings. The text also gives various examples of instances where suspects have been tricked into making admissible confessions. Furthermore, the manual actually *urges* police officers to use trickery and deceit to elicit confessions whenever necessary within the bounds of what it calls "decency."

On the afternoon of April 5, 1991, Gene Cummins would have found these simple facts about police trickery to be extremely relevant. For although he was an educated and intelligent man, one who possessed what he would have described as a healthy degree of skepticism about the police in his current situation, he had never read *Criminal Interrogations and Confessions*. He was absolutely not aware that the police would resort to blatant dishonesty. He didn't even know that this kind of deception was legal. And because of that, he never expected to sit in Jacobsmeyer's office listening politely, with his son's life hanging in the balance a few feet away, while the lieutenant looked him squarely in the eye and fed him outright lies.

Tom Cummins had not fallen ninety feet from the Old Chain of Rocks Bridge. He had fallen about fifty.

CHAPTER NINE

For Tom, the worst moment of the entire ordeal had come when his father had entered that little room and encouraged him to tell the truth. Before that moment, no matter who screamed at him or called him names, Tom had felt sure that somehow, with the help of his family, they could straighten this whole mess out. This was obviously a mistake. A giant, cosmic misunderstanding.

But with the revelation that his own father didn't believe him, Tom simply and wholly gave up hope. Sometime during the ensuing hysteria, Gene was bodily removed from his son and Tom was once again alone with Jacobsmeyer and Pappas. He didn't care what happened now. It could not possibly get any worse. He didn't care if they arrested him. He didn't even care if he got convicted. And when Jacobsmeyer hinted that confessing was better than getting the electric chair, Tom couldn't bring himself to care one way or the other. The electric chair didn't scare him — it couldn't be worse than this. He just wanted to be left alone — to cry and to grieve and to sleep.

"Let's try this again, shall we?" Jacobsmeyer said, settling into a chair opposite from where Tom sat. "This is what happened."

Jacobsmeyer again went through his various scenarios with

Tom, who sat shaking his head. But his heart wasn't in it any more. His denials were growing quieter and weaker with each new accusation, and Jacobsmeyer sensed this.

"After Robin jumped in to try and save Julie, you freaked out, ran down to the riverbank, and jumped in to look for them. When you couldn't find them, you went to seek help and that's when you flagged down the trucker to phone the police. That's what really happened. Right?" the lieutenant concluded.

Tom looked up at the ceiling and let all of the breath leave him before answering. "You know," he began slowly, with the courage born from sheer hopelessness, "you are going to believe whatever the hell you want. I've told you the truth. So if this is what you want to believe, then *fine.* Sure. Why not? That's what happened."

Confession.

"Bingo," Jacobsmeyer said, looking up at Pappas, who was in his usual spot behind Tom's chair. "We've got ourselves a confession."

Jacobsmeyer and Pappas left the room quickly, like men on a mission, and for the first time all day Tom, left alone, did not sleep. He tried to consider what had just happened to him, and the only emotional reaction he could manage was relief. He was no longer afraid. He had hit rock bottom. The word "confession" didn't scare him either. There was no tape. He hadn't signed anything. And the "confessional" phrase had been spat out contemptuously during a moment of sarcastic frustration. Now *that* was taking sarcasm to a whole new level. Robin would have been proud, he thought, and he giggled to himself. He was still chuckling at the thought when the door banged open and Pappas stuck his head in.

"Come on," he said to Tom.

Pappas took Tom down to the basement of the police station and across an ill-lit underground parking garage. An hour ago,

Tom would have been terrified at the thought of being alone in a place like this with the brutally intimidating Pappas. But now he felt confident, secure. The man wasn't screaming or glaring at him. He was walking along beside him, almost like a civilized human being, Tom thought.

"Where're we going?" Tom asked, his voice rich with a new boldness.

"To the video-recording studio," Pappas answered, less gruffly than Tom had heard him speak all day, "so we can record your confession."

It was almost as if the prospect of wrapping up the case had subdued any animosity the man had previously felt toward Tom. He didn't hate him nearly as much for being a murderer as he had before for being a liar. Tom didn't have any particular desire to stir up the man's wrath, so he raised his eyebrows and nodded, remaining quiet. He would wait until the video camera was rolling before he would proclaim his innocence again. They reached a door at the far end of the garage, and Pappas opened it for Tom. They were in yet another long linoleum-floored hallway that was strung with closed doors. Pappas led the way toward one and reached for the knob. It was locked.

"Shit," he said. "The equipment guy isn't here yet. We'll wait in here."

He turned and led Tom toward an open door at the end of the hall. Inside there were several snack and soda machines and a table with two long benches. Tom sat down while Pappas threaded quarters into one of the machines.

"You want one?" he called over his shoulder to Tom.

"Sure."

Pappas placed a cold can down in front of Tom and opened his own as he sat down.

"Cigarette?" he asked.

"Sure."

It was Tom's first cigarette all day and it did more to relax him than he had ever dreamed possible. He held the Coke in his non-smoking hand and took swigs from it in between drags. Pappas appeared almost pensive beside him, if the man was capable of pensiveness, Tom thought.

"What the hell happened up there?" Pappas asked quietly.

Tom was shocked by the utter calm of the detective's voice. It was almost uninterested. Tom shook his head and sucked on the cigarette, smiling wryly. He felt more in control than he had all day.

"You know," Tom said in a strong, clear voice, "when this video guy gets here, and the tape is rolling, I'll tell you what happened."

"Tell me now," Pappas pressed, like a teenager awaiting some juicy gossip, "What happened?"

"Okay," Tom said, nodding and finishing his last sip of Coke. "You want to know what happened? I'll tell you what happened. You guys fucked up. You have the wrong fucking guy and there are four murderers running around out there. That's what fucking happened. I'm not making any goddamn videotape and I'm not answering any more questions on the grounds that I may incriminate myself."

Tom ground his cigarette butt into the little green plastic ash-tray that sat on the table in front of him. He tried not to look at Pappas for a reaction, but he felt good about his articulation. It was a brave statement and it had said all he wanted to say. Pappas nodded beside him and mulled over the remarks.

"Okay," the detective responded dully, "I guess there's no point in waiting down here then. Let's get back upstairs and we'll see what to do next."

After a call from Gene during dinner about the news of the disastrous polygraph results, Kay spent the next half hour talking quietly on the phone in her parents' room. Tink and Kathy couldn't hear a word despite their best eavesdropping efforts at the door. Grandpa Art shooed them away every few minutes, but they crept back repeatedly. The first call she made was to Sheila at Ginna's house. Sheila seemed to be waiting by the phone.

"It's all sorted out," Sheila began — all business. "He knows that you may call, although he's not privy to the details yet. His name is Frank Fabbri."

Kay thanked her, jotted down the lawyer's number and hung up. Her next call was to Frank Fabbri, criminal defense attorney. Fabbri was cordial to Kay, but like Sheila, he was quick — very much down to business. After Kay introduced herself, he began firing off questions almost immediately. Kay answered them as best she could.

"Do you mean to tell me he's been down at that police station all day long answering questions without an attorney present?" he asked, almost angrily.

"Uh-huh," Kay answered. "He insisted on helping."

"Shit," Fabbri responded, and then, without missing a beat, he began a detailed list of instructions. "Okay, here's what I need you to do. Call your husband back at the police station. Tell him to go straight to the desk sergeant and say 'This has gone on long enough. I'm taking my son and we're leaving.' Tell him to write down exactly what the officer says, and then to call you back immediately with the response. Then call me back."

Kay listened to her instructions, growing more frightened all the time, but her fear seemed to lend her resolve. Now she finally had something concrete to do. Now she could help. The only thing that had kept her from losing her temper with the police up to this point had been her maternal instinct to support Tom. She had been disgusted by the way they had brushed her aside at the bridge that morning. They had patronized her and ignored her in turns, while speaking respectfully and urgently to her husband.

They wore their sexism as proudly as their badges, she thought. And now that they had given her a mother's reason for anger, now that they accused her son, her fury was quick and motivating. She drew in a sharp breath of determination and immediately dialed the number of the pay phone that Gene had given her. The courtesy of the extra detective's desk and phone in the homicide room had been retracted from him sometime before. He picked up the wall-mounted pay phone after half a ring.

"Okay, you're to go to the desk sergeant and tell him very deliberately that you and Tom are leaving. Write down his exact response and call me back," Kay instructed.

She hung up and waited. She jumped when the phone rang several minutes later, and she grabbed it. Gene sounded more distraught than ever.

"Are you ready?" he asked.

Kay poised her pen over the small notepad that balanced on her knee, and said she was.

"He said, 'You are welcome to go whenever you want, but Tom isn't going anywhere.'" Gene read from a notepad he had acquired during the day. There was an audible quiver in his voice and he tried to conquer it by clearing his throat. "That was kinda what I expected them to say but still, I sure didn't like the sound of it."

Kay nibbled on her bottom lip and answered her husband with as much resolve as she could muster.

"It's fine," she said, "I think it's what we all expected. I better let Fabbri know and then I'll call you back right away."

They hung up. Kay dialed more frantically this time. She couldn't help but notice the way her hand shook while she pushed the buttons. She tried to will stillness and calm into her extremities, but her whole body was shaking with fear and adrenaline.

"They said he can't leave." She spilled the information to Fabbri without even saying hello.

"All right, I'm on my way down there. You call your husband back, tell him to go back to the desk sergeant and tell him that you have retained an attorney for your son and the attorney's name is Frank Fabbri. Tell him to demand that the questioning cease immediately and to write down exactly what the officer says again. Kay, your son is so exhausted at this stage, he couldn't tell the pope what happened," Fabbri said.

Kay glanced at the clock on her father's nightstand and quickly did the math in her head. Tom must have been up for at least thirty-six hours by now.

"The next few hours are going to get a little hairy for you," Fabbri continued. "The police don't want to let Tom go, but they clearly can't keep him any longer without arresting him, so in all likelihood, he is going to be arrested. The charge will probably be two counts of first-degree murder, but it sounds to me like they don't have a leg to stand on. Really, this is just us forcing their hand, to ensure that the questioning stops immediately. So don't let it panic you. I have to get down there immediately, so I'll call you back after I've seen your son. You may want to warn your husband about what I've told you."

Kay nodded and felt her breath coming in sharp stabs.

"Thank you," was all she could think of to say.

She called Gene with his next set of instructions and asked him to ring her back immediately. When he did, he sounded almost relieved.

"Well, what'd he say?" Kay asked.

"I told them exactly what you said, that we had retained an attorney for Tom and that the attorney's name was Frank Fabbri, and the sergeant's exact words were, 'Oh shit, it's Fabbri.' I guess this was the right guy to hire. His reputation precedes him around here," Gene explained.

"Gene, I have to tell you what else Fabbri said," Kay interrupted her husband. "He warned me about a couple of things.

He says that by forcing an end to the questioning, we are kind of pushing them into making an arrest. Fabbri said that if Tom is arrested, the charge will most likely be two counts of first-degree murder."

Gene was silent. Something on the other end of the phone line was distracting him.

"Gene?" Kay said. "Gene?"

He didn't respond, but she heard the exchange of voices that took place in the police station's echoey corridor. Footsteps approached. The first voice was a deep one and Kay didn't recognize it. She couldn't make out the muffled words, but she heard Gene say, "Yes?" and then the voice came back, clearer this time:

"Your son is being arrested and charged with two counts of first-degree murder for the homicides of Julie and Robin Kerry."

Gene dropped the phone and Kay was instantly frantic. She screamed his name several times, and Tink and Kathy lost their patience, flinging open the bedroom door when they heard the terror in their mother's voice. They stood clinging to each other in the doorway and didn't move toward Kay, who didn't seem to notice their arrival. She had a wild look in her eye and she was pacing with the phone in her hand, screaming their father's name. After thirty seconds or so, Gene's choked voice came back, and he sobbed down the line to her.

"I'll have to call you back," he said.

And before Kay could respond, she was listening to a dial tone.

When Fabbri entered the little interrogation room where he knew Tom Cummins would be waiting, the sight that met his eyes was even worse than he had expected. He knew what interrogations were like, how traumatic they could be for a suspect, particularly an innocent one. But Tom Cummins looked as if he had been to hell and back. The young man's eyes were so swollen and red that he could hardly open them, and he made no attempt to speak to this new man who strode in wearing the chic Italian suit. The parade of detectives had been dressed in a virtual array of wardrobes today, everything from grunge to uniform to business casual. And when Fabbri entered, Tom assumed that he was just the latest. Fabbri crossed the small room slowly and lifted his briefcase onto the table. He sat down and looked silently at Tom for a moment. He didn't know quite what to make of the young man yet, but one thing was clear: he was miles past miserable.

"It's over," Fabbri said quietly, looking Tom straight in the eye.

"What?" Tom asked.

"It's over. All the questioning is over," Fabbri said again.

Tom blinked across the table from Fabbri. He couldn't allow himself to hope that this man was telling the truth. He shook his head. Fabbri reached slowly into the inside pocket of his suit jacket and drew out his wallet. He removed his driver's license and his Missouri Bar Association card and slid them across the table toward Tom, gesturing for him to pick them up and examine them.

"I'm an attorney," he explained slowly, "and a friend of your family's. Your aunt Sheila called me and I'm here to tell you that this nightmare of a day is over."

Tom studied the two cards, flipping them over incredulously in his hands and reading every word he could find on them. He looked back to Fabbri and remained silent.

"So we've got good news and bad news," Fabbri continued. "I've already told you the good news. No more questioning. No more lies. No more shit. I am *not* a cop. And this is the one thing that the cops are not allowed to lie about. It is illegal to impersonate an attorney. I am *your* attorney. Do you understand what I'm telling you? It's all over. I'm on *your* side. Nobody can touch you now. They can't ask you any more questions. It's all over."

Tom let the Missouri Bar card drop out of his fingers and land upside down on the table. He tipped his head back and allowed tears of relief run down his face.

"Now the bad news is that the police are going to arrest you. Here's what's going to happen. They are going to take you somewhere in this building. They are going to take your mug shots, and they are going to book you on two charges of first-degree murder."

Tom nodded. He didn't appear scared — he didn't even seem surprised. He just listened intently. Fabbri wondered if the boy was in shock.

"It's going to be okay. They kind of just *have* to do this now that I'm here. They are going to take you to a jail cell, again somewhere in this building, and you are going to have to spend the night there. I want you to know that this is all okay. This is good. This is what has to happen for right now and it's the first step towards clearing you, okay? We're going to get through this now. All your family is behind you," Fabbri said in the most conciliatory tone possible.

He was speaking to Tom as a teacher might talk to a kindergartner, and Tom didn't mind at all. In fact, it was exactly what he needed to hear, and exactly the tone in which he needed to hear it. He felt like collapsing with relief. The news that his family was behind him restored some hope to him, lifted him from rock bottom, and as a result he now felt more terrified than ever. He hadn't tried his voice in a while and he wasn't sure what kind of a squeak or tremor might come out when he opened his mouth, but Fabbri's words gave him the courage to try.

"I just want to know that you believe me," Tom said softly. "I need to know that *somebody* believes me."

Fabbri was unexpectedly moved by the boy's words. The desperation of suspects had ceased to affect him emotionally years before, but this young man was different. His plea was so genuine, his voice so purely grief-laden as he searched the face of this complete stranger for affirmation.

"Tom," Fabbri answered unwaveringly, "I believe you."

And at those four simple words, Tom collapsed into a blubbering heap on the table. His fingers gripped tightly at the hair on the back of his head while he cried and Fabbri watched mournfully. He let Tom cry for a few minutes. When he quieted down a bit, Fabbri handed him a handkerchief and explained a few more details of what to expect in the coming hours.

"You are not to speak to *anyone* tonight while you are in this building. After you are booked and taken to your cell, you may experience some further harassment. If they come for you and they start trying to question you, say *nothing.* Not a single word. Don't even tell them your name. I will be back for you in the morning."

Fabbri stood up to go and Tom felt like throwing himself at the man. He wanted to scream, "Don't go," and hug and kiss this man in the expensive suit and the silk tie. But he didn't scream or throw himself bodily at Fabbri. Instead, he stood like a man and held his hand out to his savior.

"Thank you," he said simply.

Fabbri took Tom's hand and shook it firmly.

"I don't know the details just now and I don't need to," he said before he left, "but I believe you are telling the truth. And we are going to get you through this."

Tom nodded and swallowed hard. Fabbri put his identification back into his wallet, lifted his briefcase lightly from the table, gave Tom a parting smile, and then was gone.

It was only a matter of moments before two new detectives came into the room to take Tom up to booking. Tom was a little surprised and altogether relieved that they didn't produce any handcuffs and didn't attempt to restrain him in any way. They simply opened the door and said, "Let's go."

Tom was standing flanked by the two detectives at the now-familiar elevator, waiting for the doors to open, when Fabbri and Gene emerged from the squad room. Gene looked ashen and nauseated — almost seasick, Tom thought. And when he spotted his son, he dropped the hushed conversation with the attorney and moved quickly to where Tom stood. The two detectives did not attempt to interfere as Gene threw his arms around his son in the most abandoned, most heartfelt tenderness he had ever displayed. Father and son clung to each other and wept heavily.

"I didn't do this, Dad," Tom said between sobs.

"I know, son," Gene responded. "I know."

CHAPTER TEN

Kay wasn't exactly sure what to tell Tink and Kathy, but so far today she had been painfully candid with them and they had held up remarkably well. She wasn't sure if that fact spoke more of their maturity or of their youthful resilience, but either way she was relieved. She had enough on her plate right now without having to worry about one of her daughters having some kind of a breakdown. So as she hung up the phone and looked at them, standing clinging to each other in Grandma Polly's bedroom doorway with frantic faces, she knew she had to tell them the whole ugly truth.

She walked past them down the narrow hallway into the living room and they followed her, still holding hands. Her daughters had *never* held hands before, Kay thought — they were archenemies, sworn rivals. How terrible that it took a moment like this for them to finally learn to cling to each other for support.

Kathy and Tink walked silently to the blue couch and sat down together while Grandpa Art turned off the television and Grandma Polly came in from the kitchen, wiping her hands on her apron. Kay's two brothers were there as well and their faces were filled with concern. Everyone was silent, waiting for Kay to speak. She steadied herself with her hands on the back of her father's chair and cleared her throat before she began. Her eyes were unnaturally wide and she looked as if she couldn't close them at all, they were so busy with fear and disbelief. Her brother Art Junior stood up from his chair to go and support her, but then thought that his approach might make her even more emotional, that she might not get through what she had to say, so he sat uneasily back down, ready to spring up when the real need presented itself. She cleared her throat again and found that the lump wouldn't budge — she would simply have to resolve to speak past it. So she did.

"Tom has been arrested," she began.

Tink and Kathy both bolted toward the bathroom. They didn't want to hear the rest. They didn't need to hear the rest. They both just needed to throw up the few bites of dinner they had managed to wrestle down. Kay continued.

"We've hired an attorney — Frank Fabbri — and he went down to put an end to the questioning. He said Tom was too tired . . . too tired to be of any use and that they had to stop the questioning. So they . . . they arrested him for two counts of first-degree murder and . . ." Kay's hand was in front of her mouth now and her words were becoming a garbled mess.

Art Junior rose from his seat and walked over to Kay, encircling his baby sister in his big strong arms while she wept. Grandma Polly and Grandpa Art silently reached for each other's hands, their eyes never leaving their daughter's tortured face in front of them, while Skip slipped from the room to check on his nieces.

Frank Fabbri's office was in an airy, old-fashioned home in a quiet residential neighborhood in midtown St. Louis, not far from police headquarters. It had a big stretch front porch and an oversized cherry door that hung heavily on its hinges. Gene followed Fabbri into the small, empty parking lot and parked the van haphazardly across two spaces. If Fabbri had known Gene at all, he would have recognized this as absurdly rash behavior, but he didn't know Gene. So he just assumed that the man wasn't a terribly good driver.

Gene was still intensely disturbed by the evening's events and his ever-ready handkerchief had taken about as much abuse as one could. Inside his office, Fabbri supplied a box of ordinary paper Kleenex and Gene thanked him with a loud honk and a clearing of the afflicted sinus passages. Despite the country charm of the house's exterior, the office was modern, sleek, and efficient inside. A large Cuban flag on the wall and a desk calendar of Che Guevara were the only real hints of Fabbri's personal character. There wasn't a speck of dust or a loose paper to be seen, but legal documents were stacked neatly everywhere in working piles. Fabbri sat down behind his big tidy desk, placed his speakerphone in between himself and Gene, and dialed the number of Kay's parents on Fair Acres Road.

Gene Cummins was a man of order, of organization, and of preparedness. During his long naval career, he had been known as a go-to man, the kind of person who got things done. There had been very few situations in his life that he hadn't been able to somehow climb on top of and conquer — and his family depended on him in that way. When the kids were young they had thought their dad could fix *anything*. The tape recorder that was left on the back porch during a thunderstorm? Don't worry — Daddy can fix it. The doll who got her hair cut the same day Tink did? Don't worry — Daddy can fix her. The beanbag that was leaking teeny Styrofoam balls all over the playroom? Don't worry — Daddy can fix it. And he did. He fixed all of these things and a lot more in the late evenings while his children were tucked up in their beds and his wife smiled and chuckled, calling him the Miracle Worker or Doctor Dad, depending on the job.

But now, as he sat in Fabbri's chrome and leather office, Gene was faced with an insurmountable tragedy. This type of destruction was completely overwhelming. His usual staid determination had been futile — he had been unable to gain control of the situation. Gene simply could not fix this. And this feeling of utter helplessness was new to him — he didn't know how to handle it. It became terror and unbearable frustration when he looked at it too closely, so instead he concentrated on deep breaths and answering the questions Fabbri was asking him.

During those moments when he paused to take stock of the situation, here is what he gathered: his nieces were gone, almost undeniably dead, though there was still no definite word on that front. His own two terrified daughters were at their grandparents', waiting for him to bring their brother home. And his son had just been taken away from him, taken to jail, charged with two counts of first-degree murder. He shook his head again. It was just all too much. Back to the deep breaths and the questions.

Kay's voice was on the speakerphone now in Fabbri's office. She had wanted to be present for this meeting but hadn't wanted to leave Tink and Kathy alone, so this was the result. The three-way conversation lasted over an hour and neither Kay nor Gene could remember much of what was said. Fabbri told them that Tom was being booked and placed in a holdover for the night, at which point Kay urgently interrupted.

"A *holdover?* What in God's name is that? You don't mean to tell me he's going to be kept in a cell with a bunch of criminals, do you?" she asked.

"Just overnight, Mrs. Cummins. After the hearing tomorrow —"

"Overnight! There has to be some way to get him out of there. He can't. He's only a kid, and he's not even a tough kid. He's never even been in a fistfight. What if one of these guys from last night gets picked up for drugs or something, and gets thrown in there with him? They'd kill him. You have to get him out of there!"

Kay was near hysteria.

"You know what, Kay," Fabbri said calmly, "I think you're right. I will phone the station as soon as we are finished here and tell them to put him on a suicide watch. That way they have to give him his own cell."

This served to pacify some of Kay's worries, and Gene agreed that it was a good idea. Fabbri went on to explain what he expected to happen the next day. From the time of Tom's actual arrest, the police department had twenty hours in which to procure warrants against Tom for the alleged offenses. If they were unable to acquire the warrants, they would have to let him go. But if they *did* obtain the warrants, which Fabbri felt was more likely, Tom would probably not be offered bail — he would have to stay in jail until the trial date, which could be anywhere from six to eighteen months away. Kay gasped audibly when she heard *eighteen months* and this time Fabbri had no words of comfort for her.

"Will we be able to see him?" she asked. "Will his sisters be able to see him?"

"For now, no," he answered. "We'll cross that bridge tomorrow after the twenty-hour deadline has passed. We'll have to see then what we're dealing with."

Kay and Gene sat on opposite ends of St. Louis, nodding solemnly at Fabbri's words and feeling their old life in Gaithersburg, their life from yesterday, slip further and further into unreality.

The holdover cell wasn't so bad really. Kay probably would have been mildly relieved had she actually seen it. The whole place was painted a minty, institutional green and the hard metal benches were crowded but not full. Tom looked around hazily at the other suspects in the all-metal room, but they didn't have names or faces or voices. They were just moving, breathing blobs that occupied spaces around him. He was asleep sitting up when the two arresting officers came back for him.

"Come on, get up. You're being put on a suicide watch," one of the officers said. "Apparently you're gonna kill yourself tonight. Your cousins last night, yourself tonight. You're on a roll," he sneered.

Tom trudged along sleepily beside the guard on the way to the new cell. Now that the idea of sleep had been planted firmly in his head, he seemed powerless to stay awake. The nastiness of the officer had ceased to affect him. His eyelids drooped shut as he walked automatically, following the man by the sound of his heavy, echoing footfall and the jangle of the keys on his belt.

If the communal holdover cell had rated a "not bad" on Tom's sleep-deprived comfort scale, then the new cell was definitely in the "marvelous" range. It was smaller, with two metal shelves along each wall for people to sleep on, but he was alone and it was darker and quieter. To Tom, it felt like the Ritz-Carlton. There was a commode with no seat or lid, coupled with a metal sink, in one corner. Everything in the room was painted with several flaking coats of the same industrial mint green. Sherwin-Williams must have had a sale that day, Tom thought as he collapsed onto the nearest bench. He didn't hear the ominous whir and heavy clunk of the metal cell gate as it yawned itself shut above him. He didn't feel the lice bouncing off him and nipping his skin raw as he slept. And he was only vaguely aware of the sounds of his PCP-addicted neighbor slamming himself repeatedly into the walls in his adjoining cell. Tom slept in blackness.

On Petite Drive, Ginna's house felt like an empty tomb despite the constant level of activity. After Kay and her daughters had left late that afternoon, all incoming information had pretty much seemed to dry up. People rattled around the house quietly and awkwardly, and the silence and grief pervaded everything. The television was on and there were pockets of conversation around the house, but somehow the silence seemed to thicken and harden like a film over all the quiet sounds of waiting.

When it began to get dark, Sheila and Lisa both kissed their sister Ginna, offered hugs and prayers, and then headed home to their respective families, who would no doubt be curious and hungry because of their mothers' absences. They both had over an hour's drive to get home, and kids to comfort when they got there.

Ginna's brother Kevin was at the house too, but he felt awkward and in the way. To Kevin, Ginna's house had always felt like women's territory, crowded as it always was with females. But now more than ever it felt like a feminine world. Julie's and Robin's rooms were already beginning to take on shrine-like qualities. People would wander in and sit quietly on their beds, looking around with reverence, absorbing memories and trying not to disturb anything. Ginna's friend Marianne was there too now, and all the women in the house were clucking and cooing around the tormented mother, offering her the brand of comfort that only women seem able to effortlessly conjure up.

Kevin, for his part, was having a very male reaction that felt out of place here: he was seething with rage. The thoughts of what had happened to his nieces and the suffering even now of his nephew were stirring up a wrath in him. He wanted to find these four men and rip their heads off with his teeth. He paced around the house and tried to get his head in order. Tomorrow he'd feel useful and helpful. Their parents and the remaining siblings would be flying and driving in from all over the country, and Kevin would be the airport-shuttle-bus driver and navigator. He would collect grandparents, carry suitcases, help organize sleeping arrangements. These practical thoughts calmed him while the women fussed and whispered to each other.

As the dark of the evening came down over the window

shades, Kevin too kissed Ginna good-bye and headed to his home in South County. He'd be back at the crack of dawn to help with whatever needed doing, he promised her. Everyone was finding a role.

The eleven o'clock news was, unfortunately, more eventful than the earlier broadcast. Tink and Kathy sat side by side on their grandfather's organ bench, where they had the best view of the television and where they had eaten their stir-fry dinner just the evening before. The grown-ups filled the surrounding chairs.

"The Chain of Rocks Bridge story," as their family tragedy was rapidly becoming known, was at the top of the news, and the newscaster was wearing a grim face while Julie's and Robin's photographs hovered over her right shoulder. In a clipped voice, she began reading from her typed notes.

"Alleged murderer Thomas Cummins is in custody tonight . . ."

Even the first sentence was too much for the girls to take in. Tink stood up hysterically, upending the organ bench and her sister. She couldn't speak, but she could no longer sit quietly either. She clamped her hands over her ears and began looking around wildly, her eyes spinning from the front door to the faces of her family, and across the walls of the room. Her eyes jumped on everything in sight except the television. She looked like a frightened animal seeking escape.

Skip was up from his seat in an instant and standing in front of her. He pulled her head into his chest and tried to hush her. Kathy sat stunned behind her, with glazed eyes and a stupefied expression. Skip walked Tink a few steps into the hallway and away from her sister, in case the hysteria might prove contagious. He hummed quietly into her ear, holding her tightly the whole time.

"Sshh, sshh, sshh, we all know it's not true, honey, it's okay, it's okay," Skip murmured.

It was a momentary hysteria and soon Tink and Skip returned to the room, where Tink resumed her place beside Kathy, whose expression had not changed despite the tears that were racing down her face and gathering in a puddle on her upturned hands in her lap.

"Well, if that isn't the greatest load of hogwash I've ever seen," Grandpa Art muttered angrily as he stood and slapped off the television.

Tink and Kathy sat speechlessly staring at the black screen. Grandpa Art spun toward them and marched straight up to Tink, who was still quivering in the aftermath of her outburst. He bent over her, gripped her strongly by the shoulders, and spoke forcefully into her face, almost shaking her as he talked.

"Don't you believe a single word of it. Not a single word — do you hear me?" He was almost shouting. "Your brother did not do this. He loved those girls. He is *not* a murderer. Do you understand me?"

Tink nodded lamely.

"Good girl," he finished and released his grip, patting her head before he turned to go.

Grandpa Art was such a quiet and reserved man. He had always been rather shy with his emotions and Tink was certain that she had never seen him even the slightest bit irritated. The fact that his ire had been stirred on behalf of her brother touched her very deeply, and his words were like strong hands that grabbed her under the arms and stood her up again. She snapped out of her pitiful state and almost smiled as he patted her head.

The whole day suddenly seemed like a dream. She knew that Tom was innocent, but the shock of hearing him called "alleged murderer" by some tight-lipped newscaster in a fuchsia suit had proven more powerful than she had expected. For a single, terrible instant, she had wondered what *had* happened, what the truth *was* exactly. Her grandfather's words were just the strength she had needed in that instant, and they had restored her faith as quickly as it had floundered. She took a deep breath and wiped the remaining loose tears from her face, setting her jaw at a hard angle again and resolving to be strong.

"Thanks, Grandpa," she whispered to his back.

It was a Friday night and not everybody in the St. Louis area was grieving. In Wentzville, not far from where Gene's and Ginna's sister Lisa lived with her family, there was a party going on, hosted by a friend of Danny Winfrey's. Winfrey and his three companions from the night before were all in attendance, along with about thirty other young people. The noise level in the house was high as conversations competed with music, television, and laughter.

Gray, as usual, was entertaining a rather large crowd all by himself. He hardly missed a beat when Tom Cummins's face flashed up on the eleven o'clock news. The panic that momentarily flitted across his face was immediately replaced with a smirk. He pointed at the television, laughing, and said, "Man, that fat white kid couldn't've pulled off a stunt like that. *I* did it! That shit was *my* handiwork."

"No, you didn't, you sicko," one of his friends retorted. "*I* did it."

"No it was *me,*" somebody else countered.

Three or four others chimed in, all claiming to be the murderers of the missing Kerry sisters. Julie and Robin were dead and it was a joke. Tom's picture stared grimly back at them from the television screen. He wasn't laughing. Finally, a voice of tentative reason spoke up.

"Y'all shouldn't say shit like that," somebody quietly warned. "Somebody's gonna believe you."

Danny Winfrey had listened with restrained alarm to the

ironic volley of claims, but at the tone of serious warning, he stood abruptly from his seat, knocking his beer bottle over as he stood. His girlfriend, Amanda Marshall, uprighted the nearly empty bottle and followed her boyfriend out of the room. Gray noted Winfrey's brusque departure, and in response continued his show with even greater energy than before.

In the bathroom upstairs, Winfrey sat on the edge of the porcelain bathtub and stared at his shoes. Amanda sat on the lid of the closed toilet seat and leaned forward, her elbows resting on her knees. Her face was the picture of concern.

"What is it, Danny?" she asked.

Winfrey nibbled his bottom lip and studied his sneakers with increased scrutiny.

"Whatever it is, you know you can tell me," she prompted.

So Winfrey opened the floodgates. He told her everything. When Gray's heavy knock fell on the wooden door a few short minutes later, Amanda hadn't even begun to process the story that her boyfriend had just confided in her. She didn't have time to take any of it in before Danny opened the door and Gray came barging in.

"We gotta talk," he barked at Winfrey, and then, turning to glare at Amanda, added, *"Alone."*

Amanda scooted out the door, past the intimidating figure of Gray, and went back downstairs while Winfrey took his seat again on the edge of the bathtub. Gray kicked the door shut hard and whirled around to face Winfrey.

"You have got to get your shit together," he said quietly, leaning into Winfrey's fifteen-year-old face. "Could you be any more fucking obvious? Listen, just chill the fuck out — everything's gonna be fine. They've got that rich boy in custody. They think *he* did it. There is no way in hell they're gonna find us. Besides, if anybody says anything, I'm gonna fucking kill 'em."

Gray placed his thumb under Winfrey's chin. "You hear me?" he said. "We're gonna be just fine. We stick together. We keep *calm,* and they will never catch us. Got it?"

Winfrey looked up into Gray's eyes, squirmed, and then nodded.

"Yeah, I got it," he said.

After the commotion of the newscast had passed, Kathy and Tink settled back in to their well-worn places on the couch with a deck of cards — anything to keep their minds numb and occupied. They played gin rummy, but their hearts weren't in it. Kathy was the first to spot headlights through the living-room curtains. Fair Acres Road was not a busy street, and the headlights approached and then passed the house before the brake lights came on and Gene backed the van into his in-laws' driveway.

"Dad's home," Kathy announced.

Gene couldn't bring himself to come into the house for several minutes. Kay was just considering going out to him when the front door squeaked open. Kay's parents and brothers had made themselves scarce, giving the others some privacy. Grandma Polly had invented an urgent load of laundry in the basement and Grandpa Art had suddenly remembered a new painting he wanted to show his sons.

So Kathy and Tink alone witnessed the slow, hesitant opening of the front door and their mother's anxiety as she threw her body across the room toward their father. For Kay, her husband's homecoming was the moment of release she had been waiting for all day. The emotion she had been almost successfully hiding from her daughters was now on full display and her shoulders heaved heavily and soundlessly as she wrapped herself in Gene's open arms.

Tink and Kathy were terrified by their father's face. They had never seen him look so desperate, so frightened, so helpless. They moved themselves from the couch, but everything was slow in the room, as if they were underwater or characters in a slow-motion nightmare. The carpet felt like quicksand as they crossed the room to where their parents were hugging each other.

"I'm sorry," Gene was saying, "I'm so sorry. I'm so sorry."

Kay just shook her head and clung to him, still unable to speak.

"I tried to bring him home. I'm so sorry I couldn't bring him home. They wouldn't let me bring him home."

He searched the faces of his wife and daughters for forgiveness and reassurance. Tink and Kathy squeezed themselves into the middle of their parents' embrace. The four unincarcerated members of the Cummins family huddled in the space that had been occupied by the kids' folding dinner table and six happy plates of chicken stir-fry the night before, and wept together.

Ginna was there almost immediately, it seemed to Gene. He hadn't had time to do anything. He hadn't showered or brushed his teeth or even shaved, and a one-day growth of beard on Gene was enough to solicit Chia Pet remarks from his two daughters, even in their current state of distress. His homecoming from Fabbri's office had been an emotional one and he had just sat down at the dining-room table to try to gather his thoughts when the doorbell rang. Kay's brothers had left a few minutes earlier, and Gene presumed that one of them had forgotten a wallet or something and was back to retrieve it. He heard Kathy holler, "I'll get it," and a few moments later she appeared wordlessly in front of her father and then stepped aside to allow Ginna to pass into the room. Jamie followed, looking lost but not entirely hopeless.

"Genie," Ginna whispered, holding her hands out toward her brother.

Kathy ushered Jamie quickly into the kitchen as Gene looked up at his sister and burst into tears.

"I'm so sorry, Ginna," Kathy heard her father saying, and Ginna responded:

"No, no. Sshh. There's nothing for you to be sorry about. I just came to let you know that none of us believe this. We all know that Tommy didn't do this."

Gene's and Ginna's voices dropped into the hushed tones that Kathy had grown so accustomed to hearing the grown-ups use throughout the day.

"How about a Coke?" she said to Jamie, who nodded her response.

More than anything, the Coke was just an excuse to make noise. Kathy didn't even think about the fact that before today she would not have helped herself to a Coke without asking her parents first. It was just one of the many tiny but somehow significant changes that had taken place since that morning. She and her sister Tink had both become grown-ups today, with grown-up perks like the ability to curse or drink a Coke whenever they wanted, but with grown-up responsibilities too, like trying to protect their young cousin from the uglier, more distressing scenes surrounding her sisters' violent deaths. She pulled two glasses from her grandmother's kitchen cabinet and let Jamie fill her own glass up with ice. No sooner were the girls entrenched at the kitchen table, fortified by their Cokes, than Gene and Ginna appeared in the doorway and announced a kind of makeshift family meeting.

"Why don't y'all use the game room downstairs," Grandma Polly suggested. "It's private, there are plenty of seats for everybody, and there's a phone if you need it."

So they moved downstairs. Tink, Kathy, and Jamie were invited to join the parents. Everyone seemed to recognize at this stage that, though there was the occasional need for privacy during personal moments, there was no point in trying to hide anything from the children. They were going to have to get used to this tragedy, and withholding information from them would only serve to confuse them. And to their credit, the girls had proven strong so far, apart from their collective inability to hold much food down. They had all been so good to each other today — their parents were proud of the way they were handling the whole ordeal. Tink, Kathy, and Jamie sat at the green felt–covered table where they had played poker the night before, trying not to look at the empty seats where Robin, Julie, and Tom had sat. At Jamie's request, Tink dealt a game of go fish, but they all paid more attention to their parents' conversation than they did to the game.

Ginna, Gene, and Kay sat talking quietly on the two facing leather sofas behind the girls. They talked about how everyone was holding up, and they discussed the impending arrival of their parents, who would be flying in from Florida in the morning. Gene had made that most difficult of phone calls just after Tom's arrest. Gene had always trusted in his father's strength, but nonetheless had been floored by his reaction. Gene Senior had taken the news very hard initially. He had taken down Gene's payphone number at the police station and excused himself to go have a good cry. But when he phoned back twenty minutes later, his tone had been entirely different.

"Well," he had said to his son, "your mother and I could have gotten on a late flight tonight, but I need to get to the bank in the morning before we come up there. I will be bringing the deed to my house. Tell Tommy not to worry about a thing. If he needs bail, it's covered — and he'll have the best damn lawyers that money can buy. And you're not to tell your mother about this. You know I have more than enough money in stocks to cover it. I don't want to bother her with the details."

There had never even been a question about guilt or innocence in Grandpa Gene's mind. And Gene Junior would certainly not mention this deed business to his mother. In fact, he hadn't even mentioned it to Tom or Kay or Ginna. Instead, he tried to put the whole thing out of his mind. It was just too big to talk about, too big to take in. His father's generosity and faith contrasted so starkly against the terror of the day that it was emotionally overwhelming.

So instead he kept it to himself and talked lightly of logistical things — who was going to pick up the grandparents from the airport in the morning and such. While they discussed these matters, the phone rang. It was well after midnight. All eyes in the room snapped to the phone, and the girls' cards hovered like a still life over the green felt–covered table. There were footsteps upstairs and then Grandpa Art called down.

"Ginna? The phone's for you."

Ginna stood shakily and she stepped cautiously toward the phone, a mother who was waiting for terrible, terrible news. She stood with her back to the room and lifted the receiver slowly. For the next couple of minutes the room was silent except for Ginna's occasional "mm-hmm"'s. When she put the phone down and turned back to face her brother, her face was cracked with the lines of grief. She was crying.

"I have to go . . . We have to go . . . Jamie, come on," she said.

"Wait," Gene started, confused. "What's going on? What . . ."

"That was Rick," Ginna responded. "He said he wants his daughter out of here. He said he doesn't want Jamie in the home of the man who murdered our girls."

Ginna was sobbing now as she spoke and the three girls abandoned their card game and approached the grown-ups.

"I'm so sorry, Genie," Ginna said. "He doesn't mean it, I know he doesn't, he just, he's very emotional right now."

Jamie cuddled in under her mother's arm while her mom cried and held her tightly. It was such a childlike gesture that it nearly startled Tink and Kathy, who in the course of the day had forgotten just how young Jamie was. She was so mature, so witty for her age that it was easy to forget that she was just nine years old. The unhappy party trudged up the stairs and Ginna paused at the front door.

"I'm sorry," she said again.

But Gene hushed her and they hugged for a moment. Kay kissed Ginna on the cheek and bent to hug Jamie as well. Tink and Kathy waited patiently, and when their turns came they embraced their aunt more emotionally than they ever had, as if they feared never seeing her again. Ginna clung to them and touched their hair and faces.

"You're such good girls. We're all gonna get through this, aren't we?" she said.

They both nodded and she smiled through her tears. She took Jamie by the hand and they left. Jamie looked over her shoulder as Ginna led her toward the car and waved at her cousins who stood leaning their faces against the screen door.

On the green metal shelf, without pillow or blanket or dreams, Tom slept on in blackness. The clanking approach of keys did not wake him, nor did the sound of his cell door opening, or the guard calling to him to get up. The night watchman had to actually enter the cell and physically shake Tom awake. When he did so, reality returned instantly. Tom felt no moment of confusion, no terrible shock of remembering. He knew where he was and he felt as if he hadn't been sleeping at all.

But the sleep was still heavy in his eyes and limbs as Tom stood to follow the policeman out of the dim green cell. Together they trudged down what seemed to Tom like endless hallways until they came to a small office that served as a waiting area. There was a Plexiglas window at one end of the room and a clerk was seated behind it. Tom was instructed to take a seat on a low bench along one wall that was already occupied by two other young men. After several minutes of paper-shuffling, the clerk called a name and one of Tom's companions stood and walked to the little window. After obtaining the man's name, age, and address, the clerk began to explain the charges against him.

"Grand theft auto," the clerk declared loudly, looking over the rims of his glasses before launching into a legal description of the charge.

"Lucky bastard," Tom muttered under his breath.

The kid seated beside him overheard Tom's little exclamation and glanced up nervously. He edged himself away on the narrow bench, despite Tom's attempt at a reassuring smile. The absurdity of the situation was not lost on Tom. Here he was, a nineteen-year-old fireman and Eagle Scout who had never been in any serious trouble in his life, envying a hoodlum who was charged with grand theft auto. Tom chuckled, causing his bench companion to slide even further away from him, and then he gave up, tipping his head back against the brick wall behind him.

When his name was called about half an hour later, Tom opened his eyes to find that he and the clerk in the window were alone in the room. There were guards outside, he was sure, but his criminal companions were gone. Tom wondered vaguely if they would spend the night in jail or if they had been released on bail already. He seated himself heavily across the fortified counter from the obviously disapproving clerk. The man on the other side cleared his throat and started his list of questions. Tom answered them mindlessly and only half listened while the man explained the two charges of first-degree murder, and the likelihood that Tom would not be offered bail.

The guard who came to collect Tom from the office was the same one who had escorted him from his cell, and it was no stretch to say that Tom was delighted to see him. He needed sleep, for the release as much as the rest, and he was anxious to get back to his semi-quiet cell and his PCP-addled neighbor. When they reached the guard station in the center of the building, Tom

An aerial view of the twin Chain of Rocks bridges spanning the Mississippi River and of the St. Louis Waterworks to the southwest. (Data available from U.S. Geological Survey, EROS Data Center, Sioux Falls, SD)

The entire span of the Old Chain of Rocks Bridge, taken from the Illinois bank, looking west toward Missouri. The new Chain of Rocks Bridge is visible in the background. (© 1997 Dr. Frank P. Maloney)

One of the open manholes in the road surface of the old bridge,
April 1991. (*St. Louis Post-Dispatch*)

The Cummins grandkids, autumn 1983. Top row, left to right: Kelly Thess, Tom Cummins. Middle row, left to right (all standing): Danni Thess, Buddy Thess, Kathy Cummins, Robin Kerry, Tink Cummins, Christie Southerland. Third row, left to right (all seated): Kathy Kerry, Jacob Southerland, Julie Kerry. Front row, left to right (all seated): Carrie Southerland, Daniel Southerland, Jamie Kerry.
(Olan Mills Portrait Studios)

Julie and Tom in Clearwater, Florida. Summer 1990.
(Brandon Justice)

Kathy, Tink, and Tom Cummins, 1991.
(Olan Mills Portrait Studios)

Robin Kerry, 1989. (Prestige)

Julie Kerry, 1989. (Prestige)

Robin and Jamie Kerry, April 2, 1991. (Ginna Kerry)

Tink and Tom Cummins. (Kathleen E. Lopez)

Grandpa Art Matthews examining the remnants of Julie's poem on the
post-restoration bridge. (Kay Cummins)

Julie's and Robin's quilt squares that Kay and Kathy made for a homicide
victims' quilt. (Kay Cummins)

thought it was heavily manned, especially for that time of night. He didn't remember having passed it on the way to the little office, but he had been so sleepy, he supposed that they could have walked through a minefield without his noticing. The guard who was escorting him paused at the station, where four or five of his coworkers were seated at two round tables. There were a deck of cards, several magazines, and a newspaper on one of the tables, but the graveyard-shift officers looked bored nonetheless.

"Go and stand right over there against that wall," Tom's guard instructed him.

Tom turned and walked sleepily toward the wall, feeling every eye in the room bore into his back as he did so. When he reached the thick painted brick, he leaned his back against it and brought one heel up under his bottom for support. He crossed his arms in front of him and unthinkingly inspected his shoe. He didn't dare look any of these cops in the face, give them ammunition for their hostility. But neither did he dare to close his eyes, fall asleep standing up, and risk falling over. So he examined his shoe, and when that proved useless in keeping him alert, he started counting floor tiles.

"Ain't you the big city boy that darn near fooled all us silly old farmers with your wacky story? The one's gonna kill yerself tonight?" one of the seated officers jeered in a ridiculously mock-hick accent.

Tom yawned and continued counting.

"What's wrong, sleepyhead?" one of the other cops joined in. "Did you have a nightmare or something?"

Tom smiled wryly in spite of himself. *A nightmare,* he thought. *You have no fucking idea.*

Tom stood propping the wall up like that for several minutes while the officers taunted him, but their insults didn't really bother him. He remembered Fabbri telling him not to mutter a single word, not even in his own defense, and that thought lent

Tom strength and dignity. It was easy to keep quiet, especially when he saw that his silence was causing them to lose interest in tormenting him. Still, Tom had counted every floor tile in the room and every brick in the wall opposite him, and had picked every remaining bit of sand and river sludge from under his fingernails before his guard began to saunter down the hallway without him. He turned and called over his shoulder to Tom, slapping his thigh as if he was summoning a dog.

"Here, boy," he called. "Come on, boy, let's go. That's a good boy."

The officers gathered at the two tables laughed heartily at this parting shot and one of them wished Tom "good luck with the whole suicide thing."

Tom almost thanked him, but thought better of it and kept his mouth shut. He walked between the two tables and past the night officers as if they were invisible. He didn't cry until he was locked into his cell, alone again, and the glaring overhead bulb was dimmed for the last time that night.

In the middle of the night, while Tom suffered the harassment of the guards, Jamie sat on her living-room couch with her legs folded compactly under her body, her fingers entangled and busy with a blob of pink yarn. The quiet that had been gathering all day in the house had become downright eerie with the fall of night. Jacquie sat beside her young niece with her own tangle of pink yarn while Jamie patiently and perfectly instructed her aunt in the intricacies of "finger crocheting."

"Is there anything you *don't* know how to do?" Jacquie asked admiringly.

Jamie smiled and shrugged.

Ginna and her friend Marianne had been chatting at the kitchen table ever since Ginna and Jamie had returned from their brief visit to Gene and his family. She sat shaking her head. The whole thing was so surreal, so bizarre, that she still couldn't even seem to line up the facts in her head. A few blocks away, her brother Gene was sitting in a darkened house, much like this one, without his only son. Tommy was in jail. And here she sat in her own vacant kitchen, the light over the stove providing the room's only illumination, without her daughters. Julie and Robin still weren't home.

With each passing hour, different scenarios presented themselves. *Maybe they made it to Mozentine Island in the middle of the river and are unable to swim ashore. Maybe they were too embarrassed to walk naked in the daylight and seek help. Now that it's dark — maybe they will make their way to a phone.*

But these possibilities grew less and less likely with each tick of the clock. *Maybe they're unconscious on the riverbank somewhere, or they have amnesia. Maybe they broke their legs in the fall and are unable to walk for help.*

Anything, no matter how horrible or far-fetched, was better than the looming truth: Julie and Robin were dead. They had been brutalized and murdered and they were never coming back.

"At least they were together," Ginna kept saying. "They'll be okay because they're together."

Nobody on Petite Drive slept that night. Eventually Jamie passed out on the couch. Periodically she'd awaken and occupy herself with one of her crafts or video games until she exhausted herself and passed out again. Ginna and Marianne hardly moved from the kitchen table. Some time in the middle of the night, Jacquie retired to the basement for a little while and tried to sleep on the mattress that had been the old standby for any of the various friends in need of a place to stay who Robin habitually brought home. Jacquie tossed and turned on it for an hour or two and then crept back up the steps, not altogether surprised to see Ginna still camped out at the kitchen table.

"Can't sleep, honey?" Ginna asked.

Jacquie shook her head. Ginna was the oldest girl in the Cummins family and Jacquie was the youngest. There were almost twenty years between them, and Ginna was more like a mother to Jacquie than a sister. Right now it was exactly what they both needed. Ginna needed to pamper and nurture somebody, to be a mom. And Jacquie, who was emotionally and physically exhausted, welcomed the doting.

"Milk and cookies," Ginna announced. "The combination of the milk and sugar always makes me sleepy. That's what you need. A good dose of milk and cookies."

She got up and fetched a saucer, filled it with cookies, and set it down in front of her baby sister with a tall glass of cold milk.

"Thanks," Jacquie said, and did her best to fake a smile for Ginna.

The den on Fair Acres Road was crowded with sleeping figures, or at least prone and fitful ones trying to sleep. The back bedroom where Tink and Kathy had been sleeping all week had been transformed into the stuff of nightmares for the two girls. For them, that room had been the launching point for this entire ordeal, and neither of them had even entertained the idea of trying to sleep in there tonight, or ever again for that matter. So their parents had pulled the mattress off of the foldout couch and onto the floor and then replaced the couch's exterior trappings. The two sisters lay head to toe on the couch while their parents sprawled on the mattress beneath them, and Blarney snuffled around from one body to the next, eventually curling up in a warm place beside Gene. But nobody really slept. Sure, there were moments of unconsciousness, but they were snatched and interrupted in cycles. Everyone had the same nightmare and they all took turns waking up in cold sweats, and they all took turns comforting each other.

Near dawn, Tink and Kathy awoke to find their mother sitting cross-legged in the middle of the mattress in her thin silk nightgown. Her hands covered her face and she rocked back and forth slowly. Her cry was so high and so sharp that it was soundless, but her breath somehow pierced the air nonetheless. Their father knelt in front of her with his arms helplessly around her shoulders, trying in vain to comfort her. The pink blush of reluctant dawn was creeping to the windows, and the room was thick with grief. The first night of their new life was over.

CHAPTER ELEVEN

Tom was thirsty when he woke up, and the man who was standing over him, bent at the waist and peering down into his face, was holding a paper cup of water.

"Breakfast," the man said and almost smiled.

He was an older fellow and dressed like a janitor, Tom thought. Whether he was or not, he looked like somebody's grandfather and his face was a kind one. Tom propped himself up on his elbows and slowly sat up, unfolding his joints from the metal shelf and trying to gauge the various aches and pains.

The man took a step back to give Tom some room to stretch before handing him the paper cup and a Hostess sticky bun, still wrapped in the cellophane. Tom thanked him and this time the man did smile properly. He nodded his head and shuffled wordlessly out the door, closing and locking it behind him.

Tom had no idea what time it was, but he felt somewhat refreshed by the sleep. It was impossible to read the hour by the scanty natural light provided by the room's single high window, and his watch was gone — taken by one of the four men who should be sitting there, eating a Hostess sticky bun and rinsing it down with a cup of lukewarm tap water. He supposed that if the four guys hadn't stolen his watch, the police would have taken it from him anyway, along with his belt and his shoelaces, the night before, so from that point of view it was really no major loss.

Tom finished the bun and had nowhere to throw the wrapper so he just left it crumpled on the shelf beside him. There was no breeze to stir it and it stuck in place on the shelf as if it had grown roots there. Tom crumpled it into a tighter ball and then flicked it onto the floor.

He swallowed the last of the lukewarm water and was still thirsty, so he called for a guard but no one came. He called every couple of seconds for a few minutes, but still nobody showed up.

Tom stood up from the green metal shelf and walked to the green metal sink mounted on the back wall of his cell. He turned the tap's one squeaky knob and murky lukewarm and yellowish water spewed out. He set the cup on the edge of the sink and turned the knob back off. *I wouldn't even wash my hands in that water,* he thought.

So he went to use the green metal seatless commode instead. When he was finished there, he returned to his green metal shelf and then opted for a change of scenery and switched to a different metal shelf instead. Just as he was beginning to wonder how he could spend another second alone in the cell without losing his mind, he heard footsteps approaching.

"Your lawyer's here to see you," the guard announced as he approached Tom's cell and lifted his heavy key ring to unlock the gate.

The guy wasn't exactly friendly, but neither did he seem to possess the downright animosity that Tom had experienced the night before. It was a relief, and Tom's mood lifted a bit as he stepped out of his cell and followed the not-vicious guard down the fluorescent-lit corridor toward Fabbri. *How vastly things can change in a day and a half,* Tom thought. *My God, the things I am now thankful for.*

★   ★   ★

On Fair Acres Road, the atmosphere was at its lowest yet. There was absolutely nothing the family could do now. Today they played the waiting game. Tink and Kathy both needed to shower, but the prospect of spending any chunk of minutes alone with their thoughts terrified them both into procrastination, so they resumed their places on the couch with their worn deck of cards instead. Gene and Kay paced and stalked around the house like caged wild animals while Grandma Polly puttered around her kitchen, hoping that someone would feel up to eating. Grandpa Art had looked from his watch to the clock to his watch to the clock to his watch until finally, at about eight-thirty, he could stand it no longer.

"I'm going for a drive," he announced to his wife, before slinging his keys into his jacket pocket and tottering out the door.

"Well where're you going, Art?" Grandma Polly asked from where she had appeared in the kitchen doorway with a frying pan in her hand.

But he was gone and the door was already closed behind him. When he returned about an hour later, he secretly carried the deed to his own house. Like Grandpa Gene, he was determined to provide whatever financial support his grandson needed.

The front page headline of *The St. Louis Post-Dispatch* on the morning of Saturday, April 6, 1991 read "Two Sisters Missing in N. County: Police Hold Cousin After Story of Attack." Julie and Robin looked beautiful on the front page, but their pictures were dwarfed beside a huge close-up photograph of one of the bridge's rusty gaping manholes. The police were quoted repeatedly in the article, alleging that Tom Cummins had made a sexual advance toward his cousin Julie, and that she had fallen off the bridge during an ensuing struggle. Her sister Robin had fallen too, they explained, trying to help her.

On page eight, where the story continued, there was a large

scenic photo of the bridge, and a snapshot of one of the search parties in its boat. The article briefly described the ongoing search efforts for the girls by the U.S. Coast Guard, the St. Louis Police Department, and various rescue teams from both banks. Tom was described as having "made incriminating statements about the incident." And Julie and Robin were described as "lovely girls and very excellent students." At the bottom of the article there was also a picture of one of the detectives, holding a flashlight that had been found on the bridge. The caption read, "Police believe the owner of this flashlight may have been a witness to the incident. The flashlight has HORN 1 etched into it."

The police had Antonio Richardson's missing flashlight.

Across town, on Edgewood Avenue, not far from the apartment where Richardson lived, the original owner of the mysterious HORN 1 flashlight was reading the paper, and he was baffled. Ron Whitehorn, a bus driver and former police officer, recognized his missing flashlight as the pivotal piece of evidence in the murder investigation.

Ron's daughter Stephanie and her brother had invited a few people over one evening in March while their parents were out. Antonio Richardson had been among them; Antonio Richardson had stolen the flashlight.

Ron Whitehorn immediately phoned the police with the information and identified Antonio Richardson as the potential "witness" they had been seeking since Friday.

At police headquarters, the unwashed Tom Cummins sat feeling rather itchy as he stared through the smudged and filthy screen at his impeccably dressed lawyer. The room was tiny and Tom sat on a swivel stool bolted to the floor like the ones in old greasy-spoon diners. There were none of those snazzy phones like they had on *Miami Vice,* Tom noticed, and was secretly relieved. He felt criminal enough in there without having to talk to people in the real world on a phone when he was looking right at them.

"Morning," Fabbri said, and offered Tom a smile.

"Morning." Tom smiled back, but Fabbri's was more genuine.

Fabbri wouldn't bother asking the boy how he was doing — that was a question that simply invited disaster. Fabbri had learned well the dos and don'ts of jailhouse etiquette, and what he was here to tell Tom certainly wouldn't make the young man feel any better, so there was no point wasting time with chitchat.

"I'm here to explain today's procedure to you," Fabbri began. "I didn't want to get into all this last night because you were exhausted and needed to sleep. But now that you've gotten some rest, it's time you understood what's happening."

Tom nodded on the other side of the smudgy screen.

"You know, they came for me last night like you told me they would," he blurted.

"You mean they were asking you questions and stuff, like the guys before?"

"Yeah and just kinda jeering me and being real assholes," Tom further explained.

"And you didn't say a word to them, right?" Fabbri's blue eyes were wide, his eyebrows up, arched in an expression of concern.

"Right," Tom answered, almost proudly.

"Great." Fabbri smiled, relieved. "Good job."

The little disclosure had been Tom's way of thanking Fabbri. By telling him that things had happened exactly as he had predicted, and that Tom had followed his sage advice, Tom was trying to express his gratitude. There was so much more he wanted to say before they launched into all of the legal drama and Tom's terrible future, but he was at a loss. He wanted to tell Fabbri thank you for believing him, thank you for taking him out of that nightmare yesterday, thank you for saving him. He wanted to tell Fabbri that he would do anything the man suggested, because he had saved his life the day before and Tom would trust him to save his life again at every turn from that point forward. But in the scrubbed morning light, Fabbri looked like a movie lawyer in an Armani suit and Tom sat shyly in his filthy clothes, picking at the corner of the metal screen in front of him.

Fabbri smiled warmly at him and shook his head. *Poor kid,* he thought.

"Well, I guess we should get cracking," Fabbri began, looking to Tom for confirmation.

Tom nodded and Fabbri began to explain the legal entanglements of the day. According to Missouri state law, he explained, the police had twenty hours from the time of the arrest in which to obtain warrants charging Tom with the two counts of first-degree murder against him. The police would present their evidence to St. Louis Circuit Attorney Nels Moss, and he would tell them whether or not their case was substantial enough to issue the warrants. As one of the city's best prosecutors, and the man who usually took the high-profile homicide cases, Nels Moss was also the man who would eventually litigate this case. That was bad news for Tom, Fabbri explained, because he would obviously want an airtight file against the suspect.

"I have no idea what kind of evidence the police will present, but if they've got anything at all worthwhile, Mr. Moss will want to see those warrants issued," Fabbri explained.

"Okay," Tom said, nodding. "So what happens then?"

"Well, after the warrants are issued, you will be held over until Monday for your initial appearance before the associate circuit judge. At that point, the judge will read the charges against you and discuss bail. Because murder one is a capital offense, you will likely *not* be offered bail. So, Tom, what I need you to do is start trying to get used to the idea that you may be in here for a little while. The trial could be a year or more away and you could very well be in jail until then. I know that this is an awful lot to take in, but this is your task today. I really need you to start getting used to that idea so that we can move on and become a productive team. It's not gonna be easy."

Tom folded his hands in front of him, and the calm that had accompanied his sleep fled from him. He went cold while Fabbri's voice came through the metal screen in front of him. He imagined he could feel the calm slipping from his head, sliding down his body, seeping squishily into his shoes and then sinking into a free-rolling puddle on the floor that would leave him and escape from the jail without him. His hands were freezing and trembling now and his toes felt cold and rigid in his shoes, but the rest of his body was hot and feverish.

"How's the search going?" Tom asked abruptly.

"Pardon?"

"My cousins? Have they found any trace of Julie or Robin?" Tom asked with growing desperation.

"I'm sorry, Tom." Fabbri shook his head.

"It's just that," Tom spluttered and his face grew red with shame at the pure selfishness of what he was about to articulate, "just that . . . if they found the girls. If one of them survived, they would tell them, I'd be . . ."

Tom's voice trailed off and he brought his hand up to cover his face.

"Oh God," he said quietly and the first tears of the day slid down his face.

Tink and Kathy wanted to go to Ginna's house and didn't really understand why they weren't allowed. They didn't understand the tension that had infected their family the instant that Tom was accused of murdering Julie and Robin. Gene and Kay were both in agreement that their presence at Ginna's might be problematic — for Rick and for anyone else who didn't know Tom well, who might put some stock in the allegations. So for

Ginna's sake, in an effort to be considerate in a monumentally delicate situation, they stayed away. Instead, all of the troops of aunts
and uncles and cousins came visiting Fair Acres Road in shifts.

But Tink and Kathy weren't pacified by the brief and constant
visits. They wanted to be with Jamie and Ginna — they wanted
to be there whenever news of a discovery came in. And with the
day's growing sunshine, everyone was busily hoping for some
kind of discovery. There had been an anonymous call to one of
the local news stations with a tip that someone had indeed seen
two women on the river's Mozentine Island, which is not far
south of the Chain of Rocks Bridge. The police warned the family not to get their hopes up, that legitimate tips usually came to
the police department rather than through the news media. But at
this point, hope was the only thing keeping the family afloat, so
they jumped on the rumor. Privately, many members of those
two households found quiet corners in which to kneel down and
cross their hands in front of them and whisper fervent prayers
over those rumors.

The hours passed like a kind of sickly, ticking syrup. Faces and
voices passed in and out, back and forth, between the two houses,
but for the most part, they didn't hear or see each other. They just
waited. Petite Drive to Fair Acres Road and back again. Card
game at the coffee table to throwing up in the bathroom and back
again. Nintendo to the hourly no-news update and back again.

And everyone tried desperately not to notice the absence of
the two lively, sparkly voices — those two voices that usually
laughed and teased and preached and scolded and somehow made
everything light and right.

Across town at police headquarters, Nels Moss sat with his legs
crossed at the knee, perusing the open file folder in front of him.
Moss looked young for his age, despite his white hair and the pipe
that often hung from the corner of his mouth. At forty-eight, he

was in good physical shape and kept his white beard and moustache neatly trimmed. He looked like an academic, and indeed, he had the sharp reputation to match. The Missouri Bar Association rated Moss as having very high to preeminent legal ability and very high ethical standards. Within the St. Louis Police Department, he had earned the highest level of respect along with the nickname "Boss Moss." Sergeant Nichols and Detective Richard Trevor were silent at the table across from him, waiting for him to speak. They felt confident that he would agree to the warrants they were seeking, but they knew better than to rush him.

"Okay, so what have you got, really?" Moss asked, looking Nichols directly in the eye as he spoke.

"Well," Nichols began, "We don't really have any physical evidence per se, but we did obtain a confession."

"Oh well, that should be plenty," Moss said. "Is it written or videotaped?"

"Well, neither actually."

"You *do* have it on audio tape then," Moss prompted.

Nichols shook his head and glanced at the frowning Trevor. "Uh. Not exactly," he said.

"Well, then you don't have a confession," Moss snapped. "What exactly was the nature of the statement?"

"Well . . ." Nichols hung his head a bit like a scolded child as he truthfully related the scenario that had been dubbed Tom's confession. "He said, 'If you say I did it, then fine. I did it.'"

Moss folded his arms sternly in front of him while he listened, and when Nichols was finished speaking the prosecutor slid the closed manila folder across the table and stood to go.

"You've got no evidence," he said. "No confession, no bodies, no witnesses . . . *No evidence.* Let the kid go. In the meantime, I suggest you step up your search for those two girls. Come back to me when you have something I can work with."

★   ★   ★

Tink still had Julie's red bandana tied around her right wrist. She was lying in her grandfather's recliner, listening to Simon and Garfunkel on her Walkman and trying not to feel hollow. "Bridge over Troubled Water" was playing and Tink was just considering turning it off, the irony being a bit too heavy for the moment, when the call came in. In the instant that the phone rang, the house ground to a halt so completely that it seemed to have been spinning before that moment. Outside, every bird in every tree on Fair Acres Road shut its beak and drew its breath in, waiting. Kids' wagon wheels halted in mid-turn, and water from the sprinkler next door hung suspended in midair as the world stopped.

Tink rolled her body over the arm of the recliner and stumbled toward the phone, but as she rounded the corner, her father was already there in front of her with the receiver to his ear. There was no sound. Her father's lips were moving, but there was no sound. Kathy and Kay were there too now, and they all clasped each other. The prayers that flew up from that kitchen at that moment seemed the fastest, most ardent, and most frantic prayers ever prayed.

The first sound was the slow-motion click as Gene dropped the receiver back into its cradle. His expression was impossible, unreadable. He looked sick and terrified and stunned all at once. And then he spoke.

"He's out!" Gene shouted and the tears that came loose from his eyes were tears of joy and relief. He shook his head, unable to believe the words, even as they came out of his own mouth.

"They're letting him go. The prosecutor took the warrants under advisement — said they have no evidence."

Gene held his wife's face in his hands now, and Kay was unable to speak, her lips and face a trembling mess of relief. Tink covered her head with her hands and wept, looking up at the ceiling and crying, "Thank you, thank you," until Kathy tackled her and the two sisters fell onto the floor together in a happy, blubbering heap.

Tom was the last to learn of his own freedom, and what he thought was his first of many afternoons in jail already felt like an eternity. He had never been claustrophobic before, but the green metal room had long grown to feel like a tiny tin box, and he a sardine crammed into it. He had been pacing wildly, wrestling with the idea of staying in this place and clearly losing the battle. He breathed as deeply as he could and stretched his arms and legs constantly, as if to reassure himself that he still had space enough to do those things. But it didn't help.

By lunchtime he was no closer to accepting his fate than he had been when Fabbri suggested the idea to him earlier that morning. When the grumpy-looking guard came to deliver the lunch of franks and beans and the obligatory paper cup of luke-warm water to wash it down, Tom wished he were the janitor from earlier that morning. At least that man had looked like someone with whom he could strike up a conversation. Tom looked distastefully at the paper cup as the guard maneuvered it gingerly through the bars and placed it on the stone floor inside the cell.

"Any chance I can get a Coke, or at least maybe a glass of ice?"

Tom was unaccustomed to beginning a day without any caffeine whatsoever, and his head was beginning to pound.

"No glass allowed — suicide watch," the guard explained gruffly.

He didn't seem to have an excuse readily available regarding the requests for Coke or ice, but Tom's reservoir of patient conversation had dried up anyway. He lifted the limp paper plate and began silently chewing his franks and beans. The guard left without another word. Tom finished the food in a matter of minutes and when it was gone, he wished he had drawn the eating process out a bit more. Eating was something to do and it killed time. Now that the meal was over, Tom was once again alone with his thoughts.

He dozed sporadically on the green metal shelf with no concept of how quickly or slowly the time was passing. Each time he dozed off and woke up again, he felt as if an entire night had passed. He would wake with a start, sit up abruptly, and swing his legs over the edge of the shelf, half hoping to see the friendly janitor standing nearby.

But in the small corner of his mind that was still in touch with reality, Tom knew that it must still be only early afternoon. There had been no dinner delivered, he reasoned. Tom's parents had always had a habit of equating the passage of time with the strictly scheduled intake of food, a habit that had always irritated him and his sisters. How strange, he thought, that the very same routine was like a lifeline to him now. But beyond that, Tom was also aware that before the dinner delivery would come a delivery of a different kind: the news of his warrants. The dread that had spread over him in a panic that morning had settled well into his bones now. And although he was more terrified than ever, he almost longed for the delivery. He needed the finality of the announcement and he wanted to get it over with. His stomach lurched when he thought of it so he tried to turn his mind to other things.

In a few moments he was asleep again and dreaming of driving in the Hornet with Julie, except in the dream the car was a convertible and strips of fuzzy fabric didn't hang down to clutter his ears. There was no floor in the car either, and Tom and Julie had to use their feet, Flintstones-style, to get the car to stop and go. There was no radio, but it didn't matter because Robin was singing loudly in the backseat and the three of them were laugh-

ing as the wind whipped through their hair and they rolled happily in their rickety car across the empty, sunny Old Chain of
Rocks Bridge . . .

The jarring sound of keys and footsteps awakened Tom this
time, and he was momentarily confused by the dream. He stood
and stretched as the footsteps grew closer, and when the guard appeared at the cell he opened the gate without a word. He jerked
his head at Tom in a "follow me" gesture, and Tom fell in step
with him. The hazy, happy dream had melted from his consciousness upon wakening, and the dread that replaced it was stronger
than ever in contrast. Tom followed the guard silently for a few
moments before venturing a few words of cautious inquiry.

"Is my lawyer here to see me?" he asked.

"Nope," the guard responded, without offering anything further.

"Well, what's happening then? Is this something to do with
the warrants?"

"In a way, yes," the guard answered. "The prosecuting attorney decided to take the warrants under advisement."

Tom didn't understand what this meant. He waited for the
guard to explain further.

"You're being let go," the guard said, without attempting to
mask his disgust.

Tom froze. "Let go?" he said, incredulously.

"Yup," the guard responded. "Let go."

Tom's face broke into a contorted smile and his breath failed
to come. His face turned red while his breath faltered and when
he finally gasped for air, a giant choke escaped him. His head spun
and his body felt light and twisted, as if he were growing and
stretching visibly there beside the guard in the florescent hallway
light. Tom thought he would fall to his knees and crack the
linoleum tiles beneath him with the thunderous drop. He almost

reached out to the guard for physical support, but stopped himself in time and leaned instead against the thick painted brick of the corridor wall. He was laughing and crying simultaneously now, and his hands covered his face while he tried to hold himself upright.

"Oh God," he cried. "Thank you thank you thank you."

"Don't thank *me,*" the disgusted guard spat.

Tom did his best to compose himself and straighten his body to his full height. "I wasn't," he answered, with all the false animosity he could muster. He held his chin up higher than he had ever held it before, he was sure, but allowed the tears to remain in the trails they had cut in his cheeks. He would make no apologies now. He was entitled to these tears.

"Get me the hell outta here then," was all he said.

Tom was released from jail without fanfare. The guard led him down countless identical hallways to another small Plexiglas window where he was given some paperwork to fill out. When he was finished with that, they traded him the paperwork for his shoelaces and belt and then opened the gate that separated the jail wing from the rest of the building. Tom walked through the gate alone and the guard locked himself back inside, turned, and strolled away down the long hallway.

Tom stood for a few brief moments outside the locked gate and weighed his options. He had presumed that either Frank Fabbri or his parents, or maybe even a whole party of family members, would be there to greet him for the moment of release. But instead he found himself standing alone outside a locked gate in what appeared to be some kind of a small waiting room, unsure which way would even lead him out of the building. The sparse seats in the room were mostly empty, but one was occupied by an elderly black man who looked as if he was waiting for someone.

The gentleman had smile lines etched deeply into his face and he held a softpack of menthol cigarettes in his hands, turning them over and over, fidgeting. Tom approached him.

"Excuse me, do you mind if I bum one of those?" Tom asked, pointing to the packet.

The man looked up and smiled at Tom, exhibiting all of his laugh lines in their deepest, most majestic form.

"Son," he responded, "you look like you could use the whole pack."

He laughed a deep and raspy smoker's laugh and handed the half-full pack of cigarettes to Tom, and then offered his hand for a handshake.

"Thank you, sir," Tom stammered.

He shook the proffered hand and turned quickly in an effort to spare the man a display of grateful tears. That man would never know the faith he had helped to restore in that brief moment. *After everything, I can still expect to be surprised by the kindness of a total stranger,* Tom thought, recognizing a very Julie-like and comforting naïveté in the notion.

As Tom left the little waiting room, a sense of urgency began to grow in him. This building was full of people who had clearly defined themselves as his enemies, and he felt quite sure that those people wouldn't be too happy when they got wind of his release. Tom didn't want to stick around and give them further opportunities to express their misplaced anger. He briefly thought of his four attackers, how two of them had been in that building, examining him from behind that two-way mirror just the day before. Tom still didn't know the degree of the police deception — he didn't know that those two men had never set foot in the building. So his panic at the thought of running into them was very real and terrifying.

He had to get out of there and he had to do it fast. He followed hallway after hallway toward what he thought was the front of the building until he spotted natural light streaming through a glass door. He headed for the door, breaking into a trot as he did so and glancing nervously over his shoulder to check if he was being followed. There were a few people milling around or talking quietly to one another, but no one seemed to be paying him any notice. He was relieved, but didn't stop jogging when he got to the door. Instead he flung it open and broke into a dead run, ignoring the sharp pain in his hip and the persistent aches in the rest of his body. He hadn't noticed the pains so vividly before, when he had been confined and all his movements slow and constricted.

He bounded down the steps and crossed the street without looking for traffic, lucky that it was a weekend afternoon and there weren't many cars on the road. He didn't stop until he got to the far curb. He looked back across the street to confirm that no one had followed him, and then lowered himself onto the curb to think for a few moments, acknowledging the searing pain in his right hip for the first time. He flinched, but the pain passed once he was seated and he concentrated on trying to take stock of his situation.

He was somewhere in downtown St. Louis. He was in the business district and there weren't many people around. He guessed by the afternoon light that it was somewhere between three and four o'clock. He didn't have a single penny and no one had been waiting to collect him upon his release from jail. Fabbri had been so adamant that his family was behind him, supporting him. And his father had embraced him so tenderly at the elevator the night before. But he hadn't had any direct contact with any of them since. Surely they hadn't abandoned him? Tom's life had changed so utterly in the last two days that he couldn't be sure of anything any more. Maybe they did think he was a murderer. Maybe his parents had decided that, after all, it might be better to cut their losses and leave him to get himself out of the situation he had dragged them all into. There was only one way to find out. He had to get to a phone.

He looked around and realized he was on the edge of a parking lot and that there was a pay phone not too far away. He made his limping way toward the phone, the pain in his hip demanding more delicate movement now. He didn't think about the fact that he had no quarters until he was standing in front of the phone staring at it, but that problem was easily enough solved: he would call collect. The more urgent problem, clearly, was what *number* to call collect. He knew his grandparents' address by heart but the phone number had never seemed that important before. He was usually dialing out from there, not in. Besides, Julie knew the number, so if he had ever needed to call and tell his parents he'd be home late, she had just dialed for him. He cradled the receiver against his shoulder and dialed 411 with a visibly shaking index finger.

Within a minute, the operator had connected Tom's collect call to the name and address he had supplied. Grandma Polly answered on the second ring.

"Grandma?" he said, but the operator was talking over him.

"Will you accept a collect call from Tom?" she said in a pinched and nasal voice.

"Of course!" Grandma Polly responded, and Tom's heart melted once again with relief at the sound of her voice.

"Grandma?" he said. "I got out. They let me out and I don't know where to go. Nobody was here to get me and I don't have any money for a taxi — I don't even know where I'd get a taxi and I'm afraid to go back into the police building in case they decide to lock me back up or something . . ."

Tom's words came rushing out, and if it hadn't been for the raw emotion he was feeling, he would have felt rather silly for the tumble of timid words.

"Listen to me, doll baby, everything's gonna be just fine," Grandma Polly soothed. "Your mom and dad are on their way down there right now. They just got the call about fifteen minutes ago and they rushed outta here like a whirlwind. They should be there real soon. You just sit tight, you hear? Don't worry about going back inside there. If you're scared, then you're right to be scared and you just follow your old instincts. Stay right where you are — they'll find you."

Tom picked at a sticker that was peeling from the corner of the phone box and the tears came rushing down his face while his grandmother talked. It was so good to hear her voice. And she was so loving and encouraging that all of his previous fears were allayed. He knew he should hang up soon, that this collect call would cost her a fortune.

"Okay, Grandma, I'll wait here. I guess I better go — I called collect," he said. But despite his best efforts to sound strong, the tremble in his voice was unmistakable.

"You're just gonna rush off the phone like that?" Grandma Polly teased. "You run off and have all these adventures without us, and now you won't even give me the time of day on the phone. You have an appointment or something? Something more important to do than fill old Grandma in on the happenings?"

Tom laughed, clearly relieved that she wasn't letting him go. She had sensed his trepidation and she didn't care if this call ended up costing half her life savings. She wasn't about to hang up that phone.

"Tommy, I don't know if I told you this, but I've been learning that electric slide dance? I'm getting real good at it, you know. I was showing Grandpa just the other day — I did a whole demonstration for him right there in the living room. He was sitting in his favorite chair, so I made him put his newspaper down and I put on a little country music and I did that whole electric slide for him. I just love to dance. Do you know the electric slide dance?"

"Uh, no, Grandma, I can't say that I do," Tom responded.

He knew what she was doing, trying to distract him from his predicament, but he was so caught off guard by the image of his grandmother partying around the house to Garth Brooks that the tactic was actually working. He was laughing instead of thinking about the fact that he was standing alone in a nearly abandoned parking lot with a broken hip, a broken life, and two dead cousins.

"Well, it's a date then. As soon as you get home, I'm gonna teach you the electric slide. That way, whenever one of you kids is ready to get married and we throw a big old party for the wedding, you and I can cut a rug together. What do you say to that?"

"Sounds great, Grandma," Tom answered. And he meant it.

Gene and Ginna's parents, Grandpa Gene and Grandma Maria, had arrived in St. Louis from Florida early that morning, much to the relief of the gathering siblings. Grandpa Gene had always been a force to be reckoned with. As a young man, he had studied for the Catholic priesthood for seven years before meeting his wife and falling in love. He married Maria after a whirlwind courtship and, instead of becoming a Catholic priest, he became a Catholic salesman, for John Fabick Tractor Company. But his faith in and devotion to God had never wavered over the years, even when he had chosen the marital vocation instead of the priestly one, and he had raised all of his children strictly in the Roman Catholic tradition. Even now, despite his age and arthritis, all eight of his children considered him one of the most powerful, most dedicated, and most intelligent men they had ever known. And his friends and colleagues agreed. So there was an unspoken sense among the siblings that his arrival in St. Louis would mark the beginning of the end of this tragedy. To some degree, they had maintained their own childhood mantra, "Don't worry — Daddy can fix it."

Grandpa Gene's impeccable honesty, solid work ethic, and tremendous success had earned him quite a reputation in the St. Louis business community. People knew his name and respected him. But it was his personality that people most admired. Grandpa Gene loved a good story, and was known to employ all props within reach when relating one of his tales. At the dinner table, for instance, he'd use a knife to represent whatever street he was describing, and then he'd reach for the salt and pepper shakers to stand in for the buildings. He sometimes became so engrossed in the construction of his scene that he forgot where the story was going. But he always managed to find his way back to the punch line and earn a few laughs from his listeners along the way. His quick smile and the twinkle in his sharp blue eyes hadn't faded a bit over the years, and he still used them to flirt with Maria, the love of his life.

Kevin had collected Grandpa Gene and Grandma Maria from the airport early that morning and had checked them into the local Marriott before driving them to Ginna's house. First Grandpa Gene stopped to privately speak words of comfort to his daughter and share some tears. He then made a beeline for the telephone and started dialing, calling in favors. He spent the next hour calling every contact he could think of in St. Louis — and that was no small list. Grandpa Gene had friends in the Coast Guard, friends in the police department, friends in the government. He even had friends in the St. Louis Cardinals baseball administration, although he couldn't think of any way they could be particularly useful at the moment. He called everyone he could think of, and before the hour was out, he had left a tidal wave of information-gathering, damage-controlling, eager-to-help activity in his wake. He would see to it that every possible human effort was made to find his granddaughters.

*   *   *

As they pulled into the half-empty parking lot, Kay and Gene were surprised to find their son limping to approach the van before they could even park. They had assumed he would be held inside until they arrived to pick him up. After a brief and tearful reunion, the threesome drove straight to Frank Fabbri's office. Tom wanted to know how the family was holding up, and Gene filled him in while they drove.

"I want to go and see Ginna as soon as we're done here," Tom said as they pulled into the driveway that was Fabbri's parking lot.

Gene thought for a moment before he answered. He knew that this wasn't his decision. "Okay," he responded.

Fabbri set Kay and Gene up comfortably in a separate, if similarly decorated, room across the hallway from his personal office. He supplied them with yellow legal-sized notepads and a variety of pens, suggesting that they might spend some time writing notes about their experiences over the last forty-eight hours. Anything at all they could remember about any interaction with the police would be helpful, he explained, starting with the very first moment of the ordeal, right up to the present. He offered them use of a phone if they needed it. Then he crossed the airy hallway and closed the big wooden door, shutting himself and Tom inside his chrome-and-black office where they could talk privately and at length about his circumstances. Kay started writing her notes immediately, while Gene sat down and dialed Ginna's number. His own father answered.

He was forty-six years old and he still greeted his father with "sir." Grandpa Gene listened intently while the younger Gene explained what he expected the next few hours would bring. Fabbri had insisted on seeing Tom right away, before he was taken home, he explained. And Tom was anxious to see Ginna, so they would be bringing him by on their way home.

"I'll arrange to get Tink and Kathy over here too, then," Grandpa Gene said.

Gene thought about arguing, about explaining Rick's discomfort with the situation, but he stopped himself before he started. There was no use arguing with Grandpa Gene anyway. The man was almost always right, and young Gene felt reasonably sure that this time was no exception. The decision had been made and it was final. By the time the two Genes hung up, someone was already en route to pick the two sisters up from Fair Acres Road.

The sun had set again and dusk was dropping down over the eaves of Ginna's crowded little home on Petite Drive. Tink and her cousin Danni Thess were parked on the living-room sofa, keeping a lookout for Tom's arrival. The night before they had been told he was on his way home, and the next thing they knew he had been arrested. The relief everyone had felt with the news of Tom's release had been replaced with a growing sense of unease as the day stretched into evening and Tom still made no appearance at the house.

When the big blue van finally did round the corner and approach the house under the canopy of trees, Tink slapped her cousin's leg and they both stood, pressing their faces against the darkening glass. Grandpa Gene noticed this, and within a moment he had motioned Tink and Kathy alone out onto the front step and gathered the rest of the large family into the kitchen to give them privacy.

Tink linked her arm nervously through her sister's and their two stomachs rolled in unison as the van approached the driveway and made the turn. Their father was driving and their mother sat in the passenger seat beside him. The blue polyester curtains were pulled tight over the back windows so that the seats inside were obscured from view. Kathy gripped Tink's hand as they waited for the van to stop. They prayed that the back door would open and reveal that their brother had come home.

Tink and Kathy watched as the van stopped and their parents

unstrapped their seat belts. No lips were moving in the van. Nothing was being said. But in a moment the van's back door creaked open and Tom's face appeared over the doorjamb, his eyes seeking his sisters before he even moved to climb down from the van. Seeing them, he gave a brave smile and stepped carefully down from the high step. Tom descended from the van like an old man. He put one foot and then the other shakily down onto the asphalt in Ginna's driveway before turning to walk toward the house. He left the van door standing wide open behind him and limped up the driveway toward where his sisters stood waiting for him. As he came closer they could see that his lips were white with dehydration, his filthy hair stuck up at crazy angles, cemented in place by river water and silt, and his shoulders were hopping with lice from his night in jail. He limped toward them and tried to smile, but his face was twisted with the effort and he held his arms out to them as he came nearer. Tink and Kathy enveloped him in a hug and all three of them gave over to desperate tears. The three siblings just stood gripping each other and sobbing.

"I love you, Tom," both girls said over and over again. "Thank God you're home."

"I love you guys too," he answered, burying his face between their shoulders.

CHAPTER TWELVE

Tom's reunion with Ginna was brief and fraught with emotion. He sat with her for fewer than fifteen minutes on her living-room couch, their four hands knotted together on a pillow across their laps, their faces tight with tears. Gene and Kay were anxious to get their son cleaned up and into a proper bed for the night, but they cleared the room, giving Ginna and Tom time alone together first. Ginna offered him the comfort he so needed.

"Of course you've done nothing wrong. We're going to get through this, you poor thing," she said to him.

And, at the back of his mind, behind his relief and gratitude, he marveled at her ability to console him. When he stood to go, he bent over her trembling figure and Ginna held his face in her hands. He whispered into her ear words for her alone, and he kissed her face before limping out of the house and back to the van.

It was the beginning of another long night — the second sunset without Julie and Robin. And though hope of finding them alive was waning with each passing hour, no one seemed able to foster any sense of finality without news of a discovery. The hours stretched on in limbo. Again, no one really slept much that night except Tom. But he slept deep and black enough for the whole family to draw strength from his rest.

*   *   *

When the Cummins family awoke on Sunday morning, April 7, 1991, the front page headline that greeted them invoked fresh despair. *The St. Louis Post Dispatch* printed: "Suspect In Deaths Of 2 Women Freed During Search For Bodies." Tom's name was muddier than ever.

Tom sat at his grandmother's kitchen breakfast table, enjoying his first cup of morning coffee with newborn appreciation. He leafed gingerly through the newspaper while he sipped. After reading the headline, he cringed as he turned each page, as if the words and pictures they contained actually caused him physical pain. In the end, he found they didn't. He didn't even bother reading the rest of the article in which he was labeled "suspect." Skipping it, he missed the few sentences that read, "Police had been searching Friday night for the owner of a large flashlight, inscribed 'HORN 1' that was found on the bridge. Sgt. Dan Nichols, of the homicide division, said Saturday that police knew the identity of the flashlight owner. He declined to say whether the person had talked with police."

Instead, Tom found himself drawn to a mini-article about Julie's poetry. Her photograph smiled out at him from under the headline, "Woman Who Fell From Bridge Is Recalled As Promising Poet." A chill ran down Tom's spine while he tried to shake off the headline's image of Julie falling from the bridge. One of her English professors at UMSL was quoted in the article, saying that Julie was "the most promising poet I ever taught." *Well, I could have told you that,* Tom thought. The paper had printed an excerpt of one of her poems:

Surviving on tired manuscripts
And dog-eared love letters,
We saw it coming.
We used to wait for it

In cozy cafes,
And prophesize with our pens
On paper napkins
Color it with chalk
On city sidewalks.

Tom read it over and over again, until his coffee cup was empty. The poem was no different in the paper than it had been when Julie had sent it to him in one of her letters. Sure, it was in type instead of Julie's neatly printed handwriting, but the sentiment was the same. When the splatter of his teardrops threatened to turn Julie's poem into a gray and jumbled mess, Tom closed the paper and pushed the unread article away. He cried quietly for a few moments, but his grief was confused by his fear. He was still a suspect and he was still terrified.

Detectives Trevor and Brauer didn't have to look hard for Richardson. They reached his neighborhood early in the morning hours, when people were just starting to trickle out of their homes, some in bathrobes, snapping up their morning papers. Others were in their Sunday finery, herding their families to church. The unmarked squad car crept quietly through Northwoods, failing in its efforts to appear discreet. The detectives parked at the intersection of Barken and Edgewood and double-checked their witness's address before getting out of the car.

The banging went on for a couple of minutes before a sleepy Richardson cracked the door open to peer out at the two detectives from behind the apartment's chain lock.

"Antonio Richardson?" Detective Trevor asked.

"Yeah," Richardson responded without offering more.

Trevor flipped his badge open and proffered it toward the narrowing eye behind the door.

"St. Louis police. We need to talk to you. We have reason to believe that you may be a material witness in a case we're working on. Would you mind opening the door please?"

Richardson yawned loudly and shut the door. Trevor and Brauer exchanged brief, uneasy glances but, a moment later, they heard the telltale flick of the chain unlocking, and Richardson flung the door open to them. He didn't invite them in, but turned instead and strolled back to the couch, where it seemed he may have spent the night. His T-shirt and shorts were rumpled, and the afghan on the couch curled lazily around his legs as he slumped into a reclining position. He stretched and yawned again — a typical sleepy and grumpy sixteen-year-old, unimpressed at being awakened from his Sunday-morning slumber by the police. The two detectives entered the room and closed the door behind them. They didn't intend to make themselves at home, but allowed Richardson to slump in front of them while they talked.

"Do you know anything about a flashlight bearing the inscription HORN 1, Antonio?"

A fleeting moment of panic rippled through Richardson, waking him more than the unexpected knocking had. He sat up a degree or two in his seat. His mind raced. *They must know something about it, or they wouldn't be here,* he thought. He knew he had to admit at least some connection.

"Yeah," he began sheepishly, "that was my flashlight. I lost it on the bridge a few days ago."

"That's why we're here, Antonio. There's not going to be any trouble about you stealing that flashlight from Mr. Whitehorn. But we do know that you were a witness to what went down at the Chain of Rocks Bridge on Thursday night, and we need your cooperation in that matter."

Antonio shifted uncomfortably in his seat, using one arm to lever himself into a more upright position. He chewed his bottom lip and thought it over for a moment, pulling at a loose thread on the multicolored afghan as he did so. The two detectives silently awaited his response.

"Yeah, okay," Richardson said finally. He glanced at the two men's faces before continuing. "I got important information about that actually. I know what happened. I can help y'all."

"Will you make a statement?" Brauer asked.

Richardson nodded. A few minutes later, he was dressed in a T-shirt and pair of blue jeans that were not noticeably less wrinkled than his previous ensemble, and ready to head downtown with Trevor and Brauer. Richardson was silent as they left his apartment, and he hung his head low as Brauer unlocked the squad car and opened the back door for him. He got in quickly and immediately slouched down in his seat. Trevor and Brauer weren't sure if the kid just had posture as bad as his attitude, or if he was trying to hide from his neighbors. With a potential homicide witness, just about anything was possible.

In the backseat, Richardson continued to stare moodily out the window. He already knew what he was going to say — he was just hammering out the details in his head. He would tell the truth, more or less, but only about Marlin Gray and his cousin Reggie Clemons. He'd tell them what Marlin and Reggie had done and he'd blame the whole thing on them. He'd say he was scared — that they'd threatened to kill him if he squealed. He'd say he had been a silent bystander, unable to stop the crimes because he was so young and so frightened. And he wouldn't even mention Danny — Danny was the most likely to break down. He knew that if they brought Danny Winfrey in, they'd get the whole truth out of him and that would be the end of everything.

It's gonna be all right, he told himself. *I'm gonna get myself out of this.*

For the first time in history, Tink and Kathy didn't fight their brother for time in the bathroom. Tom stayed in there for well over an hour, scrubbing and washing and shampooing and shaving and grooming. The RID that Kay had bought for him at the supermarket had been largely successful in evicting the rather persistent lice that had found a home on him during his time in jail, but he still felt less than presentable in his dress clothes for Mass. When he looked in the mirror he still saw a shambles staring back at him. His hair, annoyed at being left unwashed for so long, refused to lie down flat on his head and instead stuck up in three or four inappropriate cowlicks. His eyes were bloodshot, his shave looked prickly, and his skin still felt dirty, although in fact he was immaculate down to the fingernails. He shook his head and switched the light off.

They were all ready and waiting for him upstairs: his sisters, his parents, and his grandparents. But nobody complained that he had kept them waiting.

"Ready, son?" Gene looked at Tom, who steeled himself and nodded his head.

Grandma Polly and Grandpa Art went into the church first. They were always so considerate, Tom thought. How kindhearted and brave they were being now. He followed them, limping noticeably and flanked by Kathy and Tink. He was sure that neither of his sisters had ever held their heads so high as they did that morning, yet he caught the unmistakable trace of water in their eyes as they helped him down the aisle behind their grandparents and into the front pew. Kay and Gene brought up the rear. All seven of them knelt down and prayed. In a few moments, Kay had the Kleenex out of her purse and was quietly passing it along the pew. Tom blessed himself and sat back, and his sisters joined him.

Tink and Kathy had never been so protective of him before, and while he was touched, he was also a little worried by it. The truth was that he was more than slightly uncomfortable being out in public for the first time. Since his release the day before, he had seen his own picture on television countless times, paired with phrases like "alleged murderer" and "suspect." He was sure that everyone in the church had seen these pictures as well, and that they were now watching him, wary and disgusted. But they *were* in church, after all, he thought. Maybe he was just being paranoid. Maybe people here would give him the benefit of the doubt. He saw a few parishioners snap their eyes away when he glanced at them, and he really couldn't sort out the paranoia from the reality. He breathed deeply and tried to concentrate.

The priest talked in soothing Midwestern tones and soon Tom felt himself getting sleepy again. His energy hadn't quite caught up with him. He didn't know how he'd last the whole hour without further disgracing his family by falling asleep. He'd have to find something to keep himself alert. Just then Tink nudged him in the rib cage and showed him her hands. She was doing "Here's the church, here's the steeple, open it up . . ." She usually finished it off with an Indian burn or a middle finger or an uppercut to the jaw instead of the more traditional ". . . and see all the people." Tom looked up at his sister's face, pale pink and blue and green from the stained-glass light, and she stuck her tongue out at him and smiled. Tom chuckled quietly and if the priest noticed, from where he was preaching about four feet away, he didn't let on. Grandma Polly leaned forward in the pew and winked at the two of them. Tom's spirits lifted a little.

After several hours of questioning and a couple of taped statements from Richardson, the St. Louis Homicide Division was ready to take its investigation in an entirely new direction. It was beginning to dawn on them that Tom Cummins might actually be telling the truth. And Richardson had something further to add to Tom's seemingly unbelievable story — he had names and addresses. He knew only two of the assailants: Marlin Gray from Wentzville and Reginald Clemons from Northwoods. The addi-

tional assailant that Tom had described was unknown to Richardson. He admitted to having seen him, but he kept emphasizing
that he wasn't important. Clemons and Gray were the ringleaders.
Clemons and Gray were the rapists and the murderers.

"Surely you've seen this story on the news the past two days.
You knew those two girls were still missing, probably dead. And
that kid Cummins has been to hell and back. If you saw all this
happen and you knew who had done it, why didn't you come
forward?" Brauer pressed him after the tape recorder clicked off.

Richardson shrugged. "I was scared," he answered.

You sure as hell don't look scared to me, Brauer thought, shaking
his head.

"Antonio, we'd like for you to accompany us to the bridge this
afternoon, if you will. We're going to make a videotape, and you
can map out the sequence of events for us logistically. How does
that sound?"

"Fine," Richardson responded.

When the detectives left him alone in the interrogation room,
Richardson stretched and linked his hands behind his head. He
even risked a little smile. He had managed the performance of a
lifetime, he was sure of it. He had given them exactly what they
needed, and they didn't suspect him of a thing. Sure, he would go
along to the bridge and he would reenact the crime for them. In
fact, he was quickly getting used to the idea of seeing the whole
thing from the outside. He was warming to his role as frightened
bystander. He was going to pull this thing off without a hitch.

By the time police arrived in Northwoods to take Reginald
Clemons into custody, Richardson was back in his apartment,
socks on the coffee table, flipping through early-evening television. *Six o'clock, nothing on but news.* As he flipped channels, he
caught a brief glimpse of Tom Cummins's grim-looking face. It
was too soon for the media to have gotten wind of the new developments, and as a result Tom was still being labeled "alleged

murderer." But Richardson wasn't interested. He flipped channels again, hoping for a game show or something.

The afternoon had been another long and tense one for the Cummins and Kerry families. Everyone had gone to church, and every church in the St. Louis area was asking for prayers for the two missing sisters, Julie and Robin Kerry. When Tom and his parents had left Fabbri's office the previous evening, his final word to them had been one of caution.

"I know you're relieved right now and this is great," Fabbri had said, "but just be warned that this thing is far from over. You are still the number-one suspect, and the police are still determined to obtain evidence against you. As soon as they find a body or anything else, you should expect to be rearrested."

Tom had nodded, but inwardly he had blanched at the thought. To think that just a week before his worst fear had been heights. Now he was terrified at the thought of going to jail for murdering his cousins. So as the rest of the family spent Sunday hoping and praying for word of some discovery, Tom was torn. The families knew at this stage that there was very little likelihood of finding either girl alive, and their hopes had drifted, slowly but surely, to finding their bodies. Ginna needed closure. Tom, for his part, had to hope for the impossible. He wanted peace for Ginna, but he was sure that the discovery of a body would get him rearrested. He didn't know what to pray for. So he just held on and hoped. He barely dared to breathe.

When the phone rang early that evening, everyone jumped, as had become their habit. Later, the psychiatrists would identify this phenomenon as "exaggerated startle response." Right now however, all the Cumminses knew was that the phone would bring news, and with it heartache, hope, terror.

"Gene," Grandma Polly said from the kitchen, "the police are on the phone. They need to talk to you."

This was the phone call they had all been dreading. Tom was sure of it. They had found something. Gene's face turned sickeningly ashen as he heaved himself up from the couch and tottered dizzily toward the kitchen phone. He didn't look Tom in the eye as he went. Tink and Kathy gripped each other and tears welled up in their eyes while they waited. Tom looked wildly from his sisters to his mother and he trembled. Only Kay met his eyes.

"I won't go back," he said quietly. "I'm not going back. I'll run. Whatever I have to do — I can't go back there. Mom, you can't ask me to. I can't go back, I didn't do this."

His voice was rising in pitch and volume with each word, and by the time Kay had crossed the room and rested her hands on her son's shoulders, he was near hysteria. She sat down next to him and looked him levelly in the eyes.

"We're not asking you to go back, honey. Let's just wait and see what they have to say, okay? Try to stay calm."

Tom shook his head and leapt up from the couch to pace. The pain shooting through his hip reminded him to be careful as he did so. In the days that had passed since Tom's fall from the bridge, he still hadn't seen a doctor, still didn't know that his hip was throbbing because it was fractured. The discomfort registered low on his list of priorities.

Gene wasn't more than two minutes on the phone and when he returned, his face carried a hint of a smile. He opened his mouth to speak but momentarily faltered. It took him an additional few seconds to process his thoughts into words. Tom was in agony waiting for him to speak.

"They've got a guy in custody," Gene began simply. "I don't know how they found him, but they arrested one of the four guys this afternoon and he . . . I guess he confessed. He has basically corroborated your whole story."

Tom's gaze left his father's face and he sat down beside his mother with a thump on the blue velvet couch. He folded his hands across his lap and stared into middle space, struggling to digest this latest news. He hadn't even known that the police were investigating any other leads. His efforts at hope thus far had been extended to clearing his own name. That they would actually have found even one of the four monsters who did this had seemed too grand a possibility to even hope for. Kay was throwing her arms around him now, and he watched in stunned silence as his sisters sprang up from their seats and rushed toward him. Tom just couldn't take it in. There was a loud buzz in his ears and everything seemed slow and contorted. Until all at once, the joyful sounds of his family burst upon his ears and he crumpled, crying, while his sisters tackled him.

Gene briefly disappeared from the room, and when he returned he set two bottles of cold Budweiser on the coffee table, peeled the smiling, teary-eyed Tink and Kathy off of their brother, and handed his son a beer. Tink and Kathy looked at each other wide-eyed, but Kay shot them a warning glance before they could comment on the fact that their father had just handed their brother an actual beer. It was unprecedented. Again Gene opened his mouth to try to speak but found himself unable. There were just too many things to say. Nineteen-year-old Tom stood up and embraced his father.

"I know, Dad," he said.

It didn't take long for the euphoria to subside, as everyone's utter relief was replaced by guilt for experiencing joy while there was still no word of Julie and Robin. Still, the next hour's worth of phone calls were certainly easier than any others Gene had made in the last two days. He phoned Ginna first, then his father and brothers and sisters. The response was the same each time.

"Oh thank God," they all said.

When the six o'clock news came on, it became abundantly clear that while the police had turned their scrutiny away from Tom, the media as yet had not. The story was still at the top of every newscast. A reporter had questioned Jacobsmeyer earlier that day and Channel Four aired the interview: "Police say Cummins tried to sexually assault one of his cousins. One of the women fell from the bridge; the other fell trying to help her. Is that still what the police believe at this point?"

"Yes it is," was Jacobsmeyer's response.

"Tomorrow morning, searchers and family members will continue their agonizing wait for the bodies to surface," the reporter concluded. "In the meantime, police say, Cummins is free to return to Maryland."

The Cummins family watched the report with stony faces. Their knowledge that the truth would come to light, probably as soon as the eleven o'clock news, did little to quell their hurt and rage.

Smoothing things over with Eva had not been as easy as Gray had hoped, but as usual, his charm had won out in the end. Gray wasn't the type to waste much time with apologies or making up. He figured that Eva would either forgive him or she wouldn't, and that was it. Sure enough, in a couple of days the whole incident seemed to have blown over, and on Sunday evening the couple drove to Mike and Chrissy's to spend an evening much like the one Gray had spent there with his friends the night they killed Julie and Robin.

No one took much notice when the knock on the door came, just after nine o'clock. Mike and Chrissy's was an open household, with friends constantly dropping in unannounced. Mike handed his drink to his wife before getting up. Detectives Walsh and Trevor already had their badges out when Mike opened the door.

"St. Louis police," Trevor announced. "We're looking for Marlin Gray."

Mike, stunned, took several steps back from the door as the two plainclothes detectives, flanked by several uniformed officers with guns drawn, spilled through the doorway without awaiting an invitation.

"Um," Mike stammered. "He's in . . . he's in the bathroom."

Mike indicated the direction to the bathroom with a jerk of his head. He hadn't had a lot of dealings with the police, but he knew enough not to make any sudden movements in the presence of so many unholstered weapons.

By this time, Eva and the others were on their feet in the living room, staring openmouthed as the half dozen or so police moved through the little house, converging on the bathroom. Gray was still inside, oblivious to the fact that he had visitors. By the time the officers were stationed outside the bathroom door and knocked, somebody had switched off the television and the house was silent. Gray made some unintelligible response to the knock, but made no move to come out.

"This is the police," Walsh shouted. "You have five seconds to come out with your hands up."

Gray was silent inside. At the count of one and a nod from Walsh, the officer nearest the doorknob twisted it and pushed the door open. Three of them rushed into the little room and grabbed Gray before he could even react. They immediately frisked and handcuffed him.

"What the hell is this? What's going on?" Gray demanded.

"You are under arrest for two counts of first-degree murder," Trevor explained.

They were walking Gray toward the still-open front door and Eva followed the cluster of officers as closely as she could. Gray craned his neck around to look at her as they dragged him off.

"Eva, baby, I don't know what's going on, but you've gotta call my mom for me. Tell her I need a lawyer," he said.

Eva nodded, unable to speak. She followed the knot of people all the way out the front door and onto the lawn where she stood, hollow-eyed, and watched them duck her boyfriend into the backseat of the waiting squad car. Her usually wan face had drained completely of color, and even her lips seemed marble-like in the moonlight. Gray didn't look at her through the car window as they pulled away.

Tom absolutely hated the idea of leaving the house to go to dinner, but Grandpa Gene had been insistent. Any relief Tom had felt earlier at the announcement that the police had a suspect in custody had faded back to rock-bottom depression during the six o'clock news. It was so hard to know who was telling the truth these days. Reporters were saying one thing, police were saying another, and both of these sources had proven themselves less than trustworthy in the last forty-eight hours.

Tom was beside himself. He didn't want to go to Red Lobster. He didn't even want to go to the driveway. He didn't want to worry about police, or jail, or if people thought he was a sick murderer. He wanted to miss Julie. He wanted to weep for Julie and Robin. He wanted to curl up under some of Grandma Polly's handmade quilts on the floor in the den and cry himself to sleep. It was Grandpa Art's usual selfless diplomacy that eventually convinced him, after his father's prodding had failed.

"You know, Tom," Grandpa Art had said, "your grandparents came all the way up here from Florida so they could be here for you and show you their support. We've spent the whole week with you, and I think you owe it to them to give them a couple of hours. I know it's not what you're in the mood for. It's probably not what they're in the mood for either. That's the whole problem, nobody's in the mood for much of anything. But you have to eat anyway, and taking you to dinner is your grandpa's way of showing you he loves you and he believes in you. You really oughtta go."

So he went, if somewhat grudgingly and nervously. He didn't exactly expect to be able to hide — a table for seven can't easily be tucked away into a dark corner. But neither did Tom expect to be seated, with his sisters, parents, and grandparents, at the large room's long center table. He limped awkwardly through the restaurant, preceded by the hostess and followed by his family, and tried not to notice the several diners who stopped in mid-sentence or dropped their forks when they saw and recognized him. He averted his eyes, slid into his chair, and self-consciously opened his large menu to cover his face.

Grandpa Gene hung his cane on the back of a nearby chair before seating himself beside his grandson. He placed his large, arthritis-ridden hand on Tom's forearm and trained his piercing blue eyes on his grandson's face. Tom allowed the menu to drop a couple of inches in order to meet his grandfather's gaze. They didn't speak, but somehow Tom drew strength from his grandfather's face.

Tink still hadn't eaten anything and had no intention of starting tonight, which was probably why she hadn't protested the choice of restaurant. She was the one member of the Cummins clan who didn't love seafood. While the rest of the family ordered crab legs, shrimp cocktail, scallops, and fish, Tink ordered a burger and tried not to gag from the strong aroma of fish all around her. They chatted quietly while they waited for the food, but nobody really had much to say and the conversation was strained. When two steaming baskets of cheese bread arrived on the table, they were empty within moments; Tink only got one because Kay intercepted it for her. She placed it in the center of her daughter's little saucer.

"Why don't you try that," she said. "I think you'll like it."

Tink studied the golden bun on her plate suspiciously. She had hardly swallowed a bite since Thursday night. She looked drawn and Kay was worried about her. Tink had to admit, though, that for the first time since her world had turned upside down, she *was* actually kind of hungry. She tore off a corner of the little bun and worked it slowly into her mouth. It was delicious. Within a minute she had eaten the entire thing. Kay looked at the empty plate in astonishment.

"You want another one?" she said.

Tink nodded, so Kay searched both baskets but came up empty-handed. She was undeterred. Her daughter was eating again. Tink wanted cheese bread? Then, by God, she would have cheese bread. Kay turned in her chair and scanned the room for their wayward waitress. She was nowhere to be found. But a waitress for the next table over came by with a tray of fresh cheese bread. Kay waited until she wasn't looking and snagged one from the corner of the tray. She dropped it onto Tink's plate with a triumphant little plop. Tink laughed at her mother.

"Thanks, Mom," she said.

"Hey, where's mine?" Kathy demanded, eyeing her sister's cheese bread enviously.

"You want one too?" Kay asked.

Kathy nodded and then Tom piped up.

"Me too, Mom," he said.

Kay grinned and followed the cheese bread waitress with her eyes. Her table was ready to order; she would have to set the tray down to take it. Sure enough, a moment later, the waitress turned and set the tray of cheese bread on a nearby tray stand, just a few feet from Kay's chair. She wasted no time, but marched directly over and lifted the whole tray as if she were a waitress herself. She doled out bread until her whole family had had their fill, then returned the empty tray to its stand. The kids all giggled when the confused waitress turned back to her now-empty tray. It was a moment of genuine levity.

"Mom, you're such a hoodlum," Kathy laughed after the waitress had passed out of earshot.

"Yeah," Tink agreed, munching her third cheese bread. "The Cummins family has turned into a regular hotbed of criminal activity."

"Watch out, Mom, they're coming after you next. And the mother steals bread!" Tom said in mock horror. "It's little wonder the son turned out the way he did."

It was strange for them all to be laughing and joking and eating at Red Lobster while Julie and Robin were still out there somewhere in the dark, unaccounted for. So the moment of lightness was a brief, if much-needed one. And soon they were paying for their laughter with those terrible, heavy feelings of guilt that survivors always feel. All of the briefly smiling faces at the table turned grave. The crumbs on Tink's saucer were turning wet with the splatter of tears, and her appetite was gone again.

CHAPTER THIRTEEN

Gray sat in Tom's vacated seat in interview room number two and stared blankly at the same whirring little tape recorder on the table in front of him. It had been a long night. Detective Pappas's voice was first on the recording, announcing the time at a little past five o'clock on the morning of April 8, 1991. Pappas read Gray his rights and asked him about his involvement in the robbery, rape, and murder of the Kerry sisters and the assault of Tom Cummins. Gray's voice was tired, deep, and monotonous, fully devoid of emotion as he began to tell his story.

Brauer could barely conceal his disgust as he watched Gray coldly recite what he had done to the Kerry sisters in their last hours. He still wasn't confessing to murder. He admitted to the rapes, but swore up and down he didn't know how the two girls had wound up in the river. Nobody believed him for a minute, but a rape confession was better than no confession at all, so they had decided to go ahead with the taping. The confession lasted about forty minutes and concluded at ten minutes to six on Monday morning.

After a terribly botched start, a start where bad hunches and an emotionally crippled witness had been their only leads, the St. Louis Homicide Division was finally back on track. They had obtained two taped confessions — one from Clemons and one from Gray. Today would be another big day — they had two more suspects to arrest. When Gray and Clemons had learned that Richardson had been the one to point the finger, they had both eagerly returned the favor. Richardson had been promoted from witness to suspect.

Just as Pappas and Brauer were wrapping up their interview with Gray, Gene Cummins was packing up the family van for the second time that week. This time there would be no sarcastically tearful good-byes from Julie and Robin, he realized, and he stopped in his work to take that in. His hands rested on Kathy's suitcase, which he had been maneuvering into place between the others before tears had caused the whole scene to go blurry. He turned and sat on the van's back bumper for a moment to compose himself.

It was a crisp morning, and the dawn was beginning to light Fair Acres Road with a lilac hue as Gene turned back to his work. Tom emerged from the house behind him, hauling his suitcase and nodding to the cops in the squad car stationed across the street. They had been assigned to protect the Cummins family until they left St. Louis. The cops still weren't sure exactly what they were dealing with in this bizarre case, but one thing was clear: the media had turned Tom into quite the unpopular figure. The police were concerned for his safety.

Tom and his dad worked silently together while Blarney sniffed around in the grass seeking an appropriate spot for her morning activities. When the work was finished, they returned to the house. Inside, Gene sat down despondently at Grandma Polly's little breakfast table and sipped his thick black coffee. It was time to get his family home; he knew that. His daughters needed to get back to school, and he was anxious to get Tom beyond the jurisdiction of this police department. Tom fully intended to cooperate with the ongoing investigation, but Gene saw that his son needed an emotional break before doing so. Tom needed time to grieve for his cousins. In Vietnam, Gene had learned that time to grieve was a luxury sorely missed if denied. It was a lesson he had hoped his children would never have to learn. But everything had changed this week. None of their lives would ever be the same, Gene knew, and the expression on his son's face showed how much he had matured in the last few days. Still, they all felt reluctant to leave St. Louis, as if they thought that once they left, they might somehow be banished forever.

Gene was startled from his reverie by the doorbell. His digital watch read just after six o'clock in the morning — a bit early for visitors, he thought, as he stood nervously to answer the door. The rest of his family was bustling around the house getting ready for the journey, but everyone froze when the doorbell rang. Tink and Kathy peeped out through the front curtains and recognized Ginna's car as their father opened the door. Ginna stood motionless, cast in deep purple shadow on the step in front of him. She twisted a Kleenex round and round her fingers and her lips trembled as Gene opened the screen door and led her inside, into the warm light of the house.

"I came to say good-bye," she began, and tears joined her words, streaming loosely down her face.

The three kids gathered around her and took turns hugging and kissing her. She held their hands in turn and looked each one in the eye as she spoke to them.

"We're going to have a funeral," she announced. "Not yet of course, but when we find the girls. And I know you guys probably won't be able to make it back out for that, but I want your input. You knew them so well, and we're going to have music there — the girls' favorite songs and musicians. Would you help me pick something out?"

The three Cummins kids nodded silently and solemnly, their wet faces shining in the lamplight. They felt honored and once again awed that Ginna, at the time of her deepest sorrow, could be such a healing force for them.

"Robin once told me what kind of funeral she wanted," Ginna continued. "And I always thought she was being morbid, but now . . . now I feel so blessed that I know what she wants . . ."

When Robin was about nine years old, her class at St. Jerome's Elementary School had discussed death and dying one day. While most of the children had exhibited some initial fear or discomfort at the topic, Robin had embraced it. Even at that young age, she was at peace with the idea of her own death. That afternoon, she had gone home to Ginna and said, matter-of-factly, "Mom, I'm going to die young. When it happens, I want you to know what to do."

At the time, Ginna had been truly stunned. "Robin, don't be so morbid!" she had snapped. She had grabbed her nine-year-old baby girl and held her tight, fighting the kind of tears that only a mother can truly understand — tears of terror.

"Don't cry, Mommy," Robin had said. "I won't talk about it again."

And for years Robin didn't talk about it. But when she was fourteen, she spoke up again.

"Now, Mom, I don't want to upset you," Robin began, "but I have to talk to you about something that is really important to me. Please just humor me. This will be hard for you to hear, but just listen to me this once and I promise I will never bring it up again."

The words that mother and daughter exchanged over those next few minutes had horrified Ginna, chilled her to the very bone. But she endured them for her daughter's sake. She had no idea what a blessing they would be in just a few short years.

During that conversation, Ginna had learned that Robin had a feeling — no, more than a feeling, a *sense* — that she was going to die young. And she was okay with it. She felt at ease and she wasn't afraid to die. She hoped to make her mark on the world before she went and she hoped she would be remembered lovingly and often. Beyond that, she felt nothing formidable about her fate, certainly nothing scary.

She asked Ginna to forbid anyone from wearing black to her funeral. She wanted bright colors and balloons. She wanted happy music, people who sang about the things Robin stood for and cared about. She wanted her friends to come and tell happy memories of her and blow soap bubbles. She didn't want anyone to cry.

When Robin finished talking, she hugged her mother and kissed her face, thanking her for listening. Now, five years later, Ginna stood in a circle with her brother's family and tried to accept the fact that her beloved daughters were gone. They had been missing for three days, but Ginna still hadn't really accepted it. After all, that conversation with Robin felt as if it had happened just yesterday. She could still feel Robin's embrace, could still see the look of contentment and relief on her daughter's young face once she had finally unburdened herself of those thoughts.

Tink and Kathy fought tears while their aunt talked, but ended up sobbing while Ginna described Robin's wishes. Ginna collected her nieces into her arms, hugging them and patting their hair as they all cried together. When they settled down, she said her good-byes to Kay and Gene. Finally she turned to Tom, who held her for a long time.

Then she gave everyone a brave, tenuous smile before Gene walked her out. Five minutes later, the family was bundled silently into the big blue van. They all waved good-bye to Grandma Polly and Grandpa Art, who stood holding each other in front of their now-empty house. Gene signaled the squad car, which revved its engine and then pulled out in front, intent on its mission to escort the Cummins family safely out of St. Louis by way of the new Chain of Rocks Bridge.

The kids sprawled out in the back of the van, Tink and Kathy sitting in the bucket seats and Tom occupying the long back bench. All of the window blinds were open, and the brightening light of the morning shone in. They reached the new Chain of Rocks Bridge within fifteen minutes, and crossed parallel to the old giant steel structure, which looked monstrous and black now.

Tink leaned into the window, her breath making fog on the glass as they crossed.

Gray's friend Robert Troncalli was currently employed as a night receiver at the local Wal-Mart, and he worked hard unloading trucks while the surrounding countryside slept. He was used to sleeping late, and when his doorbell rang at about ten-thirty Monday morning, he was grumpy as he rose to answer it.

Detective Walsh introduced himself and his partner Stuart to Troncalli and explained that Marlin Gray had been arrested for murder, and that they were there in hopes of searching the home for a key piece of evidence. Troncalli found himself suddenly wide awake as he gave the detectives his permission to search. His mind was churning and he could hardly believe Marlin Gray had actually been *arrested* for the murders he had so flippantly claimed responsibility for in that very room just a few days earlier. Troncalli was stunned.

Detective Stuart flipped open his notebook and began to ask him some simple questions about his relationship to the suspect while Walsh set about the business of searching for the missing green Swatch watch that Gray had hidden in Troncalli's recliner. Troncalli watched, bewildered, while Walsh removed the cushions from all of his living-room furniture. The detective was down on his knees, elbow-deep in couch cushions, but he soon came up empty-handed. He replaced each cushion neatly when he was finished, but then picked up each piece of furniture to get a good look underneath as well.

Troncalli tried to concentrate on the questions that Stuart was asking him, but he found himself distracted by Walsh's activities. The search turned up nothing and, within a few minutes, the detectives left just as abruptly as they had appeared. Troncalli flopped clumsily into his favorite chair and fingered the card they had given him. It had a phone number on it and the detectives had encouraged him to call if he found anything unusual. He sat alone for a few minutes in his quiet little home and gazed around the room, as if looking for clues himself. On the other side of the now silent living room, Tom Cummins's green Swatch watch was still stuck well into the recliner, having been grazed but missed by Walsh during his groping inspection.

Troncalli related the whole strange incident to his wife Kendra when she came home later that day. He was still a bit bewildered by the detectives' visit, and Kendra was equally shocked when she heard the news of Gray's arrest.

"And what did they want here? With us?" Kendra asked.

"They were searching for some evidence," Troncalli explained. "Supposedly Marlin stole a watch from that Cummins kid on the bridge. If they can find the watch, they can link him physically to the crime. I don't know why they thought it might be here. I don't even want to believe any of this."

Kendra shook her head and stood up from the table, planting a kiss on her husband's cheek as she did so. She didn't know what to make of it all either. It was too much to take in. But she had too much to do to sit around pondering it all day. She began unpacking grocery bags while her husband sat still at the kitchen table, gazing absently at the business card the detectives had left him.

By the time Kendra had the groceries unloaded and was ready to move on to the next chore on her list, Troncalli had roused himself and was outside puttering around the yard. Kendra lugged her vacuum cleaner from its usual spot and dragged it into the center of the living-room floor. As she proceeded with her routine work, her mind was racing with the news that her husband had just shared. She chewed her bottom lip absently as she reached behind the couch to plug in the vacuum. When she flicked it on, its rhythmic hum drowned out the less pleasant thoughts in her head. She stooped to shove the heavy recliner aside and clean beneath it. But as she bent her weight into the chair, something dangling from a low cushion caught her eye and she froze.

She stood up and flicked the vacuum cleaner off, allowing the purring to come to a stop before she moved again. When she reached under the cushion and tugged on the mysterious article, it came tumbling into full view on her living-room carpet: Tom Cummins's green Swatch watch lay at Kendra's feet for a few moments and she eyed it coldly. She hated its import — hated the fact that this watch on her living-room floor proclaimed Marlin Gray's guilt. But she knew what she had to do.

Kendra and Troncalli sat together while he dialed the detective's number from the card.

"Detective Stuart," Troncalli said, taking a deep breath to get himself through the next sentence. "I think my wife and I found that piece of evidence you were looking for."

The *St. Louis Post-Dispatch*'s leading headline on Monday morning was "2 Suspects Arrested in Deaths of Sisters: Police Clear Cousin As Case Takes New Turn." The article briefly described the arrests of two new suspects but did not give the names Reginald Clemons or Marlin Gray.

The reporter who wrote the story questioned Jacobsmeyer as to why Tom Cummins had previously made statements implicating himself. Jacobsmeyer's response was that Tom was "obviously traumatized and confused by the entire incident." Marlin Gray had only been in custody a couple of hours when the paper went to press, so although Tom's name was being officially cleared, the information available about why was meager and unconvincing. Public opinion in St. Louis had definitely *not* yet turned to support him.

Like her cousin Tink, Danni Thess was sixteen, which made her a junior at Wentzville High School. With long blond hair, bright blue eyes, and a starting position on her school's soccer team, she was a popular kid. Her mother Lisa was Gene's and Ginna's sister, and she was extremely proud of her three kids, all of whom were smart, athletic, and well-mannered. Danni had considered arguing with her mother when she insisted that they return to school on Monday, but she knew she'd lose the battle. She had spent most of the weekend alternately hoping and grieving, and she hadn't gotten much sleep. Like the rest of the family, Danni had been utterly relieved when Tom was released on Saturday, and even further reassured by the previous day's two arrests. But her heart was still sore with grief and worry, and she was definitely in no mood for classes. She arrived at school that morning feeling tired, paranoid, and generally miserable.

For once, Daniel Winfrey was actually happy to get to school Monday morning. It had been a long and harrowing weekend, and his freshmen classes at Wentzville High School were a welcome distraction. His girlfriend Amanda still wasn't quite sure what to make of the whole story he had confided in her, but she could see that her boyfriend was under a great deal of stress. She responded by just trying to behave normally, suffering from a classic case of "If I ignore it, maybe it will go away."

Wentzville was a quiet community, so the news of Marlin Gray's late-night arrest was already buzzing around the halls of the high school early that morning. Danni Thess was uncomfortable. She knew that her friends were just trying to be sensitive, but really, she felt that even bluntness would have been better than the whispers and averted eyes she was encountering every time she turned around. She was determined to get through this day. She wasn't about to let her family's newfound notoriety take over her life, and she was starting to get annoyed. Honestly, why didn't people understand that her family's grief was more important than all the peripheral hype and sensationalism? She slammed her locker moodily, blew her bangs out of her eyes, and resolutely trudged to her fourth class of the day.

Detective Walsh shaded his eyes from the too-bright high-noon sunshine as he and Stuart pulled their car into a space in the Wentzville High School parking lot. Another car pulled in right behind them and two deputy juvenile officers for St. Charles County got out. The four men headed inside together.

A few minutes later, Danni Thess joined some of her class-mates at the window to watch as the police led the new blond-haired freshman out of the school in handcuffs. He hung his head in shame as he walked between the two uniformed officers. But Danni didn't know that the kid's name was Daniel Winfrey. And she certainly had no idea that he was being arrested for raping and murdering her cousins.

Gray's and Clemons's names were released to the press later that day. By evening, reporters were going live, swarming the sus-pects' respective neighborhoods. Jacquie and Sheila watched the NBC newscast together in Ginna's living room, feeling somewhat vindicated to see that the media were finally barking up the right tree. Several of Clemons's neighbors were interviewed, and they all expressed their shock that the quiet preacher's son had been ar-rested for such a brutal crime.

Neighbor Buffie Garnett was particularly outspoken. "He was a nice type. You know, he was real quiet. He liked to hang around everybody but he was real quiet. I just saw him the other day and he told me he had a job and everything and I just can't believe he could do something like this. He was sweet and understanding — I never did think that he could do something like this," she said.

Another neighbor, Patricia Gully, had known Clemons since he was about four years old, and she called him "a considerate, friendly child." She had never known him to argue with other children, to be vulgar, or talk back to adults. In fact, she said, he was always a perfect gentleman.

Yet another neighbor, Mardelle Meckfessel, echoed this sentiment in her stories about the many times that Clemons had helped her to mow her lawn or carry leaves for her. "And he'd never take a dime for doing it," she said.

On camera, the neighbors gathered solemnly on their doorsteps and shook their heads while the kids rode their bikes in the street and the grown-ups swapped fond memories of the suspects.

The report then switched over to a shot of an exhausted-looking Eva sitting on her front step wearing jeans and a baggy sweater. Her smile was obviously more a nervous response than anything else. Sandra Hughes, the reporter who sat beside her, was pristine in a tailored gray suit, and neither of the two women looked at ease in the other's company. Only the wreck of Eva's world and the reporter's compulsion to satisfy public curiosity brought them together.

"I don't like what he did," Eva said into the microphone's foam top while Hughes held it out to her, "but I really loved him and I guess he was just going through harder times than I really understood."

Hughes interrupted her, after a quick attempt to check her surprise at Eva's reaction. She had expected the protests of innocence these types of interviews usually elicited. Eva didn't seem convincing, or even convinced herself, about her boyfriend's innocence.

"So, do you think that he really did do this or do you think that he didn't?" Hughes pressed.

Eva faltered momentarily, wrestling with her nervous smile as she responded, twisting a strand of hair around her finger as she spoke.

"Honestly, knowing what I know of Marlin, I'd say no, it's not his personality, it's not *in* his personality to do something like this, but knowing all the facts, um . . . they say . . . um, they say that he did."

As Hughes wrapped up the interview and turned the story back to the studio, one of the anchors shook his head and remarked, "You know, Sandra, police are saying that this case has taken more turns in such a short period of time than any case they can recall."

"You're very right," Hughes responded. "It's absolutely incredible."

Tom and his family were not in St. Louis to witness the eventual public clearing of his name, and it was probably just as well. They were back in Gaithersburg by the time Thursday's *St. Louis Post-Dispatch* printed a quote from the captain of the St. Louis City Police Department in answer to a question about why an innocent person might make an admission of guilt.

"Generally speaking, it's a person with a weakness of personality or character that would do such a thing. Some people would be very easily intimidated by the police and some would not," the captain explained, trying fiercely to defend the conduct of his officers, even if such defense came at Tom's expense.

In Gaithersburg, the Cummins family had a 850-mile cushion from such insensitive remarks, and they were busy grieving and trying to piece their lives back together anyway. Their friends proved to be unequivocally supportive. Neighbors took turns bringing by casseroles and cookies. Kay's friends wouldn't let her cook, and one day three of them even showed up with cleaning supplies and gave the house a frenzied scrubbing. It didn't really need much work, but they wanted so much to show their support for the grieving family.

"We knew he didn't do it. We never questioned him for a minute," Gene's friends at church all said. "We just knew it was a terrible mistake."

And at the firehouse, Tom's shift handled the tragedy with the black humor and unflagging loyalty that only firefighters can muster.

"Oh, shit, are you back?" Tom's lieutenant teased him upon his strange and surreal return to Rescue 2. "We thought we got rid of your ass."

Tink and Kathy had a slightly more difficult time readjusting to being around other people. While their closest friends rallied around them with support, neither of the girls was immune to the whispered rumors flying around their high school. More than once they were subjected to sympathetic smiles and condolences, quickly followed by nasty remarks that were accidentally overheard in the school's crowded hallways. "Yeah, their brother molested and killed their two cousins," whispered those who had seen the early sensational coverage of the story and missed the subsequent news about Tom's innocence. The media coverage seemed to have been even more lopsided in Gaithersburg than elsewhere, where word of a local county firefighter killing his two cousins was front-page news, but the less spectacular truth that four scumbags had actually murdered the two girls merited only minor headlines.

In their backpacks, both Tink and Kathy carried prepared statements that Gene had typed up for them in case any of the ever-persistent media tried to hound them at school or at soccer practice. Kathy turned to a couple of very good childhood friends for support, while Tink became introspective and consulted her diary. Both girls found it difficult to muster any interest in the mundane world of their academics, and they rushed home daily after soccer practice, hoping for news of their cousins, instead of hanging around chatting with their friends as had been their former habit. The interests of their friends seemed petty to them now. Tink even found herself snapping at a friend one day who complained she was having the "worst day of her life" after a disappointing grade on a test, a broken fingernail, and a fender-bender. Tink glared at her friend and responded, "If this is the worst day of your pampered little life, you should count yourself lucky."

The weeks passed slowly and the Cummins family began to feel more cut off than comforted by the 850 miles that now separated them from St. Louis. Grandma Polly collected every newspaper clipping she could find and sent them weekly to Kay. All the backwards facts and misinformation she had read about her own family over the past two weeks had taught Kay to become an extremely discerning reader. Still, when she sat down with the first of her weekly installments of articles, she was comforted to see Julie and Robin characterized as "young women committed to world peace and fighting race hatred" in one *Post-Dispatch* article. And she was more annoyed than upset when she read the April 12 article under the headline, "2 Rape Suspects Charge Brutality." *Well, they should know a thing or two about brutality,* she thought bitterly.

Kay did find herself increasingly irritated at the *Post-Dispatch*'s extensive weekend coverage of the brutality charges, though. Saturday's headline read "Attorney, Mother Say Suspects Were Beaten: Two Young Men Accused Police of Brutality." By Sunday the headline was "Friends Defend Suspects in Sisters' Killings: 'Something Doesn't Add Up,' Says Stepfather of One of

2 Charged." Both lengthy articles were peppered with descriptions of Gray and Clemons, of their hobbies and personalities, and each devoted only one brief paragraph to a mention of Julie and Robin.

"Marlin Gray's song would echo in the night air as he stood on the old Chain of Rocks Bridge, high above the Mississippi River," began Sunday's article. "He loved to sing and dance there, his friends say. The echo was a big draw, and dancing was his passion. Years ago in St. Louis, he won a Michael Jackson dance look-alike contest."

Clemons was described by his friend Harold Whitener as "a good kid trying to find his place in this crazy world."

A good kid? Kay thought, as she tried to digest the article. She had two dead nieces and a broken son, one daughter who was still barely eating or talking, and another one who practically jumped out of her skin every time the phone or doorbell rang. She herself was wrestling with nightmare images that assaulted her every hour of the day. And these guys had the nerve to complain about brutality? *Get them alone in a room with me,* she thought. *I'll show them brutality.*

But the most upsetting article yet was the one entitled "Search For Sisters May Take Weeks." Kay pushed that one to the back of the stack before returning the entire collection to its fat envelope. It had already been almost two weeks since her nieces' disappearance, and hope was rapidly waning that they would ever find the girls. She dreaded Tink and Kathy coming home from school with their inevitable daily question, "Any word, Mom?" The answer was no, there was no word. And there might not be for a very long time. In fact, there might never be.

Kay felt better prepared for the next batch of articles when they arrived, and they were easier to read anyway. On the front page of *The Post-Dispatch* on Monday, April 15, a large color photograph showed a group of Julie's and Robin's friends embracing each other on the Old Chain of Rocks Bridge. The headline read "Bridge Was Special Place For Sisters: They Shared An Interest In Poetry, People." The article was a beautiful eulogy to the girls, and quoted Julie's poetry several times. It focused largely on their social activism and altruism. Ginna was also interviewed, telling some of her favorite anecdotes about her daughters and their in-exhaustible energies. The article even quoted Julie's mantra, "Who says you can't change the world?"

"Robin, who loved vintage clothing, would have made a wonderful model for Coco Chanel," the article stated. And that may have been very true — Robin, with her high cheekbones, waiflike figure, and smoldering eyes, probably would have been a great Chanel model. But if she'd been alive to hear such a com-pliment, she probably would have rolled her eyes and gagged her-self in the sarcastic horror that was her trademark.

While Kay leafed through newspaper articles in Gaithersburg, Ginna sat in her too-quiet home in St. Louis, combing through Julie's poetry. Though she had always been her daughter's biggest fan, Ginna had developed an even greater admiration for Julie's talent now, and the weight of her daughter's words wrapped her like a heavy blanket. Her poems seemed eerily prophetic:

> we are nearly saints now
> and the river is wider still
> and half the river ahead of us.
> the river cares nothing for our troubles
> the river — cold, menacing, indifferent, dangerous
> the water itself — life, baptism/rebirth, a moving
>   force, a changing presence,
>   dilutes other liquids, consumes us but it is us;
>   we are made of it
> when you watch the water while you're
> standing in it, it makes you very dizzy.

rivers are boundaries
crossing one means foreign land, strange people
         dark woods to be encountered
but it is also an escape
         from both physical and psychological
         fears, guilt, shame — all of which I have.
therefore, bridges are a good thing? if so, then
why don't we cross the river by bridge?
crossing a bridge means a new life within
         and without, means also solving problems,
         moving up in the world of maturity

crossing by foot means maybe someone is chasing
         you, maybe you're isolated and can't
         find a bridge, maybe you didn't know
         what you were getting into.

When it finally came, the news that a body had been found was received with very mixed feelings in all quarters. Three weeks after the murders, a fisherman in Caruthersville, Missouri — almost two hundred miles downriver from St. Louis — hauled the body of a young woman wearing a gold Seiko watch out of the treacherous Mississippi. The next day, Dr. Michael Graham, forensic pathologist and chief medical examiner for the City of St. Louis, used dental records to identify Julie.

The family, who had been expecting at least some degree of solace from the news of a discovery, found very little to feel relieved about. Ginna voiced what they were all feeling. "I don't know why, but I fully expected them to be found together," she said. "It never occurred to me that one would be found before the other."

She was almost angry when a reporter asked her about funeral arrangements.

"I lost two daughters," she replied. "We'll wait for Robin."

And so they waited. But when three more weeks went by and the search for Robin still turned up nothing, Ginna made the heart-wrenching decision to go ahead with a funeral mass.

The joint funeral and memorial mass was scheduled for Monday, May 20, at St. Jerome Catholic Church.

Ginna was determined to honor Robin's expressed wishes while planning the funeral, and the result was a service of which both girls would have been truly proud — a celebration of their lives. The church was packed to standing room only, with many of the attendees wearing the requested bright colors instead of the muted browns and blacks more common at such somber events. Soap bubbles were provided to everyone, and Julie's and Robin's friends were encouraged to blow them at will throughout the service. Reverend Gene Robertson, who had been one of Julie's high-school teachers, provided a eulogy.

"Maybe the world couldn't handle the Kerry girls," he said. "Maybe the world wasn't ready for them."

He finished his speech with a call to social action, encouraging the congregation to "carry the torch of justice they carried, to work against war and violence, to work for the homeless."

Before the mass ended, many of the mourners opened the single-page pastel-colored scrolls they had been given as mementos of the girls. This is what they found:

JULIE AND ROBIN KERRY

May 20, 1991
These words were taken from the walls of their rooms.
This is what they believed in.
This is how they lived.

Give to the world the best you have and
the best will come back to you.

GIVE ME A PLACE TO STAND AND I WILL MOVE THE WORLD.

Only those who risk going too far can possibly find
how far they can go.

A modest proposal for peace:
Let the Christians of the world agree that
they will not kill each other.

It will be a great day when our schools get all the money
they need and the Air Force has to hold
a bake sale to buy a bomber.

If love comes from the heart, where does hate come from?
Children aren't born knowing how to hate. They must be
taught. Therefore, the lesson is simple. Let's not teach our
children hatred and prejudice, because what they don't know
won't hurt them — or others.

PEACE IS PATRIOTIC.

Peace without understanding is merely silent hatred, and a silent war is endless, for it kills from the inside.
Silence = Death.

GIVE PEACE A CHANCE.

The future is not something we enter.
The future is something we create.

WHO SAYS YOU CAN'T CHANGE THE WORLD?

Julie was laid to rest in a shiny white casket in Calvary Cemetery in north St. Louis County later that afternoon. The procession to the graveyard stretched to well over a hundred cars and the soap bubbles could be seen floating from the open windows all along the line. At the cemetery, Ginna and Rick threw red roses onto the white coffin as it dipped into the earth. The headstone that would be erected simply read: KERRY. JULIE, DECEMBER 16, 1970– APRIL 5, 1991. ROBIN, JANUARY 27, 1972–APRIL 5, 1991. BELOVED DAUGH- TERS, SISTERS, FRIENDS. WE LOVE YOU SO MUCH.

Robin's body was never found.

The *St. Louis Post-Dispatch* headline for Tuesday, May 21, read "Kerry Sisters Remembered as Crusaders for Justice: 2 Whose Lives Ended Violently Are Mourned." After that, the frequency of headlines about Julie's and Robin's murders, or "the Chain of Rocks Bridge Murders," began to decline. It was a bittersweet phenomenon for the families. The intensity of their grief did not subside with the hoopla and sensationalism. While Ginna felt utterly relieved at the respite from the loathsome spotlight, she also began to fear that now her daughters would be forgotten.

On June 23, 1991, more than eleven weeks after Julie's and Robin's deaths, *The Post-Dispatch* ran a brief article about the indictment of Gray, Clemons, Richardson, and Winfrey. It stated that all four men were charged with murder, rape, and robbery, and that the two juveniles had both been certified for trial as adults. The article identified them as "the four suspects previously charged with the murders of Julie and Robin Kerry, who were raped and thrown off the old Chain of Rocks Bridge into the Mississippi River." For the first time in print, Julie's and Robin's rapes and murders were not labeled "alleged." St. Louis, by way of its media, had finally accepted Tom's truth.

CHAPTER FOURTEEN

Over a year later, in September 1992, Nels Moss sat in a Gaithersburg, Maryland, hotel suite on a floral-print couch with his tennis-shoed feet propped up on the crowded coffee table in front of him. The room was cluttered with manila file folders, each one containing various facts and documents related to the puzzling case he was there to work on. On his lap, one of the folders lay open, displaying photographs of the Old Chain of Rocks Bridge. He shook his head while he flipped through pictures.

"It just doesn't add up," he muttered, closing the folder and tossing it on a pile of others to answer the knock at his hotel-room door.

Tom Cummins and his father Gene stood in the narrow hotel corridor, and Moss welcomed them each with his professional smile and a firm handshake. Gene's relationship with his son had evolved dramatically in the last year; they had developed a much greater sense of equality between them. Despite that fact, Gene still felt protective of his son. Tom was clearly comfortable with Moss and eager to get to work, but Gene hesitated to leave his son alone with anyone who was on the same payroll as the St. Louis Police Department. Only after several not-so-subtle gestures from

Tom did Gene excuse himself, telling Tom to call him when he was ready for a lift home.

After Gene left, Moss remained quiet for a few moments, shuffling through file folders and getting himself organized for the interview. The official business at hand was called "witness preparation." The purpose of Moss's visit to Gaithersburg was to meet with Tom, to explore his memories in depth, and to instruct him on what to expect at the upcoming trial. Moss had first met Tom in late April 1991, over a year before, and less than a month after the deaths of the Kerry sisters. Tom had flown back to St. Louis to attend four separate lineups, and he had nailed the identification of each suspect without the slightest hesitation. So Moss couldn't explain why it was that he just didn't quite believe the kid.

In the aftermath of their arrests, Winfrey, Clemons, Richardson, and Gray had all done enough talking and finger-pointing to implicate themselves and each other. And in each of their cases there was enough evidence to corroborate most of Tom's story. But there were just so many details, so many little facts that didn't quite fit. Moss had his work cut out for him.

Commencing his interview with Tom, he took scrupulous notes and stopped often to ask for clarity as Tom related the intimate details of his gruesome story. When Tom began to describe the manhole he was forced through, and the iron bar he had used as a step in climbing down, Moss stopped him.

"Hang on a second now," he said, pitching his legal pad and ballpoint down on the couch beside him. He opened the folder containing the bridge photographs. "Describe that part to me again now."

"Well, there was a bar, like an iron bar, a few feet down under the manhole that you could step on to help yourself down. It was at an angle, sort of diagonal across the hole," Tom explained, somewhat perplexed by the lawyer's interest in such a seemingly minor detail. "And then when I jumped down, I saw my cousins lying there and I just stood there for a second until the guys told me to lay down beside them."

"Now when you say you *stood* there, were you actually kind of crouching, or you were standing to your full height?" Moss prompted.

"No, I was standing. Standing up straight," Tom responded.

Moss shook his head and scribbled furiously on the legal pad.

"What's the matter?" Tom asked.

"How tall are you?" Moss asked then.

"I don't know. Five-nine, five-ten," Tom said. "Why?"

Moss threw his pen down again.

"I've been to the manhole — I was just there a few weeks ago. The bar is not at the angle you describe and I couldn't stand up straight on the catwalk. The bridge deck was too low above my head. I had to crouch considerably. Are you sure you're remembering these facts correctly? Is any of this a bit hazy?"

Tom shook his head emphatically.

"No, there are certain moments, or certain facts that might be foggy in my memory, but this isn't one of them. The bar was at an angle — on a clock face, the angle would have been maybe eight o'clock to two o'clock or thereabouts. Like this," Tom indicated a severe diagonal with his arm. "And I definitely stood up straight. The two guys stood up straight too, when they moved us all down off the catwalk and onto the pier. Definitely — there was loads of room."

Moss shook his head again and rubbed his hands tiredly over his face. "Look," he said, passing one of the photographs to Tom. "This is me standing on the catwalk under the manhole."

Tom stared quizzically at the photo of Nels, standing bent from the shoulders beneath the low roof of the bridge deck.

"There's just no way you could have stood up under there. Is there something — anything — that you're not telling me? Or that maybe you don't remember clearly?"

Tom shook his head again, and scrutinized the photograph. He was at a loss. "Huh," he said awkwardly. "Weird."

"And see — here is the manhole as photographed from above. You can see that the position of the iron bar is clearly not at the angle you describe. It's horizontal."

Tom took the second photograph from the lawyer and studied it for a moment, noting the wrong angle of the bar, and shaking his head again. Moss passed him another photo of the manhole, this one taken from farther out and showing more of the surrounding bridge deck. Tom spotted the problem immediately. "It's the wrong manhole," he stated.

Moss looked up from his folder. "What?"

"That's the wrong manhole — you've got the wrong manhole. The one we went through had a graffiti hopscotch board leading up to it."

Moss looked skeptical, but took up his pen and started writing anyway. "I don't see how that's possible. This is the manhole that the police department has been focusing the investigation on since day one. It's the one that Richardson indicated during his early witness-style cooperation. Isn't it the same one you pointed out to the detectives on that first morning? When you did the walk-through on the morning of April fifth?"

"Nope," Tom answered. "Definitely the wrong manhole."

Moss had less than a month left before the trial of Marlin Gray was scheduled to begin. His star witness was a kid who had been the first suspect in the case and who had previously made what police now referred to as "statements implicating himself." And now, on top of everything else, that witness was telling him that the police investigation he had been relying on was, in fact, unreliable. Moss didn't know what to believe. The only seemingly indisputable facts in the case were that the Kerry sisters, who by all accounts had been remarkable young ladies, had been brutally murdered on April 5, 1991. And now it was his job to try their murderers.

Before Moss wrapped up the interview that evening, he asked Tom's opinion about the idea of offering one of the four suspects a deal. Tom was hesitant.

"Well, it's like this," Moss explained. "We've got a good case, a strong case. But I would like it to be even stronger. A jury might find your testimony to be questionable because you were the first suspect in this case. And beyond that, I have to do some further investigation into the stuff we talked about today. If we can't reconcile your details to our evidence, that's going to pose a problem. So, in order to cover all our bases, I think we should offer one of these guys a deal. Now one fact that has been consistent in every version of events from that night is that Daniel Winfrey — the youngest defendant — did not participate in the actual rapes. I'd like to offer him a life sentence and turn him state's evidence. I think he could be our nail in the coffin. Now I know the kid was no angel. But he was fifteen, and he had only met two of these other guys *that day.* He wasn't necessarily the career dirtball that the others might have been."

Apart from their names and faces, Tom didn't know anything about the four men who had murdered Julie and Robin. He wasn't interested in their personalities or résumés, and he certainly didn't like the idea of cutting any of them a deal. But after some discussion with Moss, he eventually agreed that if it was absolutely necessary, then Winfrey should be the one to get the offer. Moss left Gaithersburg to return to St. Louis the next day with plenty to keep him busy until the trial began.

When he called Tom a few days later to tell him he had been

back to the bridge, Tom wasn't at all surprised to learn that Moss had verified all of his details about the manhole. He was, however, surprised at the ever-professional Moss's sudden candor.

"I've gotta tell you, Tom," Moss said, "I had my doubts about you. In all sincerity, I was really on the fence when we talked last week and this stuff wasn't adding up. I was afraid you might have been hiding something. And this case has been so bizarre all along that I've never known quite what to believe. But I want you to know that I do believe you now — one hundred percent — and I'm placing all my faith in you. I'm sorry I doubted you. Now let's nail these bastards."

Marlin Gray's trial was scheduled to begin on Monday, October 5, 1992. Owing to the extensive media coverage of the case and widespread public sympathy for Julie and Robin, it took the prosecutors and defense attorneys four days to seat a jury. Kay, Gene, and a very nervous Tom flew into St. Louis that Thursday. Kay would be staying with her parents for the duration of the trial. Tom and Gene, who had both been subpoenaed, would stay at a hotel in downtown St. Louis, not far from the courthouse. This was not a social visit and Tom didn't want to spend time with any of his family in St. Louis while he was there. He was anxious and uncomfortable, and he was afraid that hanging out with the family might distract him from the ugly task at hand. But neither was he prepared for the loneliness and boredom of spending the entire trial cooped up in a hotel room with the company of his father being the only diversion.

Tom would only be permitted in the courtroom during his own testimony, so he and his father were not present on Friday morning, October 9, when the trial opened. But Kay sat in the packed courtroom near Jacquie, Ginna, and Sheila, and took meticulous notes during Moss's opening statement. She was struck by Marlin Gray's appearance. She hadn't expected him to be so handsome. At a trim and muscular six-foot-four, he was immaculately groomed and cut a dashing figure in his exquisitely tailored suit. He smiled charmingly and assuredly at each of the jurors as they filed in. Kay was revolted by the very sight of him. And she was almost equally revolted by the sight of his defense attorney, Dorothy Hirzy, whom Kay described in her extensive notes as "a dead ringer for Cruella De Vil."

After opening statements, Ginna was the first witness called to the stand. She was dignified and soft-spoken, and she avoided eye contact with her daughters' murderer. She talked about spending time with Julie and Robin on the evening of their murders. She talked about what they were wearing that night and about Julie's car. She didn't talk about the aching hole in her heart that had been growing for a year and a half. She didn't talk about her daughter Jamie's loneliness and confusion. She didn't talk about crying herself to sleep every night, or her very personal terror — how her trauma seemed to get worse and worse every day while the rest of the world moved on without her and somehow expected her to eventually recover.

Julie's best friend Hollee McClain took the stand later that afternoon to talk a little about her friendships with Julie and Robin. Her voice wavered momentarily as she proudly read their bridge-painted poem, "Do the Right Thing," aloud from the stand. For those in the courtroom who had previously been unfamiliar with the poem, the irony was breathtaking:

DO THE RIGHT THING
United We Stand
Divided We Fall
It's Not a Black-White Thing
We as a New Generation
Have got To Take a Stand
Unite as One

We've got II
STOP
Killing One Another
You don't have to be Black or White
To Feel Prejudice
To Fall in Love
Experience Pain
Create Life
To Kill ·
To Die
You just have to be Human
Do The Right Thing

As Hollee read the simple poem, the crowded courtroom collectively reached into purses and pockets for tissues and handkerchiefs. Family members grasped hands with each other and held their heads high while Julie's words rang out through the breathless room, and all of their thoughts drifted back to a time when both girls were alive, back to the night when Julie and Robin and Hollee had first painted that poem on the bridge. In Ginna's memory, her girls were still alive — young and vibrant and idealistic. In the picture in her mind's eye she saw them, breathing deeply, inhaling the fresh night river air as they watched the stars growing bright above them. They were champions of youth, and their lives seemed infinite like the skies beneath which they stood on their beloved bridge, painting.

Other witnesses that first day included Sam Brooks, one of the two uniformed officers who had been first on the scene that night and found Tom huddled under the stop sign at the St. Louis Waterworks. Also called to the stand was Dr. Michael Graham, the chief medical examiner who had identified Julie's body. A police technical artist and an evidence technician who had both worked extensively on the case were also on the day's roster. The testimony was often grim, but Ginna listened unflinchingly, absorb-ing every word.

The next day was Saturday, October 10, and the *Post-Dispatch* headline that morning read: "Death Penalty Sought in Killings of '2 Beautiful Young Children.'"

"Although [Cummins] was briefly a suspect in the case," the article explained, "he was scheduled to testify as one of the state's two key witnesses. His testimony was scheduled for today . . . The other main prosecution witness is to be Daniel Winfrey, who was the youngest defendant. In a deal with prosecutors, Winfrey, 17, of St. Charles pleaded guilty Sept. 30 to two counts of second-degree murder. Like the other defendants, he had been charged with first-degree murder. Winfrey also pleaded guilty to rape, robbery, assault and felonious restraint."

Because of the deal he cut, Winfrey would not stand trial. In-stead, his guilty plea would earn him a thirty-year prison sen-tence. Winfrey's family was suitably horrified at the thought of their son spending thirty years in prison, but they were even more horrified by his participation in the murders. They seemed to rec-ognize that punishment was inevitable and right, and they had encouraged him to accept the plea bargain.

Winfrey's parents had been divorced when he was a child and, although they provided him with as much love and guidance as possible, he spent a lot of his childhood bouncing back and forth between their homes. He was in the fifth grade when he started dabbling in alcohol and marijuana. But it was a terrible accident on April 22, 1988, that really launched Winfrey down the slip-pery slope to delinquency. That day, Winfrey had been attending a Boy Scout trip with St. Charles Troop #392 to Fort Leonard Wood, an armed-forces and military-police training ground, when disaster struck. Winfrey and two of his friends had been playing with an aluminum irrigation pipe and when they stood the pipe on end, it brushed a power line. The 7,200-volt shock killed one of the boys and severely burned the other one.

At the time, Winfrey was considered to be the luckiest one involved because he escaped without major physical injury. But emotionally the near-death incident was too much for the young boy to handle and it scarred him. Whether that occurrence left him with a severe case of survivor's guilt or a thrilling sense of invincibility is impossible to say, but one thing was certain: his behavior and psyche deteriorated rapidly. Soon after the accident he acquired a whole new set of friends, and he began attempting stupid and dangerous stunts in earnest. He seemed to find a thrill in anything ominous. He also began skipping school and his drug experimentation became a full-fledged drug habit.

Despite his worsening problems, on the surface Winfrey had remained as polite and pleasant as always. Both of his parents worked and they were good people with solid values. They thought of their son as a nice, smart kid who just had a few emotional problems. They kept an eye on him, but by and large they trusted him. The adults in his life took note of his issues, but the red flags were really not all that red. No one recognized the depths to which Winfrey was sinking. His assistant principal said that despite Winfrey's poor attendance and bad grades, he was smart and showed a lot of potential. In fact, when the school board discovered that he had never officially completed the eighth grade, they reviewed his case and allowed him to remain in high school, owing largely to his high level of maturity. During the months just previous to Julie's and Robin's murders (the early months of 1991), Winfrey's mother, Susan Crump, considered putting him into a drug rehabilitation program but procrastinated, hoping her son would pull himself together. She had no way of knowing that within two years, she would be feeling lucky that her child had the opportunity to accept thirty years in prison instead of going on trial for his life.

Tom knew that Winfrey had jumped at Moss's offer, and like the rest of the Cummins and Kerry family members, he had very mixed feelings about it. He knew that Winfrey's testimony would help their case, but he hated the idea that this kid was being at least partially excused for his actions. Tom also knew that in order for a jury to accept Winfrey as a believable witness, Moss would have to make him appear repentant and somewhat less culpable than the others, whether he really was or not. Either way, Tom knew that his feelings on the matter were unimportant in a practical sense — he couldn't change anything. So on that second day of the trial, Tom was up before his alarm went off, and he showered and shaved quickly. He was dressed in his best suit and tie and ready to go long before the circuit attorney's office investigator showed up to drive him to the courthouse.

Tom had requested that none of his family be present in the courtroom during his testimony. He was nervous enough without having to face the pained expressions of Rick and Ginna and the others. The year and a half that he had spent in therapy since the murders had not been terribly successful in convincing him that he was entirely blameless in his cousins' deaths. He still faced torturous questions daily: *What made me think they would let us live if we cooperated? Why didn't I do something to fight them? What if . . . What if . . . What if?* Tom wasn't ready to face the possibility of seeing these same questions, either real or imagined, written in disgust on the faces of Julie's and Robin's loved ones.

So the courtroom was quieter, emptier than it had been the day before. The morning was gray and overcast as Tom followed the investigator into the courthouse and down the long, echoey corridors to the witness room where he would wait to be called to the stand. The investigator told Tom to make himself comfortable, and left him alone in the room. Tom made a beeline for the green plastic ashtray that sat in the center of one of the round linoleum-covered tables. His first cigarette of the day was a much-needed one, and he despaired to see his hands shaking as he lit up. The hour passed like a year and he was on his eleventh cigarette when the bailiff banged on the door and opened it. It was time.

Tom stubbed out his smoke with still-shaking hands and followed the bailiff out of the room. His heart was in his throat. He stared at the bailiff's heavy black boots as they clonked down the abandoned hallway. In a moment they arrived at the heavy wooden double doors and the bailiff swung the right-hand one open for Tom, who tottered in weak-kneed. He focused his gaze now on his own highly polished shoes as he made his way toward the witness box. His tongue was heavy and tasted like tar as he promised to tell the truth, the whole truth and nothing but the truth, so help him God. *So help me God,* he repeated in his head as he stepped up into the glossy oak witness box, wishing he hadn't smoked quite so many cigarettes that morning. When he finally looked up, the only faces he recognized were those of Nels Moss and Marlin Gray.

Gray looked just as Tom remembered him, except that he was dressed in what looked to be an expensive suit. He still had the cocky air of a man who expected to be the center of attention, a man who could always win people over with a smile or a story. Gray glanced quickly and uninterestedly at Tom, as if he had never laid eyes on him before, and then returned his blasé gaze to some papers on the table in front of him. He looked almost bored, Tom thought. Almost as if this whole proceeding were just a waste of his precious time. Tom realized that any fear, any trepidation he had previously felt about facing this moment was gone, utterly replaced by a seething hatred for this man. Tom's jaw jutted out and his stomach pitched as he struggled to get hold of his emotions. He placed his hands firmly on his knees to control his sudden desire to race to the defense table and beat the living crap out of the smirking Marlin Gray. The room spun a bit, and in an instant Nels Moss was standing in front of Tom, his blue eyes piercing him, pinning him to his seat, steadying him. Tom's eyes clamped onto Moss's face as onto an anchor, a lifeline, and he focused there.

"Would you state your name for the record, please?" Moss began.

"Thomas Patrick Cummins."

Tom's testimony lasted four and a half hours. The worst moment, just as Tom had expected, came when Moss asked him about his time in the river.

"Did [Julie] get close to you at any point?" Moss asked.

Tom paused for a long moment while a lump in his throat constricted his voice and tears sprang to his eyes. He would not cry. He would not let this animal see him cry.

"Yes," he responded, with an audible crack in his voice. "After I went under the first time and I came back up. When I came up, Julie was right next to me and she grabbed ahold of me and I panicked. I . . . I shook her off. I pushed her away."

His nostrils flared as he spoke these words and he was so grateful that his family, that Ginna and Rick, were not in the courtroom to hear this confession. He wouldn't allow himself to explain that moment in any further detail. He didn't want to describe how the two of them had clung together and sunk, how he had come to within an instant of taking his lungs full of water and dying right there with Julie, embracing each other to the last. He couldn't bring himself to describe his moment of panicky awakening, how he had pushed Julie off of him just in time, shoving her toward the surface and then pulling himself up after her. In that terrible instant when he had released himself from Julie's grip, he had been wrong in his faith that she would make it, that they would survive the ordeal together. And now he didn't want to make explanations. Julie was gone, and he had survived. That was the fact. Irreversible.

The rest of his time on the stand was easy in comparison. Hirzy, despite her best efforts to rattle Tom, could not make a dent in his psyche. *If only you knew what I've been through,* he thought. *You think after all this, you can scare me?* So Hirzy's hostile questions failed to have their desired effect on Tom, who answered her calmly and matter-of-factly in every instance.

"When you met Julie down in Florida back in 1990 you spent a lot of time with her, didn't you?" she asked.

"Yes, I did."

"You became very fond of her, didn't you?"

"We became close friends."

"You wanted to have sex with her, didn't you?"

"No, I did not."

Those same questions that had seemed so jarring, so intrusive and accusatory when posed by St. Louis City's homicide detectives a year and a half before, took on an air of ridiculousness here in the crowded, fluorescent courtroom. Tom couldn't even muster any shock for them. He shook his head while he answered.

Still, he was emotionally drained by the time he was dismissed that afternoon. Tom did read the newspaper the next morning, when *The Post-Dispatch* printed the headline "Visit Grew into Night of Horror: Testimony Describes Kerry Sisters' Deaths."

Tom's subpoena kept him pacing the halls of Drury's Hotel for almost three full weeks. He had memorized the hotel restaurant's menu and the hours it was open. He lingered over his daily meals as the only breaks in the monotony. Every day he looked forward to the simple, friendly greetings of the bartenders and waitresses.

On Wednesday, October 14, while Tom chain-smoked and watched mind-numbing talk shows in his hotel room, Winfrey entered the St. Louis courthouse wearing handcuffs and shackles. Likeable he was not, but believable he was. The jurors hung on his every word while he described the night of the attacks, including his own participation, in grave detail. Gray continued to look unconcerned and focused his attention on a notepad in front of him.

Out of the four assailants, Winfrey was the only one who had publicly apologized to his victims, and to his credit, the kid really did seem genuinely regretful. But when he took the stand that morning and Moss began to question him about the attacks, any forgiveness that might have been growing in the hearts of Julie's and Robin's loved ones was frozen there.

"I threw her on her back with her coat over her face," Winfrey testified, though he could not identify the "her" as either Julie or Robin. To him, the girls were just nameless, faceless victims. "Her hair was kind of short. I got on top of her and pulled her coat over her face. Tony and Reggie told them both to shut up or they would kill them. I told them to just relax."

From her seat in the first row of the courtroom, Ginna shuddered.

Five days later, Gray took the stand himself. His direct examination proved to be uneventful — he carried himself well. The jurors saw a handsome, articulate, and soft-spoken young man who adamantly denied any involvement in the rapes and murders of the Kerry sisters. When Hirzy questioned him about his arrest, Gray even broke down and cried while he described how badly the police had treated him.

It wasn't until Moss began the cross-examination that things turned really ugly in the courtroom. Gray was too smart for his own good, and he couldn't seem to keep himself from being a smart alec on the stand. He challenged every statement Moss made, claimed that everyone from Tom to Eva to Winfrey was lying, and declared that he had been joking when he told people that he had murdered the girls. When Moss began a sentence about the girls being pushed off the bridge, Gray cut him off.

"When they were *allegedly* pushed off the bridge," he corrected the prosecutor with a smirk.

But if Gray was quick, Moss was quicker. At the conclusion of the cross-examination, Moss sought clarification about some details that had been covered earlier, and Gray became irritated and expressed his impatience.

"I'm about to lose my life and I'm up here arguing with you about the same stupid points over and over again," he complained from the stand.

"At least you have the chance to argue," Moss retorted. "Julie and Robin didn't."

Two days later, on October 21, someone identified only as a courthouse regular was quoted in *The Post-Dispatch,* saying, "Even when you separate the sin from the sinner, [Gray] came across as a terrible guy."

Tom was only halfheartedly following the case in the papers. He had developed a severe mistrust of the media over the last year and a half, and while he was anxious for the end of the trial, he preferred to wait for news from Moss rather than read a version of events recorded by an outsider. Being stuck in the hotel was really starting to grind on him, but he was wary of being accosted in public, so he suffered inside rather than chance any public excursions. So when Moss rang him the afternoon after Gray's testimony to tell him that he was free to return to Maryland, Tom was packed and en route to the airport in under an hour.

Gene and Kay planned to stay on for the conclusion of the trial and contact Tom with the outcome as soon as the verdict was delivered. The very next day, Tuesday, October 20, Moss and Hirzy made their closing statements.

"He was their leader," Moss proclaimed, stabbing a finger at Marlin Gray. "His signature is on their bodies."

The jury deliberated for just four hours and fifteen minutes before returning their verdict. Gray looked as smug as ever as he stood to hear the judgment. His smirk was quickly replaced by an expression of shock and then tears as the jury's foreman read the list of verdicts. Marlin Gray was guilty on all counts.

For the families involved, the penalty phase of the trial was awful in a surreal way. Jurors cried when Moss played a recording of Julie singing a song she had written, called "Trouble in America." The Kerry and Cummins families, along with many of Julie's and Robin's friends and loved ones, were invited to give victim-impact statements, to articulate the devastation caused by the murders. It was an impossible task. Julie and Robin were gone, and no amount of eulogizing could even begin to communicate that kind of loss. Still, they wrote letters, they read poems, they did what they could.

As the testimony continued throughout the day, the jurors learned about Julie's and Robin's attachment to organizations like Greenpeace and Amnesty International. Each bit of testimony triggered a rush of memories for Julie's and Robin's loved ones. At the mention of Amnesty International, Jacquie remembered the way the girls had actively celebrated Nelson Mandela's release from a South African prison the previous year, at a time when, to most American teenagers, "apartheid" was little more than a word on the evening news. And while the jury heard about Julie's and Robin's extensive volunteer work and the money they both scraped together to donate to their favorite causes, Sheila chose to remember their less martyr-like, more human qualities — the way Robin liked to tease her boys, for instance, and Julie's impatience.

Libby Hodges, an African-American and one of Julie's closest friends, took the stand to state that she felt "the whole black race has been betrayed" by the murders. "I feel like everything I believe in has been violated," she said.

Several weeks earlier at the desk in her college dorm room in

Towson, Maryland, Tink had sat down to try to articulate on paper what Julie and Robin had meant to her. She spent several hours musing over her cousins' altruism, but nothing she wrote down seemed to capture what she wanted to say. As the crumpled balls of paper piled up on her floor, Tink thought about Ginna's refrigerator, to which Julie had taped a checklist of how to create an environmentally friendly household. She and Robin had developed a strict recycling plan for the family; they saved Campbell's soup labels so inner-city schools could buy computers, and they exchanged old newspapers for tree seedlings to help with the ozone problem. No aerosol anything was allowed in the Kerry household, nor paper plates, towels, or napkins. Julie and Robin were practicing preachers.

But these details can't encapsulate a human. And no amount of writing, pen-chewing, scribbling, or crying could produce a victim-impact statement to satisfy Tink. Eventually she threw the pen down, climbed into bed, pulled the covers over her head and cried.

When it was Gray's turn, Hirzy turned out a parade of character witnesses, all singing his praises and begging for leniency in his sentencing. His mother, stepfather, and grandmother all took the stand to proclaim their support for Gray.

"I do not believe my son is guilty," Gray's mother testified. "If I thought my son was guilty, I would not be supportive. We as Christians believe if you sin, you must pay."

Several friends testified on his behalf as well, describing Gray as the perpetual entertainer, always singing and dancing and telling stories and jokes. But it was Eva who may have inadvertently sealed her boyfriend's fate.

"I love him," she said. "I still care about him. I don't feel any differently toward him."

That was the moment when Nels Moss stepped up to the stand.

"Has Marlin Gray ever hit you?" he inquired.

"Yes," Eva responded. "But never in the face."

Tom answered the phone on the second ring. His father's long-distance voice crackled down the line to him.

"Well, the verdict is in," Gene told his son from a pay phone at the courthouse in St. Louis, "and the sentence is death."

There were no words on the line, but Gene thought he could hear his son expelling a deep breath on the other end.

"Son?"

"Yeah, okay," Tom responded in a slow, stunned voice.

"You okay, kid?" Gene asked.

Tom was quiet for another moment. The rush of emotion he had expected did not come. He did not feel elated, avenged, or even particularly relieved. What he felt was numb.

"I'm just glad it's over, Dad," he said.

Three months later, on Wednesday, February 3, 1993, Tom testified at Reginald Clemons's trial. The trial was held in the same courtroom, and he sat in the same witness box. He probably even laid his hand on the same Bible when he was sworn in.

Nels Moss prosecuted the case, and Tom's testimony was almost identical to that of the first trial. Sure, some of the surrounding faces were different and Clemons certainly appeared less cocky, more frightened than Gray had.

But the only major difference in the two cases was in the strategy of the defense attorney. Clemons's attorney, Robert Constantinou, seemed intent on creating doubt by casting any and every fact of the case into question. He questioned whether the prosecution's two main witnesses were telling the truth. He questioned whether the body that had been found and identified as Julie was *really* Julie. He blamed the press for blowing the case out of proportion. And he even accused Julie and Robin of "living life in the fast lane" and jumping willingly off the bridge.

All he succeeded in doing was infuriating the jury. Moss closed the trial with these simple words: "These young ladies, filled with so much promise, so much hope, are gone. These young ladies are dead forever."

This time, it only took the jury three hours to return a verdict of guilty on all counts.

Despite Constantinou's abrasive legal strategy, public sympathy for his client was much greater than it had been for the irrepressible Gray — and that fact was owed in large part to his family. His parents were extremely articulate and outspoken regarding their unwavering support for their son. They were positive that Clemons was innocent, that he was incapable of these atrocities.

His stepfather Reynolds told a story about an occasion when Clemons had gotten in trouble as a young child. As punishment, Reynolds had told the young Clemons that he would not be allowed to come along on a family visit to his grandmother's house. On seeing the child's distress, Reynolds had been moved with pity, but he hadn't wanted to be inconsistent, to be a pushover parent. So he had struck a deal with his son: if Clemons could memorize the Ten Commandments in the forty-five minutes before the family was to leave for the trip, he could come along. An hour later, the smiling young Clemons was sitting in the back of the family car headed for his grandmother's house. He had memorized the Ten Commandments and, Reynolds thought, he had also learned a valuable lesson about compromise and forgiveness.

These warm memories of Clemons's loving, Christian upbringing sparked some compassion for his family in the media. In an editorial column that appeared in *The St. Louis Post-Dispatch,* Bill McClellan described his own commiseration with the family. He said Clemons "seemed like a good kid who had fallen under the influence of Gray, four years his senior. Every parent's nightmare, I thought. My heart ached for Clemons' mother."

But that empathy was not enough to outweigh the jurors' shock at Clemons's barbaric crimes. Less than a week after the trial closed, all twelve jurors agreed that Clemons's crime was "wantonly vile" and "unreasonably brutal." They recommended his execution.

A month before Antonio Richardson's trial was scheduled to begin, the prosecution decided to offer him a deal. Despite the convictions of both Gray and Clemons, Moss was hesitant to pursue the death penalty for Richardson because of his age at the time of his crime. So after much deliberation, the state approached Richardson's lawyers. Richardson could plead guilty to two counts of murder in the first degree in exchange for a life sentence. Richardson's court-appointed attorney, Kris Kerr, advised him that under the circumstances it would be very much in his best interest to accept the deal. Richardson agreed.

On the morning of February 19, 1993, on the very day that Richardson was prepared to accept the deal, a man named Bob Williams came to visit him in jail. Williams represented a group that called itself the Coalition for Justice. This group was promoting the idea that Gray, Clemons, and Richardson were all innocent victims of a racist, unjust legal system. Williams cited the fact that Winfrey — the only white assailant charged — had gotten off with a lesser plea than Richardson was being offered. He ignored the fact that Winfrey hadn't participated in the rapes, and convinced Richardson that the difference in the two offers was racially motivated. Williams also focused a great deal of energy directing blame at Tom Cummins. Richardson liked Bob Williams's arguments, and in court later that afternoon, he rejected the deal.

A month later, Richardson's trial began and Williams was on the courthouse steps armed with flyers that read NO STRUGGLE NO PROGRESS in huge block capitals. The flyer had a cartoon depicting a giant named "The Justice System" wielding a whip over the cowering masses. It referred to Julie's and Robin's murders as the "Chain of Rocks Bridge Mystery Case." The text, complete with typos, read:

> *Antonio Richardson's, like the others, is a political trial where the rules of evidents do not apply. Where the juries were allegedly controlled; where the facts about the trial have not been reported in neither the newspaper nor on television, in order to hide the truth from the public.*
>
> *Antonio Richardson, last of the defendants, who's fighting back against the ruling class frame-up trials of these young working class youths: three who are African- Americans, and one is white.*
>
> *They are all innocent. . . . Thomas Cummins the first cousin of the two sisters who disappeared, cannot walk on water. He could not have survived a fall of 70–90 feet into 54 degree water of the Mississippi River, swim for 30 minutes and suffer no ill effects.*

The flyer would serve to set the tone for the trial and enrage everyone who had known Julie or Robin. Tom, who had developed an extremely thick skin by this point, simply scoffed at the ridiculous developments. In his heart he knew that he and Julie and Robin embodied the ideals of the "working class" more than anybody, and he wasn't about to let an idiot like Bob Williams take that knowledge away.

On the morning of Monday, March 22, Tom sat filling his usual ashtray in the witness room and making small talk with Ron Whitehorn, owner of the infamous flashlight. Ron's daughter Stephanie was on the stand testifying while Tom and her father sat chatting. Ron had just told Tom how glad he was that this was the last trial and his daughter could put this all behind her after today, when the door opened and a bailiff escorted the shaking Stephanie Whitehorn into the room.

As soon as the bailiff was gone, Stephanie bent to whisper something furtively into her father's ear. Tom looked away and took a deep drag on his current cigarette. The girl was obviously distraught about something and wanted a private conversation with her father. He didn't want to eavesdrop. But Ron's next comment was impossible not to hear.

"I'll kill the little fucker," he shouted.

Tom looked up and caught the look of crazed anger on Ron Whitehorn's face. Stephanie looked more terrified than ever, but Ron pulled her close and hugged her.

"You're gonna be all right, baby girl," he said in a much quieter voice. "Don't you worry about a thing — I won't let anything happen to you. We'll get this sorted out."

Stephanie just nodded and snuffled against her father's shoulder.

"Would you mind getting the bailiff?" Ron said to Tom then.

When Tom and the bailiff returned to the witness room about a minute later, Stephanie still looked rattled but she was considerably more composed.

"What's going on?" the bailiff asked as he entered the room.

"That monster in there threatened my daughter on the stand," Ron replied.

The bailiff looked at Stephanie.

"What happened?"

"He mouthed the words, *I'm gonna get you,*" she explained.

"I'll get the prosecutor," the bailiff said, and he banged open the door and was gone.

After a stern warning from the judge, the remainder of

Richardson's trial passed without further interruption. The trial was the shortest of the three, with testimony lasting only three days. On Thursday, March 25, 1993, less than two weeks before the second anniversary of Julie's and Robin's deaths, the last of their murderers was convicted. Antonio Richardson would join Clemons and Gray on Missouri's death row.

CHAPTER FIFTEEN

om didn't exactly expect his life to get back to normal after
the last trial. There could be no normal for him now, or ever
again. He had been enrolled in an intensive counseling program
since 1991 with a wonderful therapist whom he had come to
trust and admire. Her specialty was dealing with the survivors of
violent crimes and their families, and Tom had come to depend
heavily on her wisdom and words. When he brought up the idea
of returning to school, she encouraged him. And about a year
later, Tom enrolled himself in the criminal justice program at the
University of Maryland. He wanted to be Nels Moss. Julie would
be proud, he thought.

In early April 1995, four years to the week of Julie's and Robin's
murders, Tom settled a civil lawsuit against the city of St. Louis for
an undisclosed amount of money. The police, who were accused
of trying to force Tom to confess, settled the suit out of court
when they learned that Nels Moss intended to testify on Tom's behalf. The settlement, much like the death warrants, did little to
satisfy Tom. As far as he was concerned, the damage was irreversible
and the settlement was nothing but blood money. But Tom got
something much more valuable than money out of the lawsuit: a
friendship with his civil attorneys Pete Bastian and Frank Carlson.

Tom had first met the two lawyers back in 1992, during the long days of his confinement in Drury's Hotel for Marlin Gray's trial. He was a little embarrassed to admit how much he had enjoyed their company — not just because they were such a welcome respite from the tedium, but also because, when Tom told them his story that first night, Pete and Frank seemed to understand what he had been through. Tom never did achieve the title of "victim" in the media, and he had actually long since given up wanting it. But the refreshing thing about Pete and Frank was that they regarded him not only as a victim, but as a survivor of extraordinary circumstances.

"Tom, you gotta stop beating yourself up over this," Frank said to him over their steaks. "The fact of the matter is — you survived. And it's a good thing you did, or no one would ever have known what happened to Julie or Robin. These four monsters would still be walking around out there. You survived in that river. You survived the police. You survived the media. And *you* are the one whose testimony is going to send these four guys where they belong. You oughtta be damn proud of yourself."

They were words of encouragement that Tom sorely needed to hear. He was sure that neither Frank nor Pete had any idea how much their support helped him to heal. But over the years, every time Tom visited St. Louis, he made sure he called them. He came to depend on them for their company and friendship as much as for their legal advice. On the night they settled his civil suit, they took him to their favorite local bar and fed him a lot of Guinness in their attempts to make the mood a celebratory one. Tom swallowed the stout and his tears and felt grateful for the support of his two lawyers, his friends.

After that, the legal developments slowed to a crawl. Attorneys for Clemons, Gray, and Richardson issued appeal after appeal on behalf of their clients, but little would change for years on end.

Tom worked at the firehouse and attended his criminal-justice classes. He bought himself a house not too far from his parents'. After four years he earned his degree.

Then, in May 1998, Tom received a long-dreaded phone call from St. Louis. Daniel Winfrey was up for parole. As had become his habit whenever something disconcerting happened in his life, Tom picked up the phone and called both of his sisters and then his parents. After he filled the whole family in on the update, it was decided: Tom and Tink would be the family representatives to fly to Missouri and give a statement to the judge.

While Tom had flown in and out of St. Louis countless times in the last seven years, for Tink it would be the first trip back. She was twenty-three years old now, and she had never been to her cousins' grave. It was an emotional homecoming, to say the least. Their first port of call was the Old Chain of Rocks Bridge. The intervening years had been kind to the old bridge and Tom hardly recognized it when they pulled up. There was a trailer perched on the edge of a small parking area, and a sign that said VISITOR'S CENTER. The bridge had been converted into a state park — a walking and bike path for families. There wasn't a trace of the dense undergrowth that Tom, Julie, and Robin had fought their way through all those years ago. The whole structure had been patched and painted. The manholes in the roadway were now filled and the surface of the bridge was newly paved. Tom was dismayed.

"We won't be able to see the poem," he said softly as he and his sister took their first tentative steps onto the bridge.

The pair were silent and solemn as they made their way along the bridge, past moms pushing strollers and dads carrying toddlers on their shoulders. A few kids laughed and darted about in the sunshine, but Tom and Tink had heavier hearts as they paced the old structure, eyes downcast. When they came to the spot where

Tom thought the poem had been, they paused and stood by the railing for a few moments. There wasn't much to say. But then something caught Tom's eye.

"Holy crap, look at that!" he said.

Tink's eyes followed where her brother pointed, a few feet away on the bridge deck. She could make out the faintest trace of a *J* shining unmistakably through the new layer of pavement. It was Julie's *J.* Beside it, her peace symbol was also largely intact. For the most part, the rest of the poem was illegible, but they were able to make out partial words here and there. They both felt comforted that a bit of the poem, a piece of Julie and Robin, was still visible at their beloved old bridge.

From there, Tink and Tom drove straight to Calvary Cemetery, stopping only at a florist's shop on the way. When they got out and found their cousins' shared headstone, the tears they had been saving all day finally came. Tink knelt and placed two red roses beside the names of Julie and Robin Kerry. Her brother knelt beside her to make his own offering: he left them two Marlboro Lights. They both spoke a few private, tear-choked words to their cousins in the quiet of the old graveyard, and bent to kiss the headstone before leaving.

Tom and Tink's meeting with the judge in Jefferson City, Missouri, was scheduled for the next day. Their aunt Jacquie and cousin Gabbi attended with them. The judge was very kind. The families would not be permitted to testify at the actual parole hearing, he explained, because Winfrey had been moved to a secret location. Winfrey's demographics and the crimes he was charged with had made him the perfect target for jailhouse torment. His seven years in jail so far had been extremely hard-served, and the authorities had had to move him more than once because of his treatment by fellow inmates. Tink and Tom couldn't muster a whole lot of sympathy for him.

"The main point that I want to articulate," Tom said, beginning his address to the judge, "is the fact that, despite his cooperation with the investigation, despite his testimony at trial, despite his lesser culpability, Winfrey is a double murderer, and he's only served seven years. He was *not* just a good kid who accidentally stumbled into a scary situation. I understand that he kinda came across that way at trial; he had to. But he made comments during the crime that indicated he was excited and that he enjoyed what was happening. The whole thing was just one big adrenaline rush to him. While those animals were raping Julie and Robin, this kid actually sat on my back, laughing and telling me it was a good thing his buddies weren't gay or they would probably rape me too."

Tink's mouth hung open speechlessly while her brother talked. She had never really been exposed to the details of the case. She had never wanted to be — and she was visibly stricken by her brother's words. The judge stood up from behind his big mahogany desk and offered her a tissue. She gratefully accepted, noticing for the first time that there were silent tears sliding down her cheeks.

"And what do you have to add to this, young lady?" the judge asked her as she dabbed at her wet face.

"Well, obviously I wasn't there that night," she began, clearing her throat to compose herself, "so anything I have to say is more in the way of a victim-impact statement."

After her multiple failed attempts at writing victim-impact statements during the three trials, Tink was finally having her moment.

"I guess mainly I just want to express what wonderful people my cousins were and how deeply they affected my life. I'm a writer now — um, an aspiring writer — and I really feel that I have Julie to thank for that. She was the first one to encourage and inspire me. I always wanted to write, but she was actually doing it,

you know? She was studying English in college and she was published. She was the first person who ever said to me, 'Never mind
practicality — do what you love. You want to be a writer? Then
write.' So that's what I'm doing. I guess I just want you to know
that there are so many people, so many lives that were touched by
those two girls and destroyed by their deaths. Daniel Winfrey has
only served three and a half years for murdering each of my
cousins. I don't think that's anywhere near enough time. Julie and
Robin aren't coming back."

Gabbi and Jacquie made similar statements on behalf of the
girls and the family. Jacquie talked a little bit about her sister
Ginna and how desperate and isolated her life had become after
her daughters' deaths. For Ginna, the roller coaster had never
stopped in the ensuing years. While Tom had somehow pieced his
life back together, Ginna's grief remained an ever-present daily
monster in her life. The grief cycles of anger, guilt, denial, and
acceptance seemed to have become a never-ending emotional
merry-go-round for her. Every time she thought she was about to
break through to some kind of peace, the ride would start up
again and her grief would loom up in front of her, as fresh and
unconquerable as it had been the day her daughters were murdered. Jacquie also talked a little bit about the bonds of family that
had been strengthened by the collective loss; she talked about the
difficulties Jamie faced growing up in an environment that was
constantly overshadowed by loss. But she didn't presume to speak
for any of the Kerry family — their suffering being unique and
inconceivable. Even a close outsider could not articulate their anguish.

The judge listened respectfully and patiently the whole time,
his hands clasped in front of him on the large desk and an expression of concern lining his face. When the little group was done
talking, there were more than a few wet tissues wadded up in fists,

and everyone felt collectively drained. The judge stood up to walk them out.

"Thank you very much for coming," he said, shaking hands with each one in turn. "I will definitely take your statements under advisement. Just the fact that you've taken the time and come all this way speaks volumes about those two girls, and how much you loved them."

The judge's words brought a whole fresh round of tears that Tink was barely able to suppress until the elevator doors opened and the foursome waved good-bye to the judge and stepped inside. As the doors slid shut all four of them began to cry. They all held hands walking out to the sunny parking lot, and once there they stood quietly hugging each other for a long time.

A few days after Tom and Tink returned to the East Coast, they received the news: Daniel Winfrey had been denied parole. His case would be reassessed in the year 2004. The families heaved a sigh of relief. For a time, things were quiet again.

Then, at Christmastime 2000, two producers working on a documentary about Richardson for Court TV contacted Tom and asked for his participation in their project. Tom was naturally wary, but he agreed to meet with them. He traveled to New York, where Tink was now living, to meet with the producers, and he invited his sister along for moral support and advice. The intention of the show, they explained, was to explore the widespread impact, or what they called the "ripple effect," that one night of violence can have.

"The effects of one violent act can reach into the lives of dozens of human beings and last for decades," the producers said. "That's what we want to expose — that the consequences reach further than the criminals and their victims."

When the Cumminses asked the producers why they had cho-

sen to focus on Richardson rather than any of the other perpe-
trators, the answers were unclear.

"Well, we chose to focus on Antonio because he's a teen on
death row. It's just an additional dimension to the —"

"He's not a teen," Tom interrupted. "The man is twenty-six
years old."

The producers glanced at each other.

"Yes, we understand that," one of them began diplomatically.
"But the fact that he was a teen when he committed the crime —
that's what we mean. And we don't intend to make this a one-
sided fanatical view of the death penalty. That's why your involvement is so important to us. We need to show how much
damage this guy is responsible for. We don't want to just create a
blanket of blind sympathy for him."

"So it's not going to be an anti–death penalty show, then?"
Tom asked pointedly.

"I don't intend for it to come across as pro- *or* anti-." The second producer answered him this time. "I want it to be strictly
fact-driven — for the audience to draw their own conclusions.
But in order to accomplish that, we need to involve all parties affected — everyone whose life has been devastated by this crime.
And that includes you. I don't know if you guys are aware that
Ricki Lake is doing a show on Antonio?"

From the blank stares on the Cumminses' faces, it was clear
that they were certainly *not* aware of the Ricki Lake show.

"Well, her people have been pestering us for your contact information," the producer continued, without waiting for a verbal
response from the stunned brother and sister. "Don't worry — we
won't give it to her. Their show will be extremely one-sided.
She's not a real journalist and she has no intention of trying to be
evenhanded. It's her once-annual attempt at a serious topic. People won't take it seriously. But the fact is that this guy *is* getting
media attention and that will drum up a certain degree of sympa-

thy. So what we're offering you is an opportunity to counterbalance that with your own story. We want the whole truth — not just one side."

The conversation continued in that vein for the better part of an hour. After a couple of drinks and a lot of reassurances, Tom and Tink agreed to appear in the documentary. Within a couple of months, a film crew traveled to Maryland and spent a day filming the Cummins family in what would be their first cooperative effort with the media since the day of the murders.

By February 2001, Tom was still working as a full-time firefighter, but he had also used his pre-law degree to land himself a part-time gig with the FBI, which he was enjoying immensely. He came home from a hard day of FBI work one evening and was greeted lovingly by his two cats, Guinness and Cider. It was freezing outside, even for the middle of winter, so as soon as he had his coat off, he picked up Cider to warm his hands. He flicked the kitchen light on, tossed his mail on the table, and went to the fridge. On the way by, he hit the flashing light on the answering machine and listened to it beep while he peered into the fridge, hoping for a miraculous dinner idea.

The voice that filled the kitchen from the tape machine made Tom stand up straight and close the refrigerator door. Kay Crockett was the Victims Services coordinator for the state of Missouri, and she had been an enormous help to Tom over the years — a seemingly tireless source of energy and information. He walked back to the counter where the answering machine was still clicking and whirring, and he hit the rewind button while Cider squirmed in his arms. He set her on the counter and leaned onto his elbows, for steadiness as much as for concentration. Crockett repeated her message. Yep, Tom had heard right. They had set an execution date for Antonio Richardson. And it was less than a month away.

Tom sat down at his shiny wooden kitchen table and listened to his two cats mewing for their dinner. He lit a cigarette he hadn't intended to smoke and tried to take in the enormity of what he had just heard. Antonio Richardson would be executed in exactly four weeks. *I guess I've got a lot of arrangements to make,* he thought, shaking himself from his reverie and standing up from the table. The cigarette had burnt to ash in his fingers — he had hardly taken three puffs from it, he realized now as he stubbed the remainder of it out. He walked back to the counter, lifted the phone's receiver, and hit three on the speed dial.

"Dad?" he said. "I'm going back to St. Louis again."

The news of Richardson's execution spread to all corners of the Cummins and Kerry families, and sent everyone reeling unexpectedly. In New York, Tink replaced the phone and flopped zombie-like onto her couch, too stunned to relay the news to anyone just yet. In Gaithersburg, Kathy and Tom went for their weekly beer at their local bar, Mrs. O'Leary's. There wasn't much to be said this particular evening. Even their favorite bartender, Mac, couldn't do much to cheer them up — they were both just too confused by the rather surprising onslaught of emotions they were experiencing. In Missouri, Ginna, Rick, and the now nineteen-year-old Jamie hunkered down against the inevitable rush of unwelcome media attention that they knew would follow the announcement. They had four weeks to prepare themselves. The execution was set for March 7, 2001, at one minute past midnight. It would happen on the night of Ginna's birthday.

During the decade that had passed since Julie's and Robin's murders, every member of the Kerry and Cummins families had been redefined, both internally and in the eyes of those around them. Not a single member of either family was the same person he or she had been on April 4, 1991. Each of them was now what the state would call a "homicide survivor," though the title was insufficient; there were no varying degrees within that definition to depict: mother, sister, cousin, friend. Nevertheless, each of their personalities had been drastically and permanently altered by the loss of Julie and Robin.

Few of these transformations had been as dramatic as Kay's. For Kay, the utter helplessness and subsequent anger she had experienced during the immediate aftermath of her nieces' deaths had lit a fire in her that would never be quenched. When she had returned to Gaithersburg from the horrors of St. Louis all those years before, her initial feelings of ineffectiveness were immediately replaced by an itching, driving, completely motivating impatience to *do* something. So she took a page from the way her nieces had lived their lives and, at the age of forty-four, Kay — housewife, registered nurse, mother of three — transformed herself into an activist. When a friend referred her to the county's Victim Advocate Program for counseling, Kay wasted no time in becoming a veritable fixture at the offices. Within a couple of months, she and a few members of her support group had founded the *Wings of Hope* newsletter for crime victims and their families. In less than three years, the newsletter received the governor's award for "outstanding contributions in the field of victim rights or services, in recognition of exemplary humanitarian support, loyalty, devotion, and caring in serving crime victims."

But Kay wasn't satisfied. The following year, she petitioned her city and received an official proclamation by the mayor and city council that April 21–27 would now be designated "National Crime Victims' Rights Week." Later that year she was invited to the U.S. Capitol to attend a press conference about a proposed constitutional amendment for a crime victims' bill of rights. There she met John Walsh of *America's Most Wanted* and had a videotaped conversation with him that was later aired on his show. Her kids finally noticed her ambitious activities. Over the next few years Tom, Tink, and Kathy watched with bemused pride while their middle-aged mom took her newfound expertise into the legislative arena. By 1999 she had been instrumental in establishing laws on both the state and county levels to provide help for crime victims with financial burdens like funeral expenses, counseling, and lost wages.

But despite the ever-mounting successes, Kay was insatiable. Because each time she won a small public battle for victims' rights, Kay felt a profound and private victory somewhere for someone else's Ginna.

Three weeks after the announcement of Richardson's pending execution, Tink left her job at a publishing house in downtown Manhattan a couple of hours early. She was feeling a little under the weather. It was getting dark when she arrived at her apartment in Queens, and she flipped lights on around the house as she went. *A cup of tea is what I need,* she thought. *That'll make me feel better.* She turned the television on in her bedroom and made her way to the kitchen to put the kettle on. The tea was ready in a few short minutes and she returned to her bedroom, holding the steaming mug with both hands. She took two steps inside her bedroom door before the face on the television made her stop dead in her tracks. Antonio Richardson was in her bedroom, via *The Ricki Lake Show.*

She had known in the back of her mind that this day might come, but she hadn't heard another word about it since the initial warning from the Court TV producers a few months before. The reality of it now was utterly shocking, and she shrieked before slamming her mug down, slopping boiling tea over the edges as she did so. She lunged at the television, slapping the power button to turn it off. Now the black screen stared mockingly back at her.

"Get out! Get out of my room!" she shouted crazily at the television, disintegrating into tears. "Oh God, why did I come home early?"

She only allowed herself a few short moments of self-pity before pulling herself back together. She glanced at the clock and realized that her sister Kathy might be home from work by now. She ventured to the living room and dialed her sister's number before cautiously turning on the television there. Despite her initial revulsion at seeing Richardson, she realized that something was compelling her to watch.

"Kath?" she said as her sister answered the phone. "Um. Turn on channel five."

Her sister was quiet for a few moments and then answered her, "Okay . . . *Family Feud*. Is there something special about this particular episode?"

"Shit," Tink answered. "I've got *Ricki Lake* on my channel five right now."

"Ah," Kathy responded with sarcastic recognition. "Fine-quality television viewing, that."

"No," Tink said, "it's Antonio Richardson. He's on *Ricki Lake*."

Tink heard her sister take in a sharp breath over the phone line.

"I didn't want to watch it alone. But I can't seem to turn it off."

"Yeah, I can understand that," Kathy responded. "You want me to stay on the line anyway?"

"No," Tink answered. "Thanks. I'll . . . um . . . Nikki will be home soon anyway probably. Or I'll give Joe a ring."

"Okay — if you're sure," Kathy said. "But call me back if you need anything. I'm gonna try to find out when it's on here and tape it. I'm gonna need some company when I watch it too, I'm sure."

The sisters hung up and Tink immediately dialed her boyfriend Joe's cell phone. He was a construction foreman and he was working on a job in the city. By the time he answered his phone on the fourth ring, Tink was in bad shape again. The background portion of the show was finished and the interview segment was beginning. Ricki Lake was standing to shake

Richardson's hand. Her voiceover came on and said, "Before we could begin, [Antonio] had something to get off his chest." Then the film cut to a close-up of Richardson, looking propped up and not entirely successful in suppressing the wildly inappropriate smirk that seemed to play on his lips. Perhaps it was nerves, but it completely destroyed any credibility his words might have had.

"Before I do this interview with you, I'd like to, um, you know, apologize to the Kerry family — the victims' family — about this whole situation. I'd like to apologize to my family for the changes that they have been going through since I've been in-carcerated."

"When you came to prison, you were just a kid in an adult prison." Ricki Lake began the interview then, cocking her head thoughtfully to one side as she spoke. "What was that like for you — being so young?"

Richardson went on to relate the horrors that he had seen in prison. He talked about watching people get beaten up and raped. Tink could hear Joe's voice on the phone, prompting her to speak, but she couldn't at first. Finally, she managed, "Joe? Antonio Richardson is on TV. Antonio Richardson is on *The Ricki Lake Show.* Right now. I'm looking at his face right now," she said, all in a rush.

"Oh no," Joe responded. "Are you okay?"

Tink nodded, but her voice was gone again. All she could manage was a giant sniffle.

"I'll be right there," Joe said. "I'm leaving the job right now — I'll be over as soon as I can."

Tink tried to argue that she was fine, that he didn't need to leave work, but Joe wouldn't hear of it. And when he hung up, she was glad he was on his way. The show got worse before it was over. Richardson accused Tom of perjury and called him a liar. And he rounded out his "apology" to the family with a flat denial of any involvement in the crime. He admitted being at the Chain of Rocks Bridge that night, but he claimed that, like Winfrey, he had been a frightened observer.

Then came the icing on the cake. Ricki leaned in and asked him what had gone through his mind when the judge announced the death-penalty sentence. Tink couldn't even listen to his response. She stood up and paced the length of the room, all the way down the hallway, into her bedroom and back.

"Why don't you ask him what went through his victims' minds before he killed *them?*" she muttered bitterly as she paced.

Her anger was swift and unexpected. She didn't even consider herself a death penalty advocate. In fact, she had very mixed feelings on the subject. But something about the sympathetic tone in Ricki Lake's voice, something about Richardson's attempts to appear pathetic while at the same time denying all responsibility for what he had done, infuriated her. She stalked back to the couch and sat down in time to hear him say, "I did a lot of things in my past, but I'm no rapist and I'm no murderer," he said.

"Then what the hell did you just apologize for, you asshole?" Tink shouted at the television.

But Richardson didn't hear her.

"My life right now is a living hell," he was saying.

And then the show cut to commercial and Tink sat speechless, with the remote control in her hand and her mouth gawping. Ricki's voiceover came on and asked, "Do you know two people who went on a horrible date? If you want one of them to get a makeover so you can send them on a second-chance date, you could be a guest. Call 1-800-GO-RICKI."

She threw the remote control across the room, brought her knees up to her chest, and indulged in a fresh round of tears. She was still crying when her roommate Nikki came home a few minutes later.

"What's up — you okay?" Nikki asked, tossing her keys down and approaching her friend on the couch.

Tink nodded and wiped her face on her knees. "Yeah, just a bit stunned," she responded. "Antonio Richardson's on television."

Nikki looked at the TV and back to Tink.

"On *Ricki Lake?*" she asked incredulously. "What's she gonna do — give him a makeover before they execute him?"

Tink laughed in spite of herself.

The next week was a downward spiral of frenzied media activity and emotional mayhem for all the Cumminses and Kerrys. After ten years, their case was back on the front pages. In the days leading up to the execution, Richardson's current attorney, Gino Battisti, began an intensive, media-savvy campaign to drum up public support for his client. It worked. On February 26, *The Post-Dispatch* printed the headline: "Anti-death Penalty Group Urges Holden to Halt Execution."

A group called Missourians to Abolish the Death Penalty was quoted in the article claiming that Richardson's IQ was "about 70," which would qualify as borderline mentally retarded. In fact, Richardson's IQ was higher than that and he did not meet other criteria to be considered legally mentally retarded. Certainly his rather eloquent *Ricki Lake Show* interview was evidence enough that he didn't have any trouble at all with verbal communication.

Battisti was also quoted, saying, "We have a 16-year-old who in essence was just a 7-year-old at the time of the offense." The facts stated in the article were misleading at best, and to make matters worse, Julie and Robin weren't even mentioned by name until the seventh paragraph.

Over the next few days, people began writing editorials to local papers, calling for clemency for Richardson. Students on the campus of the University of Missouri at St. Louis, where Julie and Robin had been students and where Jamie was now studying, organized protests on Richardson's behalf. Groups like the American Civil Liberties Union and the European Union began writing letters of protest to the Missouri governor. But the most distressing protest, for the Cumminses and the Kerrys, was the one organized by members of Julie and Robin's beloved alma mater, Amnesty International.

Sixty-two students from the organization's University of Missouri at Columbia chapter planned a three-day hunger strike on Richardson's behalf. The event was not sanctioned by Amnesty International, but that didn't stop the media from naming the participants as members of the organization. Other volunteers at the Columbia campus organized "die-ins," where students around campus played dead at various intervals during the day.

Jacquie, who had been working at the school for several years as a graphic designer, would avoid the campus and stay home that day. She wasn't sure she'd be emotionally fit to handle watching zealous eighteen-year-olds who didn't even know Julie or Robin playing dead on behalf of one of their murderers.

When Tink read the article in *The Columbia Missourian* online detailing these protests, she envisioned Amnesty International's candle wrapped in barbed wire — the same one that meant Bobby Sands, and justice, and Julie and Robin to her — and she thought about Antonio Richardson using that candle, bending it and distorting it and perverting it for himself. The betrayal stung her more deeply than she would have imagined possible and she wept from the sheer heaviness of it. And then she did what she always did when she felt helpless or disgusted: she sat down to write a letter. When it was finished, she mailed it to the chapter president, the regional president, and the national president of Amnesty International. Here is part of what it said:

> . . . *Mr. Noah Jennings was quoted in the* Digital Missourian, *saying, "We thought this was an exceptional case, a case where we could turn up the heat." He was right. This is an exceptional case.*

I wonder if Mr. Jennings knows the names of Antonio's two rape and homicide victims. I do. They were Julie and Robin Kerry and they were my cousins. They were members of Amnesty International and compassionate young college students, just like most of these protestors.

I believe in the brave tenets set forth by Amnesty International and I applaud the efforts of its many tireless members. But I also believe, in your zeal to make a positive difference in our society, you occasionally rally around the wrong banner. I think this is one of those times.

Here, Tink spelled out some of the many inaccuracies that had been vigorously adopted and then regurgitated as fact in the recent media. But she didn't waste much time on those fact-based arguments because this letter wasn't about facts. She concluded as follows:

Amnesty International is a powerful and well-respected organization and as such, your role of social responsibility is a heavy one. I respectfully urge you to take caution when choosing your battles. Things are not always as they appear in the headlines.

Julie and Robin Kerry still have many friends and family members in the St. Louis and Columbia areas, many of whom are active in campus life. These are largely people who support Amnesty International and fondly remember the girls as members of your organization. For their sake, I ask you to exercise your greatest sensitivities regarding this case. Please do not make us feel any further ostracized. If you intend to persist in your support of Antonio, please at least reconsider your methods. "Die-Ins" and similar protests on behalf of the man who murdered my cousins really are difficult to stomach. This man continues to display a flagrant disregard for human life; his victims spent their brief time on this planet fighting for human rights, until he took the battle away from them. You are on the wrong side of the fence on this one.

The letter said everything Tink wanted it to say, and when she put the stamps on the envelopes later that afternoon she felt an enormous sense of relief. She didn't expect that her words would accomplish anything really, but she felt better for having written them.

She was more than a little surprised a couple of weeks later when she received personal, empathetic responses from all three recipients of her letter. She felt as if she had, in a small way, reclaimed Amnesty International for its rightful owners.

On March 5, *The New York Times* lent its voice to the growing public fracas, printing an editorial entitled "Cycle of Death" that argued that "by killing [Richardson] we'll succeed only in diminishing ourselves." The article also reprinted several of the erroneous factoids, spin-doctored by Battisti, that had begun to permeate every article on the subject. Julie's and Robin's loved ones watched in stricken silence as the groundswell of support for Antonio Richardson flooded the media.

No one seemed to notice the ample legal documentation, including Richardson's own clemency application, that contradicted many of the "facts" being reported in the media. The story told in the legal documents revealed not the kindhearted, mentally disabled lost soul the media had created, but rather, the true Richardson: a very disturbed and angry young man who had led a miserable life since the day he was born.

According to his own clemency application, Richardson's father, Archie Richardson, was never married to his mother Gwendolyn and was not active in any of his three sons' lives. But while Archie acknowledged paternity of Richardson's two brothers, he persistently refused to acknowledge that Antonio Richardson was his son. He and Gwendolyn had not been getting along well during the period of time in which Richardson was conceived and born. As a result, Archie was convinced that the child was the product of Gwendolyn's unfaithfulness. So even on those rare occasions when he would spend time with the boys, he overtly rejected his middle child, allowing the other two to call him

"Father" while snubbing Richardson. The young boy had not understood the spitefulness being passed back and forth between his parents, but he did comprehend the utter rejection.

When Richardson was six years old, Archie married another woman and dropped out of his sons' lives almost entirely. For Richardson, the damage had already been done. By the time he was enrolled in the first grade, he was displaying severe behavioral problems. A report from the Missouri Division of Family Services in 1981 indicated that Gwendolyn was "having trouble" with Richardson, and that his "academic progress was poor — his report card for the first grade was mostly D's and unsatisfactory marks for social behavior." His teacher from that same year mentioned that the child would not sit still; he was always moving around, fighting, throwing crayons, and stealing from his classmates.

When Richardson was seven, his mother was diagnosed with severe kidney problems, and he and his two brothers began a permanent shuffle from one relative's home to the next. Gwendolyn would spend weeks at a time in the hospital, and in between her medical difficulties, the young mother developed a serious drug and alcohol habit. She would abandon her children for weeks at a time when she went on a binge. Often the boys didn't know where their mother was, and if or when she was coming home. She would spend her Social Security payments on drugs for herself and her boyfriends and, as a result, Richardson and his brothers frequently went hungry.

Further court documents indicated that it was "the severity, frequency, and consistency of the student's behavioral problems" and not any kind of mental retardation that resulted in Richardson's placement in a special school district for students with severe academic impediments. Richardson's educational problems had nothing to do with his purported mental retardation. He was simply a neglected, angry, uneducated, and violent kid who, without the benefits of sufficient love or guidance in his life, grew up to become an angry, uneducated, and violent man.

On the morning of March 5 the online edition of *The Post-Dispatch* printed an article with an unforgivable typo: Ginna Kerry was mistakenly identified as "Ginny Richardson." From her desk in New York, Tink fired off a scathing voice mail to the article's author, Paul Hampel, and set to work on another letter, this time to the editor of *The Post-Dispatch*. In St. Louis, James Kerry — an uncle of Julie and Robin's — did the same. Nels Moss was already putting the finishing touches on his.

Tink was more than a little surprised when Paul Hampel from *The Post-Dispatch* telephoned her about fifteen minutes after she had e-mailed her letter to the editor. He felt terrible about the reprehensible typo in the morning paper, and he wondered if she might be willing to do an interview. He said he would very much like to write an article supporting the victims' families. Tink was wary — her family had been burned by the media so many times before, and when they weren't being burned, they were being resolutely ignored, while Antonio basked in the spotlight performing in his now firmly established role as victim of the system. She told Hampel she'd have to think it over and call him back.

She hung up and immediately opened her electronic phonebook. Tom was first on the list, but two hours later, Tink had spoken to no fewer than half a dozen family members, all of whom agreed that she should grant Hampel the interview. After all, they couldn't very well continue to complain about the one-sidedness of the recent media coverage if nobody from their side was willing to give an interview. So after much nail-biting and second-guessing, Tink called Hampel back and nervously agreed to do the interview that evening. Despite her initial wariness, Tink warmed to Hampel and they spent nearly two hours on the phone that evening. At the end of the conversation, he thanked her.

"I've learned a lot today, about how to treat people — how to treat crime victims and their families, and I just want to thank you for giving me a second chance. My e-mail has been jammed all day with messages from Julie and Robin's family and loved ones. Those two girls really were incredible people and their story has been overlooked during the past few weeks. You have my word, I'm going to do my best to right that wrong tomorrow."

Hampel's front-page *Post-Dispatch* headline the next morning, March 6, read "Killer's TV Appearance Infuriates Relative Of Victims." Tink was extensively quoted in the article, debunking many of the myths that had somehow evolved into "fact" in recent media coverage. It was the first article the paper had printed in years that focused on the victims rather than on their murderers.

That same day, *The Post-Dispatch* prominently printed the three letters to the editor from James Kerry, Tink Cummins, and Nels Moss.

James Kerry's letter was extremely well thought out and passionate in its arguments.

> *First, there are no doubts as to his guilt. Also, contrary to the false implication of the headline on the March 2 editorial, the state would not be executing a juvenile. He is 26. He was 16 when he committed multiple rape and murder — very adult crimes committed in a very deliberate, very vicious, very violent, very determined, very adult manner.*

Moss's letter was no less impassioned.

> *This case was probably the most callous and wanton homicide of two young people I ever saw. Make no mistake, it was Richardson*

and Clemons who raped and pushed their nude victims into the
cold waters of the Mississippi River to drown.

I have had extensive experience with mental defenses, in-
cluding retardation, and Richardson is not mentally retarded in the
true meaning of the diagnosis. Mere poor scores on IQ tests or read-
ing deficiencies do not amount to mental retardation.

Richardson has excellent verbal skills, common sense and street
smarts far above those of a mentally retarded person. He made a
videotaped statement claiming others performed the actual murder,
and he was articulate and logical in his attempted deception. He
made a reasoned choice to go to trial.

The backlash was finally underway.

★   ★   ★

What Tink did not realize when she granted Hampel the interview was that her participation would earmark her as the
spokesperson for at least the Cummins side of the family. It was
a role she did not feel either qualified for or entitled to, yet despite her reluctance, she was swamped with phone calls by mid-
morning.

The reasons the Cummins and Kerry families had remained
largely silent during the ten years since Julie's and Robin's murders were multiple. For Tom, it was as simple as this: he didn't
trust the media. Time and time again he had seen innuendoes,
half truths, and errors printed about the case, and he simply didn't
want any part of it. For the Kerry family, it may have been that
their grief was just too large to voice. For the others, the large extended families — the aunts, uncles, cousins — well, they each
had personal reasons. Some felt that these deaths were private —
that their grief was nobody's business. And those in the family
who did get angry at the lopsidedness of the media and did want
to speak out were afraid of upsetting the others. Nobody really
felt it was his or her place to step up and start talking to the press.

After all, in such a large family, it was only natural that there would be a multitude of differing opinions on issues like the death penalty. And nobody wanted the responsibility of being labeled the "voice of the family."

So when Tink found herself seemingly at the top of the "to-do" list of every reporter in the country, she was more than a little uncomfortable. But after much ongoing discussion and encouragement from several family members, she agreed that she would talk to some members of the press. At the outset of each media conversation, she explained that she was speaking only for herself, not for the whole family. And she was adamant that she would not talk about her feelings on the issue of the death penalty. The only point that she really wanted to get across was this one: *Haven't we forgotten something? What about the victims?*

But if Tink felt overwhelmed as she juggled incoming calls from reporters and advice-seeking calls to her family, it was nothing compared to what the family members in St. Louis were facing. As the date of the execution drew near, all the family members were taken by surprise by the intensity of emotion that surrounded the impending event. The advent of another death ultimately resulting from that horrifying night in April 1991 stripped any scar tissue off the wounds of grief.

For Ginna, there were no scars — the wounds had never healed. And for the rest of her family, on March 6, 2001, while the media swarmed and the protesters worked themselves into a camera-worthy frenzy, the memories and the anguish were as raw as they had been ten years before.

Tom swung his rental car into his grandparents' driveway — the same driveway he had sneaked away from all those years before on that terrible night — pulled the handbrake, and looked over at his aunt Jacquie in the passenger seat beside him. He took a deep breath, but before he had a chance to say anything, his mother had appeared at the front door and was beckoning them inside. Kay had taken an earlier flight in order to spend an extra night with her parents. They had a few hours left before the three of them — Tom, Jacquie, and Kay — would make the drive to Potosi State Penitentiary where, at one minute past midnight, they were scheduled to witness the execution of Antonio Richardson by lethal injection.

The three hadn't talked much about why they were going. In truth, Kay and Jacquie were both just going to keep Tom company. Neither one of them had any desire to witness the execution for herself; they just felt that Tom needed their support. Ginna had never had any intention of attending the execution, and though Rick had considered it, he had eventually decided against it as well.

Tom spent the remainder of the afternoon at his grandparents' home. He even let Grandma Polly dote on him more than usual and feed him, though his stomach was so queasy and jittery he was almost afraid to eat.

Just before four o'clock, Jacquie's cell phone rang and Kay Crockett delivered the news that the Eighth Circuit Court had issued Richardson a temporary stay. The execution was off. Tom was too stunned to even respond.

Crockett advised Tom that the state was appealing the decision to the U.S. Supreme Court, and that there was a very good chance it would be overturned before midnight. So after watching Tink's interview on *Catherine Crier Live* from New York, Tom, Kay, and Jacquie piled into the rental car to make the drive to Potosi. They had barely checked into the Holiday Inn where they would be staying the night when Jacquie's cell phone rang with the latest update: Supreme Court Justice Clarence Thomas had vacated the stay. Richardson's execution was back on for one minute past midnight.

Tom felt as if he were in some kind of really twisted, demented episode of *Candid Camera*. The emotional ups and downs were almost too much to take and, by this time, he was asking himself the same questions countless people had asked him when he had made the decision to come out here, to be a witness to the execution. *What do I hope to get out of this? What the hell am I doing here?*

At about ten fifteen P.M., Tom pulled into a gas-station parking lot a few miles outside the penitentiary. He went to the pay phone and dialed Crockett's number with a finger that went numb from the cold by the time he reached the third digit. He just wanted to make one final check with her before they arrived and be sure that everything was on track. It was dark outside, much darker than it ever got in the city, and between that and the cold weather Tom was beginning to wonder if the people who planned these things didn't actually conspire to make the atmosphere as creepy as possible. He shook the thought away as soon as it popped into his head. He couldn't even begin to imagine what it was like for the people who actually planned these executions.

When Crockett answered the phone, she sounded uncharacteristically tired. "You're not going to believe this, Tom," she began. "The execution has been stayed again. I'll explain all the details as best I can to you when you get here. But basically, the Supreme Court has agreed to temporarily stay the execution pending the outcome of a trial in North Carolina involving a mentally retarded man."

"But . . ." Tom began.

"Yeah, I know," Crockett cut him off. "Richardson's not mentally retarded. Doesn't really seem to matter. His lawyers are basically saying, if there's a *chance* their client *might* be even *mildly* mentally retarded, then there's a chance the outcome of the case *might* affect him. It's enough for a stay. It won't hold up in the long run."

Tom nodded. "All right, we're just a couple of miles down the road. What do you think we should do?"

"Why don't you come on in and you can sit down for a while with Dora Schriro. She's the director of corrections for the State of Missouri. She should be able to answer any questions you might have. We also have some psychiatric counselors on hand if you'd like to talk to any of them."

Even with the prison under complete lockdown and security at its tightest, Tom and his mother and aunt were in and out of Potosi in under an hour. The cameras and the press didn't spot him on the way in, but mobbed him on the way out. Guards surrounded him and walked him all the way to his rental car, with Kay and Jacquie in tow. He remained silent — didn't even provide them with the "No comment" that would have earned him a spot on the nightly news.

At the Holiday Inn, an exhausted and emotionally drained Kay hit the sack as soon as they walked in the door. Tom and Jacquie lit cigarettes and stayed up all night remembering Julie and Robin.

Two days later, Tom did his best to settle into his airline seat as his plane taxied down the St. Louis runway for takeoff. The events of the last week had laid to rest a lot of unanswered questions for him. A month ago when he had planned this trip, people had started to ask him, "Just what do you hope to accomplish by going out there, by witnessing the execution?" And Tom really hadn't known how to answer that question. He had just felt compelled. It had never dawned on him *not* to go. But when the question came up, he began to soul-search and agonize over it. Why *did* he want to go? Did he really just want to watch this man die? No. That definitely wasn't it. He wasn't bloodthirsty. In fact, the idea of actually, physically watching the execution had not appealed to him in any way. It revolted him. And neither had he hoped for closure, or finality, or any of those comforts that survivors sometimes fool themselves into believing they can obtain by watching their tormentors die. He knew he wouldn't walk out of the penitentiary after witnessing *another* death and think to himself, *Wow. I feel better now.*

So what had he been hoping for? As the plane sped up and revved its engine for ascent, Tom finally recognized his one desire, his driving reason for coming there that week. He had been hoping for an apology. One tiny, neglected corner of his mind had been holding out a sliver of hope that Antonio Richardson, when faced with his own mortality, would come clean. That he would realize in the last moments before his death that he wasn't getting anywhere in this world, and that the best he could hope for would be to make peace with his Maker before he went into the next. *That* was what Tom had been hoping to witness. In the unlikely event that Richardson repented and sought forgiveness at the very last minute — just in case he decided that after all these years, he really *was* sorry — Tom wanted to be standing by. Tom wanted to forgive him.

As the plane reached its level flying altitude and Tom left St. Louis behind, he made a decision — to leave the unrealistic hopes he had brought there behind as well.

Tom's newfound peace allowed him to shrug off the "documentary" when it aired on Court TV later that year. The rest of his family wasn't quite so blasé about it. Instead, they were furious. The ninety-minute show included none of the footage that the crew had shot of the Cummins family. All the scenes of Tom at the firehouse, along with the footage of the family telling funny stories and sharing memories about Julie and Robin, had been omitted from the show. The final product focused entirely on Richardson's family and on his lawyer.

A film crew had recorded the family and their lawyer, Gino Battisti, during the last weeks and moments leading up to the night scheduled for Richardson's execution. They had captured every tear, every heartbreaking conversation, every excruciating facial expression they could gather during the Richardson family's terrible ordeal.

The Cummins and Kerry families were nowhere to be seen. Apparently the documentary producers had decided that *their* torment was inconsequential to the story.

But the real slap in the face came toward the end of the ninety-minute piece. The footage showed a frazzled-looking Battisti pacing the length of his office and running his hands through his hair, waiting for the phone to ring. When it finally did, he pounced on it and the cameras zoomed in on the one-sided conversation. The joy was immediately visible on the man's features and he collapsed into his chair, laughing with relief. It was the news he had hardly dared to hope for — Richardson's execution had been stayed. When he hung up, he looked into the camera and, smiling, said, "So the story has a happy ending after all!"

In the family room at the Cummins house, every mouth hung open in silence.

Around that same time, while Battisti celebrated his "happy ending," the Cummins and Kerry families prepared to mark the tenth anniversary of Julie's and Robin's deaths. Tom and Kathy planned their weekly beer night to coincide with the anniversary, and Tom invited his new girlfriend along. He had been dating her for only a few weeks, but he had high hopes for this one, and he knew he was going to have to explain his history to her sooner or later. After all, the facts of the story were the Legos of his life — the blocks that had, for the last ten years, been largely responsible for building the person Tom Cummins had become. And the new girlfriend, Whitney, couldn't really be expected to know or understand Tom until she knew his terrible story, until she knew about losing Julie and Robin.

So he took her to Mrs. O'Leary's early that night, an hour before they were supposed to meet Kathy and her husband. Tom took her hands in his and told her what he had come to think of as his life story. He was nervous, and he stuttered and paused along the way, taking sips during the longer gaps to fill the silence. After all, he had told these truths countless times over the span of ten years, and the reactions he had received varied from hyperventilation to disbelief to complete indifference. Tom had only recently come to understand that this moment, the moment when he shared his story, was the most important and most telling moment he experienced in *every* new relationship. The listener's reaction to his tale would provide a kind of a lens into her soul, a microcosm of everything she was as a person.

When Tom finished his story, Whitney stared back at him with wide, waterlogged eyes. "Whatever you need, if you need anything at all, I'll understand," she said.

And Tom knew that his years of therapy had finally ushered him across a very important threshold. For the first time in a decade, Tom was really, truly making a fresh start. He hoped that one day maybe Ginna could do the same, but even as he wished for that, he recognized how different, how consuming her pain was. Tom was finally making peace with his lot in life. His therapist was right, dammit: this wasn't his fault. It didn't matter what other people thought. It didn't matter that the media still referred to him as only "the victims' cousin." He knew he was a victim in his own right. He knew it, his family knew it, and now his new girlfriend knew it too.

For the first time since April 5, 1991, Tom felt free of blame, of self-reproach, of anxiety over what others thought of him. And in place of all those demons, the small shoots of grief were springing up in him. But they were the seeds of a pure grief, not laced with rage or distorted by fear. He was finally free to just miss his cousins without any other baggage disrupting that. And it almost felt good. He really *missed* Robin. And, oh God, how he missed Julie.

When Kathy and her husband appeared a few minutes later, Tom ordered drinks for them and then dialed Tink's cell-phone number in New York. He instructed Tink to find herself a drink, and they all waited while Tink popped the cork on a bottle of red wine in her apartment.

"Are you ready?" Tom asked, into the phone.

He lifted his shiny glass then, clinked his sister's in midair, and let a single tear slide down his cheek unchecked.

"To Julie and Robin," he said.

AFTERWORD

We forget our victims.

As a society, we have a certain fascination with murder and violence. It's not necessarily unhealthy — we are a curious people. We want to know why atrocities happen; we want to understand the causes of wickedness. We go looking for answers in books, in therapy, in our media. Unfortunately for the answer-seekers, corpses can't talk. The dead can't tell their own stories.

So instead, as Doug Magee so eloquently explains in the introduction of his book *What Murder Leaves Behind*,

> *In the aftermath of murder, we turn our attention to the murderer. That, of course, is where the action is. The chase, the arrest, and the trial are all served up to us as the story, and we rarely protest . . .*
>
> *In the time immediately after the murder we may catch a minute or two of a husband or a wife or a parent, squinting in the hot television lights, pausing to cry, and then trying to put words to some of the worst feelings imaginable. But we usually only glimpse these families and we only do so when they fit in with the larger story; the families remain peripheral to the activity surrounding the murder.*

It's true. But the larger social injustice is not that the victims' families are peripheral to our attentions. The larger wrong is that, because of their death-imposed silence, we forget about the victims themselves.

On April 5, 1991, Julie and Robin Kerry died. That is the singular monumental fact of this story. As such, it should remain pivotal to all pertinent discussions. Yet during the ensuing years, my family has watched helplessly while the press has demoted Julie and Robin to little more than background details. Meanwhile, their murderers became media darlings.

I wrote this book because I felt incensed. I wrote it because I wanted to do *something* to try to change the reality that Julie and Robin's rightful place in our collective memory is being usurped by the very thugs who killed them. This is a huge injustice in our society — and it's one that I only noticed because it happened to *my* family, to people whom I love and miss.

Trying to voice that message by writing this book is one of the scariest things I've ever done, and I've questioned myself at every turn. I've questioned my ability to sufficiently express these issues, and more important, I've questioned my *right* to do so. I know that, by the very nature of what is written in these pages, this book is inherently upsetting to some of the people who knew and loved Julie and Robin most in the world, and the last thing I wanted to do was to cause more pain to people who have already endured such staggering sufferings.

But in the end, I was bound by my feeling that Julie and Robin had been reduced to nothing more than "victims" in the media, that apart from the people who did know and love them, the only thing people remember about them is that they were raped, and they were killed. I felt that by writing this, I might be able to portray their love and the dignity with which they endured that horror. But even more important, I thought that in a very small personal way, I could give them back some of the details they were so proud of in their lives. Maybe this is one of my lofty pipe dreams, but I still believe in it. I wanted people to hear the names Julie Kerry and Robin Kerry, and to learn a little bit about them, even if that little bit was merely a shadow of the real Julie and Robin. So I pray that somehow, Julie's and Robin's loved ones will understand that those are the reasons I was compelled to speak up, the reasons I *had* to write this book. In the meantime, I need to be very clear about the fact that this is *my* version of events; this is *my* very personal memory stone to my cousins. I do not for a moment endeavor to speak on anyone else's behalf.

Capital punishment is a giant and terrifying issue. Its ramifications are truly unknowable, and so, shrouded in darkness, it looms over our national consciousness like the Grim Reaper. Although I never had the opportunity to discuss the death penalty with Julie or Robin, I know that they were both against it. What no one can ever know is whether that terrible night would have altered those views or not. There's no point in wondering.

What I *do* know, however, is how the issue affects those of us who are still here. I've struggled with it myself over the years. I've had many moments when all I wanted in the world was five minutes alone in a room with a butcher knife and my cousins' rapists. But I also faced the moment, worse even than those vengeful ones, when Richardson's execution was imminent. There was no peace in that impending death for me. I was horrified by the thought of him dying. Yet when his execution was stayed, I raged again — I wanted him dead. And then moments later, I hated myself for my own viciousness. The emotional roller coaster is indescribable.

The worst thing an oppressor can ever do to a victim is to inspire such hatred within the victim that she becomes capable of the same kind of monstrosities that oppress her. This threat of an alteration in the victim's very soul is far more terrifying to me than any potential physical brutality. If I allow my revulsion for my cousins' murderers to dictate a blood lust to me, then the thugs of the world have won. And the Julies and Robins have lost.

So I don't desire Richardson's, Gray's, or Clemons's execution — I don't want to watch these men die — but it's no feeling of mercy for *them* that keeps me on this side of the fence. As far as my concern for them goes, I'd be content to know that they had been locked away all those years ago and that they would never get out, that they would never rape or murder anyone again. I'd be equally content if I found out they all dropped dead in their cells one day. I don't care what happens to them. Julie and Robin aren't coming back.

But the sad fact is that death row keeps these men present in our lives. If Antonio Richardson were serving life without *any* possibility of parole, Ricki Lake wouldn't want to interview him. Court TV would have no reason to do a ninety-minute special on him. *Nobody* would feel sorry for him, and he would not be allowed to cast himself in the role of victim the way he has.

I can't argue against the death penalty out of compassion for these men because I haven't really managed to find any compassion for them yet. Maybe I would if I thought they were sorry — if they expressed any real remorse for what they've done. I can only say that capital punishment hasn't solved anything for me. It hasn't helped me heal, and I don't expect it to.

Yet the traditional rhetoric frustrates me. We're still putting the focus in the wrong place. Maybe the death penalty is wrong, not just because of the humanitarian issue, but because it further alienates the families who have already suffered so much. Because it rubs salt in the wounds of grief. Because it trivializes the people who should matter the most. Because it allows the murderers the opportunity to wear a badge they don't deserve — the badge of the victim.

★　　★　　★

I don't want to end this book on an angry note. I'm not all that angry any more. Writing this has allowed me to move past a lot of that. Now I fling it out there in hopes that it will be received the way I intended it — as a love letter to my cousins, as a voice for my brother. Along the way, if it contributes any small change to the way a reader thinks about victims, well, then I'd like to think that Julie and Robin would be proud. After all, who says you can't change the world?

Kisses and Revolution.

Jeanine Cummins lives in New York City, where she is working on her first novel. You can check her Web site, www.ripinheaven.com, for further updates on her family and their case.